Bertha A. McNeal
in loving memory of
her husband
Rev. George R. McNeal

1988

JOHN A. W. HAAS
Muhlenberg

# DANIEL BLUM'S

# THEATRE

# WORLD

## SEASON 1953-1954

### NEW YORK

### GREENBERG : PUBLISHER

TO THE MEMORY OF VERNON RICE

a loyal friend and delightful companion

whose life was dedicated to the theatre

# TABLE OF CONTENTS

Editorial Assistant: John Willis
Staff Photographers: Louis Melancon, Earle Forbes,
Guy Gillette, Sedge Le Blang

# THE NEW YORK SEASON

The number of new plays produced during the 1953-54 season was the lowest total in Broadway's history. While the quantity was meager, the quality was encouraging. Among the 39 new straight plays to reach the Broadway boards were such successes as "The Teahouse of The August Moon" which won both the Pulitzer Prize and the Critics Circle Award, "The Caine Mutiny Court Martial," "Tea and Sympathy," "Ondine" and "The Solid Gold Cadillac." Among the musicals, "Kismet" and "The Pajama Game" were the outstanding money-makers.

Most of the moderate successes were comedies such as "Oh, Men! Oh, Women!," "Sabrina Fair," "The Remarkable Mr. Pennypacker," "King of Hearts" and "Anniversary Waltz."

There were quite a few plays of high caliber that rated more prosperous engagements than accorded them. These include "Take A Giant Step," "In A Summer House," "The Prescott Proposals," "End As A Man," "The Immoralist," "The Ladies of The Corridor," "The Trip To Bountiful" and "The Confidential Clerk."

The season was also sprinkled with some unusually fine stellar performances by Lloyd Nolan, Lillian Gish, David Wayne, Ina Claire, Judith Anderson, Geraldine Page and Josephine Hull. Among the Broadway debuts, Deborah Kerr enhanced "Tea and Sympathy," Louis Jourdan contributed a fine sensitive performance in "The Immoralist," Hermione Gingold was a delight in "John Murray Anderson's Almanac," and Gig Young enlivened "Oh, Men! Oh, Women!"

Among the miscellaneous events was a repertory of nine plays by the Spanish Theatre headed by Alejandro Ulloa, a limited engagement by the Azuma Kabuki Japanese Dancers and Musicians, and solo shows by Ruth Draper, Ethel Waters, and Victor Borge who held the stage alone in what he called "Comedy In Music."

Not since the days of the Washington Square Players or the Provincetown Playhouse of O'Neill's early years or the "Grand Street Follies" has there been a season with so much activity or excitement as displayed in the Off-Broadway theatre. "End As A Man," "Bullfight," "The Threepenny Opera," "The Girl On The Via Flaminia," "The World of Sholom Aleichem," and a revival of "Othello" with Earle Hyman in the title role, were all theatre attractions at their best. The Phoenix Theatre on Second Avenue made an auspicious beginning with revivals of "The Sea Gull" and "Coriolanus," the first New York presentation of Sidney Howard's "Madam, Will You Walk," and a musical, "The Golden Apple." "End As A Man," "The Girl On The Via Flaminia" and "The Golden Apple" were transplanted, not too successfully, to Broadway.

Holdovers from the past season included two comedies, "The Seven Year Itch," "The Fifth Season," and two musicals, "Can-Can" and "Wonderful Town" with Carol Channing replacing Rosalind Russell in the latter.

The City Center winter season was a field day for José Ferrer who starred in four revivals: "Charley's Aunt," "Cyrano de Bergerac," "The Shrike" with which he duplicated his former Broadway success, and "Richard III" which he had never played in New York and which was not too well received. In the spring, the Center revived "Show Boat," "Fledermaus" and "Carousel." The latter opened the new season and, with great acclaim, it showed every sign of spanning the summer.

# BROADWAY CALENDAR

## JUNE 1, 1953 to JUNE 1, 1954

## VANDERBILT THEATRE

Opened Monday, September 7, 1953.*
Eastman Boomer and Arthur Klein present:

# ANNA RUSSELL AND
# HER LITTLE SHOW

Music and Lyrics by Miss Russell; Lighting by
Ralph Alswang; Musical Arrangements by Arthur
Harris; Staged by Arthur Klein; Choreography by
Lorenzo Fuller.

### ACT I

1. Overture: Jane Ashlock and Arthur Harris, Duo Pianists
2. Arthur Barnett
3. Jean Leon Destine and Company with Yolande Gaffne
   Drummers: Alphonse Cimber, Ti-Marcel in "The Spider and The Lady"
4. Paul Duke assisted by Doris Haley "A Symphony in Smoke"
5. Arthur Barnett
6. Anna Russell (assisted by Joseph Scandur) "Habanera," "O Night! O Day!," "Da Nyet, Da Nyet!," "Anameia's Death Scene," "I Gave My Love A Cherry," "The Prince of Philadelphia," "Les Cigarettes," "Trink."

### ACT II

1. Arthur Barnett
2. Anna Russell "The Bagpipes"
3. Jean Leon Destine and Company "The Witch Doctor"
4. Paul Duke assisted by Doris Haley "Magic In Rhythm"
5. Arthur Barnett
6. Anna Russell "Hello! Hello! Oh, A Jolly Good Show," "Guarda La Bella Tomato," "Night and Day"
7. The Decline and Fall of The Popular Song (as witnessed by Miss Russell) "Feeling Grand," "I'd Be A Red Hot Momma," "Chlorophyll Solly," "Miserable," "Mad"
8. Pianists
9. Finale

*General Manager:* ARTHUR KLEIN
*Press:* JOSEPH HEIDT
*Stage Manager:* MILTON STERN

* Closed Sept. 19, 1953. (16 performances)

ARTHUR JACOB PHOTOS

Anna Russell (Also Right and Top)

8

Opened Tuesday, September 8, 1953.*
Paula Stone and Mike Sloane and Burke and
Van Heusen present:

# CARNIVAL IN FLANDERS

Book by Preston Sturges; Based on "La Kermesse
Heroique" by C. Spaak, J. Feyder and B. Zimmer;
Lyrics by Johnny Burke; Music by James Van
Heusen; Scenery by Oliver Smith; Costumes by
Lucinda Ballard; Musical Director, Harold Hastings;
Vocal Arrangements by Elie Siegmeister; Orchestra-
tions by Don Walker; Carnival Ballet and Musical
Numbers Staged by Helen Tamiris; Directed by
Preston Sturges.

### Cast

| | |
|---|---|
| Siska | Pat Stanley |
| Jan Breughel | Kevin Scott |
| Tailor | Paul Reed |
| Butcher | Paul Lipson |
| Barber | Bobby Vail |
| Innkeeper | Lee Goodman |
| Mayor | Roy Roberts |
| Cornelia | Dolores Gray |
| Martha | Dolores Kempner |
| Courier | Matt Mattox |

Mourning Women: Sandra Devlin, Julie Marlowe,
Lorna Del Maestro

| | |
|---|---|
| 1st Officer | Ray Mason |
| 2nd Officer | George Martin |
| 3rd Officer | Jimmy Alex |
| The Duke | John Raitt |
| 1st Citizen | Wesley Swails |
| 2nd Citizen | Norman Weise |
| Lisa | Jean Bradley |
| Katherine | Undine Forrest |
| Orderly | William Noble |

**Dancers:** Lorna Del Maestro, Sandra Devlin, Pat
Ferrier, Patti Karkalits, Mary Alice Kubes, Julie
Marlowe, Billie Shane, Emy St. Just, Elfrieda
Zieger, Jimmy Alex, John Aristides, Harry Day,
Ronnie Field, Skeet Guenther, George Martin, Greg
O'Brien, Paul Olson, Richard Reed, Michael Spaeth.

**Singers:** Jean Bradley, Jean Cowles, Undine Forrest,
Dolores Kempner, Mara Landi, Mary Stanton,
Gloria Van Dorpe, Lee Barry, Fred Bryan, Bill
Conlon, Stokley Gray, William Noble, Dick Stewart,
Wesley Swails, Norman Weise.

**Musical Numbers:** "Ring The Bell," "The Very
Necessary You," "It's A Fine Old Institution,"
"I'm One Of Your Admirers," "The Plundering of
The Town," "The Stronger Sex," "The Sudden
Thrill," "It's An Old Spanish Custom," "A Seven-
teen Gun Salute," "You're Dead!" "Rainy Day,"
"Take The Word of A Gentleman," "The Carnival
Ballet," "A Moment of Your Love," "How Far
Can A Lady Go?."

A Musical Comedy in two acts. The entire action
takes place in and around the town of Flacksenburg
in Flanders in 1616.

General Manager: SAMUEL H. SCHWARTZ
Press: KARL BERNSTEIN, HARVEY SABINSON,
ROBERT GANSHAW
Stage Managers: FRED HEBERT, DENNIS MURRAY,
AL CHECCO

* Closed September 12, 1953. (6 performances)

PHOTOS BY EILEEN DARBY

Dolores Gray, John Raitt (Also Top)
Center: Kevin Scott, Pat Stanley
Left: Matt Mattox

William Martel, Effie Afton
Top: Mary Alice Moore, Hans Josef Schumm
Left Center: Spencer James, Effie Afton,
William Remick
Top Left: Howard Smith, Effie Afton,
Winston Ross

**ROYALE THEATRE**
Opened Monday, September 14, 1953.*
Bruce Fagan presents:

## A RED RAINBOW

By Myron C. Fagan; Directed by the author; Setting by Louis Kennel.

### Cast

| | |
|---|---|
| Inspector Scanlon | Howard Smith |
| Boris Sarno | Hans Josef Schumm |
| District Attorney Britt | Winston Ross |
| Gorman | William Martel |
| Roxy Gainsborough | Effie Afton |
| Major Robert Brainard | William Kemp |
| Arline Mason | Mary Alice Moore |
| Jensen | William Remick |
| Senator Derlin | Fred Irving Lewis |
| Mrs. Russell Meadow | Ruthelma Stevens |
| J. Kerrigan Kane | Robert Middleton |
| Congressman Felz | Spencer James |
| Rourke | William Adler |

A Drama in three acts. The entire action takes place in J. Kerrigan Kane's penthouse on Park Avenue, New York City, in the Spring of 1946.

*General Manager:* Louis Cline
*Press:* Thomas Barrows
*Stage Managers:* Al Jones, William Adler
\* Closed Sept. 26, 1953. (16 performances)

Mary Alice Moore, William Kemp

PHOTOS BY TALBOT

**THE PLAYHOUSE**
Opened Thursday, September 17, 1953.*
Nancy Davids presents:

## A PIN TO SEE THE PEEPSHOW

By F. Tennyson Jesse and H. M. Harwood;
Adapted from Miss Jesse's Novel of the same name;
Setting by Ariel Ballif; Lighting by Feder; Costumes by Ruth Morley; Directed by Peter Cotes.

### Cast

| | |
|---|---|
| Julia Almond | Joan Miller |
| Anne Ackroyd | Martha Farrar |
| Herbert Starling | Claude Horton |
| George Almond | Bill Griffis |
| Mrs. Almond | Eva Leonard-Boyne |
| Dr. Ackroyd | Basil Howes |
| Elsa | Joy Saunders |
| Lily Kitt | Valerie Cardew |
| Bertha Starling | Margaretta Warwick |
| Marian Lestrange | Marie Paxton |
| Gipsy Danvers | Winnifred Cushing |
| Captain Embury | Frederic Warriner |
| Leo Carr | Roger Moore |
| Police Constable | James Morley |
| Another Constable | Pat Malone |
| Police Inspector | Ronald Long |
| Matron | Nell Clarke |
| Mr. Ringwood | Jerome Kilty |
| Dr. Ogilvie | Frederic Warriner |
| A Wardress | Shirley Gale |

Prison Officials and Others: Winnifred Cushing, Pat Malone, Richard Towers, Len Bensow, Charles Shelvey, Crandall Diehl, Richard Lederer.

A Drama in two acts and thirteen scenes. The action takes place in London during 1916 through 1923 in St. Clement's Square, the parlour of Mrs. Almond's, a dress shop on Bond Street, the sitting-room of the Starling's flat, a police station, a waiting-room in a prison, the doctor's room in the gaol, and the condemned cell.

*Company Manager:* CHARLES STRAKOSCH
*Press:* RICHARD MANEY, FRANK GOODMAN
*Stage Managers:* LEN BEDSOW, BETTY ANN METZ

\* Closed September 17, 1953. (1 performance)

PHOTOS BY EILEEN DARBY

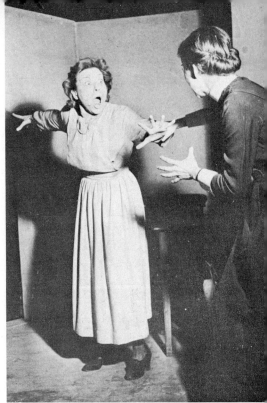

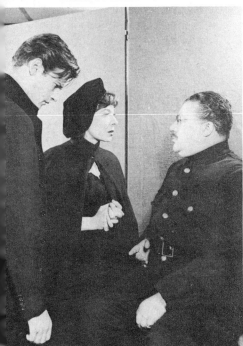

Roger Moore, Joan Miller, Ronald Long

Joan Miller, Roger Moore
Top: Joan Miller

11

Frederick O'Neal, Louis Gossett
Top Left: Louis Gossett, Pauline Myers
Left: Louis Gossett, Frank Wilson, Hel
Martin, Margaret Williams, Pauline My
Maxwell Glanville, Jane White

LYCEUM THEATRE
Opened Thursday, September 24, 1953.*
Lyn Austin and Thomas Noyes present:

## TAKE A GIANT STEP

By Louis Peterson; Directed by John Stix; Setting
and Lighting by Eldon Elder; Costumes by Ruth
Morley.

### Cast

Spencer Scott ..................................... Louis Gossett
Grandmother ............................... Estelle Hemsley
Tony ..................................................... Fred Vogel
Iggie .................................................. Bernard Rich
Frank .................................................. Frank Wilson
Man ............................................. Maxwell Glanville
Violet ............................................... Pauline Myers
Poppy ................................................. Helen Martin
Rose .......................................... Margaret Williams
Carol ..................................................... Jane White
Lem Scott .................................... Frederick O'Neal
May Scott ........................................ Estelle Evans
Christine ....................................... Dorothy Carter
Gussie ............................................... Robert Brivic
Johnny Reynolds ......................... Warren Berlinger
Bobby Reynolds ................................... Tarry Green

‹ A Comedy in two acts and six scenes. The action
takes place in a town in Connecticut at the present
time in the Scott home, a bar in the Negro section,
Violet's room, Spencer's bedroom.

General Manager: MAX ALLENTUCK
Press: BARRY HYAMS, MARTIN SHWARTZ
Stage Managers: DAVID KANTER, CHARLES PRATT, JR.

* Closed Nov. 28, 1953. (76 performances)

Frank Wilson, Helen Martin, Margaret Williams, Pauline Myers, Louis Gossett

PHOTOS BY JOHN ERWIN

Louis Gossett, Fred Vogel, Robert Brivic,
Tarry Green, Bernard Rich, Warren Berlinger

Louis Gossett, Jane White

Louis Gossett, Estelle Hemsley

Philip Bourneuf, Dennis King, Frederick Rolf, Victor Francen

Nils Asther, Victor Francen

PHOTOS BY ALFREDO VALENTE

BROADHURST THEATRE
Opened Tuesday, September 29, 1953.*
Walter P. Chrysler, Jr., presents:

## THE STRONG ARE LONELY

By Fritz Hochwalder; Adapted by Eva Le Gallienne; Directed by Margaret Webster; Scenery and Costumes by Rolf Gerard; Incidental Music by Lehman Engel.

### Cast

Alfonso Fernandez (Father Provincial) ............
Victor Francen
Ladislaus Oros, S. J. ........................ Wesley Addy
Rochus Lieberman (Father Superior) ................
Earl Montgomery
Candia .............................. Edward Groag
Naguacu ................................. Junaluska
Andre Cornelis ................................ Nils Asther
William Clark (Father Procurator) ................
Paul Ballantyne
Don Pedro de Miura ........................ Dennis King
Sergeant of The Guard ................. Stuart Vaughan
Captain Villano ............................. Martin Rudy
Captain Arago ............................ Frederick Rolf
Lorenzo Querini ......................... Philip Bourneuf
Carlos Gervazoni (Bishop) ........ Kermit Murdock
Jose Bustillos .............................. John Marley
Garcia Queseda ............................. Dion Allen
Alvaro Catalde ............................. John Straub
Father Reinegg ............................ Joseph Dooley
Father Torres ................................ Ray Rizzo
Father Claussner ............................ Dion Allen
Acatu ................................. Kuruks Pahitu
Barrigua ...................................... Dehl Berti
Young Indians .................Ernesto Gonzalez, Tuktu
Soldiers .................. Robert Ludlum, Wyatt Cooper

A Drama in two acts and five scenes. The action takes place July 16, 1767, in the study of the Father Provincial in the College of the Jesuit Fathers at Buenos Aires.

*Company Manager:* JOE ROTH
*Press:* BILL DOLL
*Stage Managers:* THELMA CHANDLER,
STUART VAUGHAN, JOSEPH DOOLEY
* Closed October 3, 1953. (7 performances)

John Kerr

Deborah Kerr
Top: Deborah Kerr, John Kerr
in "Tea and Sympathy"

Leif Erickson

Deborah Kerr, John McGovern, John Kerr
Top: Deborah Kerr, Leif Erickson

John Kerr, Dick York

Deborah Kerr, Florida Friebus

John Kerr, Deborah Kerr

Deborah Kerr, Leif Erickson

Arthur Steuer, Alan Sues, Dick York
Top: Leif Erickson, John Kerr

**ETHEL BARRYMORE THEATRE**
Opened Wednesday, September 30, 1953.
The Playwrights' Company in association with
Mary K. Frank present:

## TEA AND SYMPATHY

By Robert Anderson; Directed by Elia Kazan;
Setting and Lighting by Jo Mielziner; Clothes designed by Anna Hill Johnstone.

### Cast

| | |
|---|---|
| Laura Reynolds | Deborah Kerr†[1] |
| Lilly Sears | Florida Friebus |
| Tom Lee | John Kerr†[2] |
| David Harris | Richard Midgley |
| Ralph | Alan Sues |
| Al | Dick York |
| Steve | Arthur Steuer |
| Bill Reynolds | Leif Erickson |
| Phil | Richard Franchot |
| Herbert Lee | John McGovern |
| Paul | Yale Wexler |

A Drama in three acts and four scenes. The action takes place in a dormitory in a boys' school in New England.

*Business Manager:* VICTOR SAMROCK
*Press:* WILLIAM FIELDS, WALTER ALFORD,
PATRICIA BUTLER
*Stage Managers:* SEYMOUR MILBERT, YALE WEXLER

† Replaced June 1, 1954 by: 1. Joan Fontaine,
2. Anthony Perkins

PHOTOS BY SLIM AARONS

Deborah Kerr, John Kerr

17

Anne Vernon, Colin Gordon, Roland Culver, John Granger

Anne Vernon, John Granger

Colin Gordon, Roland Culver

Colin Gordon, Anne Vernon, Roland Culver, John Granger
Below: Roland Culver, Anne Vernon

## CORONET THEATRE

Opened Wednesday, October 7, 1953.*
John C. Wilson and H. M. Tennet, Ltd.,
present:

### THE LITTLE HUT

By Andre Roussin; Adapted by Nancy Mitford;
Decor by Oliver Messel; Directed by Peter Brook;
Costumes supervised by Frank Thompson.

#### Cast

| | |
|---|---|
| Henry | Colin Gordon |
| Susan | Anne Vernon |
| Philip | Roland Culver |
| A Stranger | John Granger |
| Second Stranger | Ray Gil |

A Comedy in three acts. The scene is a desert
island at the present time.

*General Manager:* C. Edwin Knill
*Press:* Willard Keeffe, David Tebet
*Stage Managers:* Samuel Liff, Erik Kristen

* Closed October 31, 1953. (29 performances)

Roland Culver, Colin Gordon, Anne Vernon

19

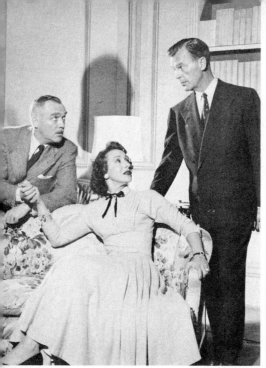

Frank Albertson, Arlene Francis, Neil Hamilton. Right: Lucile Watson, Ann Dere, Arlene Francis. Top Right: Cliff Robertson, Elizabeth Montgomery

**NATIONAL THEATRE**
(Moved to Booth Theatre, Nov. 9, 1953)
Opened Tuesday, October 13, 1953.*
Michael Abbott presents:

## LATE LOVE

By Rosemary Casey; Setting and Lighting by Stewart Chaney; Costumes by Frank Thompson; Associate Producers: Howard Erskine and Bonnie Alden; Staged by John C. Wilson.

### Cast

| | |
|---|---|
| Billy Gordon | Frank Albertson |
| Matthew Anderson | Cliff Robertson |
| Sarah | Ann Dere |
| Graham Colby | Neil Hamilton |
| Janet Colby | Elizabeth Montgomery |
| Mrs. Colby | Lucile Watson |
| Constance Warburton | Arlene Francis |

A Comedy in three acts. The action takes place in the living-room of the Colby home in Connecticut, early in September of the present year.

*Company Manager:* IRVING COOPER
*Press:* PHYLLIS PERLMAN, MARIAN BYRAM, DAVID POWERS
*Stage Managers:* WARD BISHOP, ROSEMARY PRINZ
* Closed January 2, 1954. (95 performances)

**20**     PHOTOS BY TALBOT

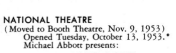

Neil Hamilton, Elizabeth Montgomery, Frank Albertson, Lucile Watson, Ann Dere.

Lucile Watson, Arlene Francis, Neil Hamilton
in
"Late Love"

Paul Richards, Ben Gazzara, Mark Richman, Anthony Franciosa

Pat Hingle, Arthur Storch, Ben Gazzara

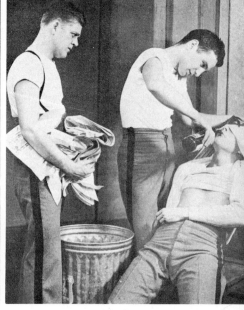

Pat Hingle, Ben Gazzara, Albert Salmi

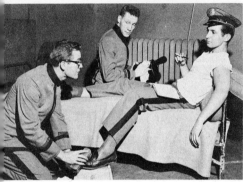

Arthur Storch, William Smithers,
Ben Gazzara
Top: Albert Salmi, Ben Gazzara

**VANDERBILT THEATRE**
(Moved to the Lyceum, Dec. 17, 1953)
Opened Wednesday, October 14, 1953.*
Claire Heller presents:

## END AS A MAN

By Calder Willingham; Directed by Jack Garfein; Production Designed by Mel Bourne.

### Cast

| | |
|---|---|
| Robert Marquales | William Smithers |
| Maurice Maynall Simmons | Arthur Storch |
| Harold Koble | Pat Hingle |
| Jocko De Paris | Ben Gazzara |
| Perrin McKee | Paul Richards |
| First Orderly | Eli Rill |
| Second Orderly | Richard Vogel |
| Starkson | Anthony Franciosa |
| Larrence Corger | Mark Richman |
| General Draughton | Frank M. Thomas |
| Roger Gatt | Albert Salmi |

Cadet Officers: Mickey Cohen, Steven Ross, Richard Heimann, Robert Dirk, Harry Gardino, Martin Greenlee

A Drama in three acts and five scenes. The action takes place in a military college in the South.

Company Manager: PAUL VROOM
Press: MAX EISEN, JOSEPH LUSTIG
Stage Managers: IRVING BUCHMAN
ANTHONY FRANCIOSA

* Closed January 16, 1954. (113 performances)
Moved to the Vanderbilt Theatre from the Theater De Lys where it opened September 15, 1953.

Ben Gazzara    LOUIS MELANCON
PHOTOS

Harry Jackson, Paul Ford, Larry Gates, David Wayne, John Forsythe, Mariko Niki

24

Mary Ann Reeve, Yuki Shimoda, William Hansen, Chuck Morgan, Haim Winant, Mariko Niki, David Wayne, John Forsythe, Larry Gates

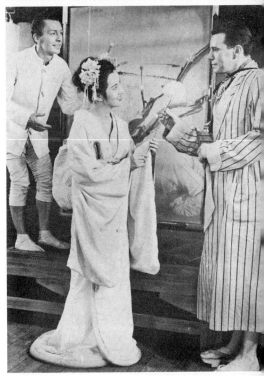

## MARTIN BECK THEATRE

Opened Thursday, October 15, 1953.
Maurice Evans in association with George Schaefer presents:

# THE TEAHOUSE OF THE AUGUST MOON

By John Patrick; Based on Novel by Vern Sneider; Directed by Robert Lewis; Settings and Lighting by Peter Larkin; Costumes by Noel Taylor; Music by Dai-Keong Lee.

### Cast

| | |
|---|---|
| Sakini | David Wayne |
| Sgt. Gregovich | Harry Jackson |
| Col. Wainwright Purdy III | Paul Ford |
| Capt. Fisby | John Forsythe |
| Old Woman | Naoe Kondo |
| Old Woman's Daughter | Mara Kim |
| The Daughter's Children: Moy Moy Thom, Joyce Chen, Kenneth Wong |
| Lady Astor | Saki |
| Ancient Man | Kame Ishikawa |
| Mr. Sumata | Kaie Deei |
| Mr. Sumata's Father | Kikuo Hiromura |
| Mr. Hokaida | Chuck Morgan |
| Mr. Seiko | Haim Winant |
| Mr. Oshira | William Hansen |
| Mr. Omura | Kuraji Seida |
| Mr. Keora | Yuki Shimoda |
| Villagers: Jerry Fujikawa, Frank Ogawa, Richard Akagi, Laurence Kim, Norman Chi |
| Miss Higa Jiga | Shizu Moriya |
| Ladies League for Democratic Action: Vivian Thom, Naoe Kondo, Mary Ann Reeve, Mara Kim |
| Lotus Blossom | Mariko Niki |
| Capt. McLean | Larry Gates |

A Comedy in three acts and ten scenes. The action takes place in Tobiki Village.

*General Manager:* ROBERT RAPPORT
*Press:* SOL JACOBSON, LEWIS HARMON
*Stage Managers:* BILLY MATTHEWS, TOM HUGHES SAND, YUKI SHIMODA

Top: David Wayne, John Forsythe

David Wayne, Mariko Niki, John Forsythe
Top: William Hansen, David Wayne, Chuck Morgan, Saki, John Forsythe, Larry Gates

John Forsythe, David Wayne, Mariko Niki,
in
"The Teahouse of the August Moon"

Anthony Ross

Anthony Ross, Hiram Sherman

Hiram Sherman, Kevin Coughlin,
Barbara Baxley

**BROADHURST THEATRE**

Opened Tuesday, October 20, 1953.*
Lyn Austin and Thomas Noyes in association
with Robert Radnitz and Robert Sagalyn
present:

# THE FROGS OF SPRING

By Nathaniel Benchley; Staged by Burgess Meredith; Setting and Lighting by Boris Aronson; Costumes by Alvin Colt.

### Cast

| | |
|---|---|
| Kay Allen | Haila Stoddard |
| Virginia Belden | Barbara Baxley |
| Danny Shaw | Kevin Coughlin |
| James Allen | Anthony Ross |
| Alice Kemp | Mary Grace Canfield |
| Charles Belden | Hiram Sherman |
| Bobby Belden | Billy Quinn |
| Chris Allen | Kenneth Kakos |
| John Allen | Malcolm Brodrick |
| Dr. Lindquist | Roland Wood |
| Asa McK. Gelwicks | Jerome Kilty |
| Luther Raubel | Fred Gwynne |

A Comedy in three acts and six scenes. The action
takes place during six days in the garden behind the
Allens' and Beldens' apartments in New York at
the present time.

*General Manager:* PHILIP ADLER
*Press:* BARRY HYAMS, MARTIN SHWARTZ
*Stage Managers:* ROBERT SAGALYN,
ROBERT RADNITZ

* Closed October 31, 1953. (15 performances)

PHOTOS BY ALFREDO VALENTE

27

Shepperd Strudwick, Frances Starr, June Walker, Vera Allen.
Top Left: Edna Best, Walter Matthau.
Top Right: Frances Starr, Shepperd Strudwick

Lonny Chapman, Betty Field

Margaret Barker, Edna Best, Clement Brace, Carol Wheeler

**LONGACRE THEATRE**
Opened Wednesday, October 21, 1953.*
Walter Fried presents:

# THE LADIES OF THE CORRIDOR

By Dorothy Parker and Arnaud D'Usseau;
Directed by Harold Clurman; Settings and Lighting
by Ralph Alswang; Costumes by Noel Taylor.

### Cast

| | |
|---|---|
| Mr. Humphries | Robert Van Hooton |
| Mrs. Gordon | June Walker |
| Mrs. Lauterbach | Vera Allen |
| Mrs. Nichols | Frances Starr |
| Charles Nichols | Shepperd Strudwick |
| Harry | Lonny Chapman |
| Casey | Louis Criss |
| Lulu Ames | Edna Best |
| Sassy | Tassle |
| Mildred Tynan | Betty Field |
| Robert Ames | Clement Brace |
| Betsy Ames | Carol Wheeler |
| Constance Mercer | Margaret Barker |
| Irma | Kate Harkin |
| Paul Osgood | Walter Matthau |
| Tom Linscott | Donald McKee |
| Mary Linscott | Harriet MacGibbon |

A Drama in three acts. The action takes place
during the course of a year in the Hotel Marlowe
in the East Sixties in New York City.

*Press:* BARRY HYAMS, MARTIN SHWARTZ
*Stage Managers:* JAMES GELB, LOUIS CRISS,
NORMA HAYES

* Closed Nov. 28, 1953. ( 35 performances)

PHOTOS BY JOHN ERWIN

**Edna Best, Walter Matthau**
**Center: Betty Field**

Brenda Bruce, Joyce Heron, Andrew Duggan

Mabel Taylor, Anthony Oliver,
Brenda Bruce, Andrew Duggan

## GENTLY DOES IT

By Janet Green; Directed by Bretaigne Windust;
Designed and Lighted by George Jenkins; Costumes
by Virginia Volland;

### Cast

| | |
|---|---|
| Monica Bare | Phyllis Povah |
| Emmie | Mabel Taylor |
| Philip Mortimer | Andrew Duggan |
| Edward Bare | Anthony Oliver |
| Freda Jeffries | Brenda Bruce |
| Charlotte Young | Joyce Heron |

A Mystery in three acts and six scenes. The action
takes place in November in the sitting-room of
Monica Bare's house at the top of Sunrise Hill,
just outside a small market town in Kent, England.

Company Manager: GEORGE BANYAI
Press: MADI BLITZSTEIN
Stage Managers: DANIEL S. BROUN, RICHARD CASEY

\* Closed Nov. 28, 1953. (37 performances)

Brenda Bruce, Joyce Heron

FRED FEHL PHOTOS

Phyllis Povah

Brenda Bruce, Andrew Duggan,
Anthony Oliver, Joyce Heron

Anthony Olive

Paul McGrath, Janet Blair

Janet Blair, Tod Andrews, Joan Wetmore

**ROYALE THEATRE**
Opened Thursday, October 29, 1953. *
Richard Aldrich and Richard Myers in association with Julius Fleischmann present:

## A GIRL CAN TELL

By F. Hugh Herbert; Staged by Mr. Herbert; Settings by Stewart Chaney; Costumes by Edith Lutyens.

### Cast

| | |
|---|---|
| Hannah | Eulabelle Moore |
| Nancy | Natalie Trundy |
| Vernon | Barry McGuire |
| Jennifer Goodall | Janet Blair |
| Artie | Marshall Thompson |
| Mr. Benton | Paul McGrath |
| Mrs. Benton | Lulu Mae Hubbard |
| Bill | Tod Andrews |
| Freddie | Donald Symington |
| George | Dean Harens |
| J. G. | Jack Whiting |
| Natasha | Joan Wetmore |
| Emmett | William Kester |

#### Phone Voices

| | |
|---|---|
| David | Bill Windom |
| D. F. | Henry Hart |

A Comedy in three acts and six scenes. The action takes place in the Bentons' living-room, Washington Square; an executive office in midtown Manhattan; the living-room of Bill's bachelor apartment.

*General Manager:* CHANDOS SWEET
*Press:* RICHARD MANEY, FRANK GOODMAN
*Stage Managers:* NICK MAYO, CHARLES VOCALIS,
PATON PRICE

* Closed Dec. 19, 1953. (60 performances)

PHOTOS BY EILEEN DARBY

Donald Symington, Janet Blair, Tod Andrews

ean Harens, Janet Blair

Barry McGuire, Natalie Trundy

Donald Symington,
Janet Blair

31

Thomas Gomez, Mary Orr

Jarmila Novotna, Basil Rathbone,
Chester Stratton

**CENTURY THEATRE**
Opened Friday, October 30, 1953.*
Bill Doll presents:

# SHERLOCK HOLMES

By Ouida Rathbone; Based on five stories by Sir
Arthur Conan Doyle; Staged by Reginald Denham;
Scenery and Costumes by Stewart Chaney; Incidental
Music by Alexander Steinert.

### Cast

| | |
|---|---|
| Dr. Watson | Jack Raine |
| Sherlock Holmes | Basil Rathbone |
| Mrs. Hudson | Elwyn Harvey |
| Rt. Hon. Trelawney Hope | John Dodsworth |
| Arthur Cadogan West | Richard Wendley |
| Lady Hope | Eileen Peel |
| Eduardo Lucas | Gregory Morton |
| Anna | Margit Forssgren |
| Count de Rothiere | Chester Stratton |
| Irene Adler | Jarmila Novotna |
| Walker | Terence Kilburn |
| Lestrade | Bryan Herbert |
| Miss Alice Dunbar | Mary Orr |
| Andrew | Evan Thomas |
| Professor Moriarty | Thomas Gomez |
| Hugo Oberstein | Martin Brandt |
| Capt. von Herling | Ludwig Roth |
| Prince Bulganin | St. John Phillipe |
| Gregson | Arthur N. Stenning |
| Villard | Alfred A. Hesse |

A Melodrama in three acts.

*Company Manager:* Ben Boyar
*Press:* Robert Ullman
*Stage Manager:* George Greenberg

* Closed October 31, 1953. (3 performances)

Basil Rathbone

32

**Lillian Gish**
in
"The Trip to Bountiful"

**HENRY MILLER'S THEATRE**
Opened Tuesday, November 3, 1953.*
The Theatre Guild and Fred Coe present:

## THE TRIP TO BOUNTIFUL

By Horton Foote; Directed by Vincent J. Done-
hue; Settings by Otis Riggs; Costumes by Rose Bog-
danoff; Lighting by Peggy Clark.

### Cast

| | |
|---|---|
| Mrs. Carrie Watts | Lillian Gish |
| Ludie Watts | Gene Lyons |
| Jessie Mae Watts | Jo Van Fleet |
| Thelma | Eva Marie Saint |
| Houston Ticket Man | Will Hare |
| A Traveler | Salem Ludwig |
| Second Houston Ticket Man | David Clive |
| Harrison Ticket Man | Frederic Downs |
| Sheriff | Frank Overton |
| Travelers: Patricia MacDonald, Neil Laurence, Helen Cordes | |

A Drama in three acts. The action takes place in
a Houston, Texas, apartment; on a bus; at a country
place.

Company Manager: RICHARD SKINNER
Press: NAT AND IRVIN DORFMAN
Stage Managers: HENRY WEINSTEIN, DAVID CLIVE
* Closed December 5, 1953. (39 performances)

Top: Jo Van Fleet, Gene Lyons, Lillian Gish
Right Center: Frank Overton, Lillian Gish;
Will Hare, Lillian Gish
Right: Jo Van Fleet, Gene Lyons

PHOTOS BY EILEEN DARBY

Gene Lyons, Jo Van Fleet. Lillian Gish

Lillian Gish, Eva Marie Saint

34

**Mary Martin, Charles Boyer**
in
"Kind Sir"

Margalo Gillmore

Frank Conroy, Dorothy Stickney,
Charles Boyer, Mary Martin

Dorothy Stickney

**ALVIN THEATRE**
Opened Wednesday, November 4, 1953.*
Joshua Logan presents:

# KIND SIR

By Norman Krasna; Directed by Joshua Logan;
Settings and Lighting by Jo Mielziner; Costumes by
Main Bocher; Associate Producer and Director, Marshall Jamison.

### Cast

| | |
|---|---|
| Anna Miller | Margalo Gillmore |
| Margaret Munson | Dorothy Stickney |
| Jane Kimball | Mary Martin |
| Alfred Munson | Frank Conroy |
| Philip Clair | Charles Boyer |
| Carl Miller | Robert Ross |

A Comedy in two acts and six scenes. The action
takes place in the New York apartment of Jane
Kimball.

*Company Manager:* ABE COHEN
*Press:* LEO FREEDMAN, ABNER D. KLIPSTEIN
BETTY LEE HUNT
*Stage Managers:* ROBERT LINDEN, DOUGLAS McLEAN
* Closed March 27, 1954, (165 performances)
SLIM ARRON PHOTOS

Charles Boyer

Frank Conroy, Dorothy Stickney,
Margalo Gillmore, Mary Martin

Mary Martin

Josephine Hull
in
"The Solid Gold Cadillac"

Josephine Hull, Vera Fuller Mellish, Loring Smith.

Charlotte Van Lein, Reynolds Evans

Top: Geoffrey Lumb, Henry Jones, Josephine Hull, Mary Welch

BELASCO THEATRE
  Opened Thursday, November 5, 1953.
  Max Gordon presents:

## THE SOLID GOLD CADILLAC

By Howard Teichmann and George S. Kaufman;
Staged by George S. Kaufman; Settings by Edward
Gilbert.

### Cast

| | |
|---|---|
| T. John Blessington | Geoffrey Lumb |
| Alfred Metcalfe | Wendell K. Phillips |
| Warren Gillie | Reynolds Evans |
| Clifford Snell | Henry Jones |
| Mrs. Laura Partridge | Josephine Hull |
| Miss Amelia Shotgraven | Mary Welch |
| Mark Jenkins | Jack Ruth |
| Miss L'Arrière | Charlotte Van Lein |
| Edward L. McKeever | Loring Smith |
| Miss Logan | Vera Fuller Mellish |
| The A. P. | Carl Judd |
| The U. P. | Al McGranary |
| I. N. S. | Howard Adelman |
| A Woman | Gloria Maitland |

News Broadcasters

| | |
|---|---|
| Bill Parker | Henry Norell |
| Dwight Brookfield | Mark Allen |
| Estelle Evans | Lorraine MacMartin |
| Narrator | Fred Allen |

A Comedy in two acts. The action takes place in
New York and Washington.

  *General Manager:* AL GOLDIN
  *Press:* NAT AND IRVIN DORFMAN
  *Stage Managers:* JOSEPH OLNEY, CARL JUDD,
        HOWARD ADELMAN

op: Reynolds Evans, Wendell K. Phillips,
osephine Hull, Geoffrey Lumb, Henry Jones

FRED FEHL PHOTOS

Josephine Hull, Henry Jones.
Center: Jack Ruth, Mary Welch **39**

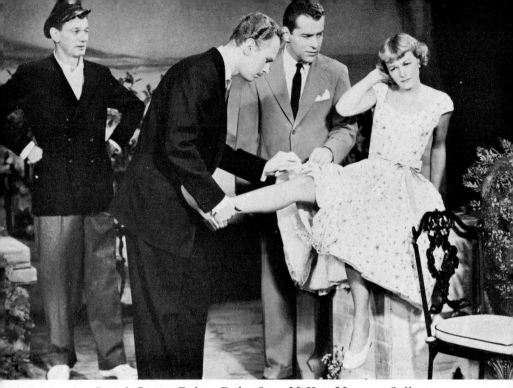

Joseph Cotten, Robert Duke, Scott McKay, Margaret Sullavan

Cathleen Nesbitt

**40**

Margaret Sullavan, Luella Gear,
Scott McKay, Cathleen Nesbitt

John Cromwell

Luella Gear, Cathleen Nesbitt, John Cromwell, Joseph Cotten, Margaret Sullavan, Russell Collins

## SABRINA FAIR

By Samuel Taylor; Directed by H. C. Potter; Setting and Lighting by Donald Oenslager; Costumes by Bianca Stroock.

### Cast

| | |
|---|---|
| Maude Larrabee | Cathleen Nesbitt |
| Julia Ward McKinlock | Luella Gear†1 |
| Linus Larrabee, Jr. | Joseph Cotten†2 |
| Linus Larrabee | John Cromwell†3 |
| Margaret | Katharine Raht |
| David Larrabee | Scott McKay |
| Gretchen | Ruth Woods†4 |
| Sabrina Fairchild | Margaret Sullavan†5 |
| Fairchild | Russell Collins |
| A Young Woman | Harriette Selby |
| A Young Man | Gordon Mills |
| Another Young Woman | Loraine Grover |
| Another Young Man | Michael Steele |
| Paul D'Argenson | Robert Duke |

A Comedy in two acts and four scenes. The action takes place at the Larrabee home on the North Shore of Long Island.

*Company Manager:* BEN ROSENBERG
*Press:* WILLIAM FIELDS, WALTER ALFORD, PATRICIA BUTLER
*Stage Managers:* DAVID GRAY, JR., MICHAEL STEELE

† Replaced by Edith Meiser from April 26 to May 24. The following assumed the roles on May 29th: 2. Tod Andrews, 3. Frederick Worlock. 4. Jayne Heller, 5. Leora Dana, and understudy Diana Douglas was replaced by Joan Morgan.

Margaret Sullavan

Joseph Cotten

Joseph Cotten, Margaret Sullavan
in
"Sabrina Fair"

Murray Matheson, Margery Maude, Roddy McDowall, Brian Aherne, Ursula Jeans

**FORTY-EIGHTH STREET THEATRE**
Opened Wednesday, November 18, 1953.*
Alfred de Liagre, Jr., and Roger L. Stevens
with Henry Sherek present:

## ESCAPADE

By Roger MacDougall; Directed by Alfred de Liagre, Jr.; Production Designed by Donald Oenslager.

### Cast

| | |
|---|---|
| Stella Hampden | Ursula Jeans |
| Mrs. Hampden | Margery Maude |
| Peter Henderson | Murray Matheson |
| William Saxon | Peter Pagan |
| Sir Harold Cookham | Arthur Marlowe |
| John Hampden | Brian Aherne |
| Walters | John Moore |
| Dr. Skillingworth | Melville Cooper |
| Miss Betts | Marie Paxton |
| Paxton | Rex Thompson |
| Daventry | Roddy McDowall |
| Andrew Deeson | Felix Deebank |
| Molly | Carroll Baker |
| George | Nicholas Howard |

A Comedy in three acts and five scenes. The action takes place in and nearby London at the present time, in The Hampdens' living-room and in Dr. Skillingworth's Study.

*General Manager:* C. EDWIN KNILL
*Press:* BEN WASHER
*Stage Managers:* WILLIAM CHAMBERS,
ARTHUR MARLOWE

* Closed Nov. 28, 1953. (13 performances)

PHOTOS BY VANDAMM

Brian Aherne, Rex Thompson, Ursula Jeans,
Melville Cooper

43

Alejandro Ulloa as Don Juan

Francisca Ferrandiz, Alejandro Ulloa

## BROADHURST THEATRE
Opened Thursday, November 19, 1953.*
Domingo Blanco and J. G. Del Pozo present:

# THE SPANISH THEATRE
### in repertory
# DON JUAN TENORIO
(Don Juan the Lover)
By Jose Zorrilla. Presented for six performances.

### Cast

Don Juan Tenorio .......................... Alejandro Ulloa
Buttarelli ...................................... Manuel Calzada
Ciutti ............................................ Miguel Garcia
Don Gonzalo .................................. Rafael Calvo
Don Diego Tenorio .................... Emilio Menendez
Capt. Centellas ............................ Enrique Cerro
Avellaneda .................................... Jose Poveda
Don Luis Mejia ................................. Pedro Gil
Gaston ...................................... Francisco Camacho
First Policeman ............................... Luis Garcia
Second Policeman ............................... A. Mendez
Dona Ana ...................... Rosario De La Torre
Brigida ........................................ Pilar Olivar
Lucia ...................................... Carmen Pradillo
Abadesa ........................................ Laura Bove
Dona Ines ........................... Francisca Ferrandiz
Hermana Tornera ...................... Rosario Torre
The Sculptor ................................. Luis Torner

Presented in two acts and seven scenes. The action
takes place around 1545 in and around Seville,
Spain.

# EL ALCALDE DE ZALAMEA
(The Mayor of Zalamea)
By Calderon; Adapted by Thomas Borras. Pre-
sented for 4 performances.

### Cast

Isabel ................................... Francisca Ferrandiz
Ines ............................................ Maria Rollan
Pedro Crespo ......................... Alejandro Ulloa
Juan Crespo ........................... Enrique Del Cerro
Sergeant ................................. Emilio Menendez
Captain ........................................... Pedro Gil
Chispa ................................... Carmen Pradillo
Rebolledo .................................. Miguel Garcia
Don Lope De Figueroa ................... Rafael Calvo
The Notary .................................... Luis Torner
1st Soldier ............................... Manuel Calzada
2nd Soldier ......................... Francisco Camacho
King Philip II ............................... Jose Poveda

Presented in three acts. The action takes place in
Zalamea, Spain.

# LA VIDA ES SUENO
(Life Is A Dream)
By Calderon; Adaptation by A. Garcia; Direction
and Mounting by Alejandro Ulloa; Decor by Ramon
Batlle. Presented for 5 performances.

### Cast

Rosaura ................................. Francisca Ferrandiz
Clarin ....................................... Miguel Garcia
Prince Segismundo ................... Alejandro Ulloa
Clotaldo ............................... Emilio Menendez
Prince Astolfo ................................ Pedro Gil
Princess Estrella ..................... Carmel Pradillo
Basilio ........................................ Rafael Calvo
Captain ................................... Enrique Cerro
Noble ........................................ Jose Poveda
Soldier ...................................... M. Calzada

Presented in three acts and five scenes. The action
takes place on the Polish frontier and in Warsaw,
Poland.

# REINAR DESPUES DE MORIR
(Rule After Death)
By Luis Velez de Guevara; Adaptation by Fernandez Villegas; Direction and Mounting by Alejandro Ulloa; Decor by Ramon Batlle. Presented for
4 performances.

### Cast

Prince Don Pedro ...................... Alejandro Ulloa
Brito ......................................... Miguel Garcia
King Alonso of Portugal .................. Rafael Calvo
Dona Blanca .......................... Carmen Pradillo
Dona Ines de Castro .............. Francisca Ferrandiz
Violante ...................................... Pilar Olivar
Egas Coello ................................... Pedro Gil
Alvar Gonzalez ......................... Enrique Cerro
The Constable ...................... Emilio Menendez
Nuno De Almeida ....................... Jose Poveda

Presented in two acts and six scenes. The action
takes place in Coimbra, Portugal, during the 16th
Century.

Alejandro Ulloa as Cyrano De Bergerac

# LA OTRA HONRA
(The Other Honor)

By Jacinto Benavente; Direction and Mounting by Alejandro Ulloa; Decor by Ramon Batlle. Presented for 4 performances.

## Cast

Don Vicenta ....................................... Laura Bove
Carmen ...................................... Carmen Pradillo
Manuel ........................................... Rafael Calvo
Victor ......................................... Alejandro Ulloa
Julia ..................................... Francisca Ferrandiz
Carlos ............................................... Pedro Gil
Servants ................... Manuel Calzado, Luis Torner

Presented in three acts. The action takes place at the present time in Madrid.

# EL CARDINAL
(The Cardinal)

By Luis N. Parker; Spanish Adaptation by Linares Rivas and Reparaz; Direction and Mounting by Alejandro Ulloa; Decor by Ramon Batlle. Presented for 3 performances.

## Cast

Pedro ...................................... Manuel L. Calzada
Benita .................................. Rosario De La Torre
Magdalena ...................................... Pilar Olivar
Honoria ................................. Leonor Hernandez
Beppo ........................................ Miguel Garcia
Claricia De Medici ........................... Laura Bove
Julian De Medici ........................... Enrique Cerro
Cardinal Juan De Medici .......... Alejandro Ulloa
Bartolome Quiggi ..................... Emilio Menendez
Baglione ........................................ Rafael Calvo
Andrea Strozzi ...................................... Pedro Gil
Abad De Ramsad .............................. Pedro Calis
Filiberta ............................... Francisca Ferrandiz
Luis ............................................... Luis Torner
Francisco ......................................... Jose Poveda

Presented in four acts. The action takes place in Rome in the 14th Century in the Palace of the Medici's.

# CYRANO DE BERGERAC

Adapted from Edmund Rostand's original for the Spanish stage by the Senores Vila Y Tintore; Direction and Mounting by Alejandro Ulloa; Decor by Ramon Batlle. Presented for 3 performances.

## Cast

Cyrano De Bergerac ..................... Alejandro Ulloa
Roxana ................................. Francisca Ferrandiz
Conde De Guiche ................................. Pedro Gil
Cristian De Neuvillette ................. Enrique Cerro
Rageuneau ..................................... Miguel Garcia
Le Bret .................................... Emilio Menendez
Capitan Carbon De Castel-Jaloux ...... Rafael Calvo
Vizconde De Valvert .......................... Luis Torner
La Duena ......................................... Pilar Olivar
Lisa ...................................... Carmen Pradillo
La Alojera ....................................... Maria Rollan
Marques .......................................... Jose Poveda
Ligniere ........................................... Rafael Calvo
Montfleury ............................... Manuel Calzada
Bellerose ......................................... Luis Calvo
Cuigy ............................................... Pedro Calis
Brissaille ......................................... Jose Poveda
Un Ratero ...................................... Antonio Mora
Un Capuchino .......................... Manuel Calzada
Cadets: Jose Poveda, Luis Vinas, Manuel Alvarez, Francisco Camacho, Luis Torner, Manuel Sanchez

Poets ................. Francisco Camacho, Luis Rosson

Presented in five acts. The action of the first four acts takes place in 1640, the fifth act in 1655.

*Manager:* MANUEL ALVAREZ

*Press:* ANNE WOLL

*Stage Managers:* PEDRO CALIZ, ALFREDO VERA

* Closed Dec. 12, 1953. (27 performances)

jandro Ulloa as The Mayor of Zalamea

Steve Reeves, Alfred Drake
Top: Alfred Drake, Joan Diener
Center: Alfred Drake

Opened Thursday, December 3, 1953.
Charles Lederer presents Edwin Lester's production of:

# KISMET

Music from Alexander Borodin; Musical Adaptation and Lyrics by Robert Wright and George Forrest; Book by Charles Lederer and Luther Davis; Based on Play by Edward Knoblock; Orchestral and Choral Arrangements by Arthur Kay; Production Directed by Albert Marre; Dances and Musical Numbers Staged by Jack Cole; Settings and Costumes Designed by Lemuel Ayers; Lighting by Peggy Clark; Musical Direction by Louis Adrian.

## Cast

Imam of The Mosque ............... Richard Oneto[1]
Muezzins: Gerald Cardoni, Kirby Smith, Ralph Strane, Louis Polacek
Doorman ..................................... Jack Mei Ling[2]
1st Begger ..................................... Earle MacVeigh
2nd Beggar ..................................... Robert Lamont
3rd Beggar ..................................... Rodolfo Silva
Dervishes ...................... Jack Dodds, Marc Wilder
Omar ..................................... Philip Coolidge
Public Poet, Later Called Hajj ......... Alfred Drake
Marsinah ..................................... Doretta Morrow
A Merchant ..................................... Kirby Smith
Hassan-Ben ..................................... Hal Hackett
Jawan ..................................... Truman Gaige
Street Dancers ........ Florence Lessing, Ethel Martin
Akbar ..................................... Jack Dodds
Assiz ..................................... Marc Wilder
Bangle Man ..................................... Richard Oneto[1]
Chief Policeman ...................... Tom Charlesworth
2nd Policeman ..................................... Hal Hackett
The Wazir of Police ...................... Henry Calvin
Wazir's Guards ...... Stephen Ferry, Steve Reeves[3]
Lalume ..................................... Joan Diener
Attendants ......... Mario Lamm, John Weidemann
Princesses of Ababu: Patricia Dunn, Bonnie Evans, Reiko Sato[4]
The Caliph ..................................... Richard Kiley[5]
Slave Girls: Carol Ohmart, Joyce Palmer[6], Sandra Stahl, Lila Jackson[7]
A Peddler ..................................... Earle MacVeigh
A Servant ..................................... Richard Vine
Princess Zubbediya of Damascus .... Florence Lessing
Ayah to Zubbediya ...................... Lucy Andonian
Princess Samaris of Bangalore ......... Beatrice Kraft
Ayah to Samaris ..................................... Thelma Dare
Street Women ...... Jo Ann O'Connell, Lynne Stuart
Prosecutor ..................................... Earle MacVeigh
Widdow Yussef ..................................... Barbara Slate
Diwan Dancers: Neile Adams, Jack Woods, Marc Wilder

**Singers:** Gerald Cardoni, Robert Lamont, Richard Oneto[1], Louis Polacek, Kirby Smith, Ralph Strane, Richard Vine, George Yarick, Anita Coulter, Thelma Dare, Lila Jackson[7], Jo Ann O'Connell, Barbara Slate, Sandra Stahl, Lynne Stuart, Erica Twiford, Doris Yarick, Loren Driscoll.

**Dancers:** Neile Adams, Patricia Dale, Devra Kline, Ania Romaine, Vida Ann Solomon, Roberta Stevenson, Prue Ward, Pat Lynch.

**Understudies:** Earle MacVeigh for Mr. Drake and Mr. Calvin; Jo Ann O'Connell for Miss Morrow; Carol Ohmart for Miss Diener; Richard Oneto for Mr. Kiley; Richard Vine for Mr. Coolidge; Kirby Smith for Mr. MacVeigh and Mr. Charlesworth; Gerald Cardoni for Mr. Hackett; Neile Adams for Mlls. Dunn, Evans and Sato; Ethel Martin for Beatrice Kraft.

**Musical Numbers:** "Sands of Time," "Rhymes Have I," "Fate," "Bazaar of The Caravans," "Not Since Nineveh," "Baubles, Bangles and Beads," "Stranger in Paradise," "He's in Love!," "Gesticulate," "Night of My Nights," "Was I Wazir?," "Rahadlakum," "And This Is My Beloved," "The Olive Tree," "Ceremonial of The Caliph's Diwan," "Presentation of Princesses," Finale.

A Musical Arabian Night in two acts and fourteen scenes. The action takes place in Baghdad.

Company Manager: HARRY ESSEX
Press: BARRY HYAMS, MARTIN SHWARTZ
Stage Manager: PHIL FRIEDMAN

†Replaced by: 1. Gerald Cardoni, 2. Ronnie Field, 3. Al Smith, 4. Neile Adams, 5. Richard Oneto, 6. Jeane Williams, 7. Ingeborg Kjellsen.

Joan Diener (also at top with Alfred Drake).
Center (l–r): Richard Kiley, Doretta Morrow; Beatrice Kraft, Doretta Morrow, Florence
Lessing; Doretta Morrow, Alfred Drake.

47

**Alfred Drake**
in
"Kismet"

Hermione Gingold
in
"John Murray Anderson's Almanac"

Nanci Crompton, Billy De Wolfe, Hermione Gingold, Elaine Dunn,
Carleton Carpenter, Polly Bergen. Top: Harry Mimmo, Orson Bean,
Nanci Crompton. Center: Billy De Wolfe, Hermione Gingold

IMPERIAL THEATRE

Opened Thursday, December 10, 1953.

Michael Grace, Stanley Gilkey and Harry Rigby present:

# JOHN MURRAY ANDERSON'S ALMANAC

Entire Production Devised and Staged by John Murray Anderson; Music and Lyrics by Richard Adler and Jerry Ross, Cy Coleman, Michael Grace, Joseph McCarthy, Henry Sullivan, John Rox, Bart Howard; Sketches by Jean Kerr, Sumner Locke-Elliott, Arthur Macrae, Herbert Farjeon, Lauri Wylie, Billy K. Wells; Sketches Directed by Cyril Ritchard; Dances and Musical Numbers Staged by Donald Saddler; Scenery by Raoul Pene Du Bois; Costumes by Thomas Becher; Musical Director, Buster Davis; Orchestrations by Ted Royal; Vocal Arrangements by Buster Davis; Dance Music Arranged by Gerald Alters.

## Cast

| | |
|---|---|
| Hermione Gingold | Billy De Wolfe |
| Harry Belafonte | Polly Bergen |
| Orson Bean | Nanci Crompton |
| Carleton Carpenter | Harry Mimmo |
| Elaine Dunn | Celia Lipton |
| James Jewell | Kay Medford |

and Lee Becker, Imelda DeMartin, Dorothy Dushock, Greb Lober, Illona Murai, Margot Myers, Gwen Neilson, Gloria Smith, Jimmy Albright, Hank Brunjes, Ronald Cecill, Dean Crane, Ralph McWilliams, Gerald Leavitt, Jacqueline Mickles, Colleen Hutchins, Monique Van Vooren, Tina Louise, Larry Kert, Bob Kole, George Reeder, Jay Harnick, Kenneth Urmston, Toni Wheelis, Siri, Millard Thomas.

**Musical Numbers:** "Harlequinade," "The Coronation," "You're So Much A Part of Me," "I Dare To Dream," "Mark Twain," "The Nightingale and The Rose," "My Love Is A Wanderer," "Tin Pan Alley," "Ziegfeldiana," "Which Witch?," "La Loge," "Fini," "Acorn In The Meadow," "When Am I Going To Meet Your Mother?," "Hold 'Em Joe," "The Earth And The Sky," Finale.

**Sketches:** "My Cousin Who?," "The Cello," "Don Brown's Body," "European Express," "Hope You Come Back," "Cartoon," "Dinner For One," "La Pistachio."

A Revue in two acts and twenty-five scenes.

Company Manager: MANNING GURIAN
Press: SOL JACOBSON, LEWIS HARMON
Stage Managers: ARTHUR BARKOW,
PERRY BRUSKIN, DENNIS MURRAY

Top Right: Carleton Carpenter

Right: Billy De Wolfe, Hermione Gingold

Nanci Crompton

Elaine Dunn, Carleton Carpenter

Orson Bean

Harry Belafonte

51

Top: Lorne Greene, Ben Astar, Minoo Daver, Katharine Cornell, Roger Dann, Felix Aylmer.
Center: (Left) Felix Aylmer, Katharine Cornell. (Right) Katharine Cornell, Roger Dann

**BROADHURST THEATRE**
Opened Wednesday, December 16, 1953.*
Leland Hayward presents:

# THE PRESCOTT PROPOSALS

By Howard Lindsay and Russel Crouse; Directed
by Howard Lindsay; Settings by Donald Oenslager;
Costumes by Main Bocher.

## Cast

| | |
|---|---|
| Mary Prescott | Katharine Cornell |
| Kathleen Murray | Emily Lawrence |
| Emma | Helen Ray |
| Elliott Clark | Lorne Greene |
| Jan Capek | Bartlett Robinson |
| Sir Audley Marriott | Felix Aylmer |
| Paul-Emile D'Arceau | Roger Dann |
| Dr. Ali Masoud | Minoo Daver |
| Alexis Petrovsky | Ben Astar |
| Miguel Fernandez | Edward Groag |
| Alan Draper | Robert M. Culp |
| Miroslav Babicka | Boris Tumarin |
| Russian Aide | Jan De Ruth |
| British Aide | J. P. Wilson |
| Precis-Writer | John Drew Devereaux |

Experts and Aides to the United Nations Delegates:
Bijou Fernandez, Joe Masteroff, John Leslie, Shep-
pard Kerman, Richard Bengali, Ward Costello,
Bernard Reines, Hubert Beck.

A Drama in three acts and four scenes. The action
takes place in Mary Prescott's apartment and in a
committee room at the United Nations.

*Company Manager:* Edgar Runkle
*Press:* Leo Freedman, Abner D. Klipstein,
Betty Lee Hunt
*Stage Managers:* Edmund Baylies, Ross Hertz

* Closed April 3, 1954. (125 performances)

Felix Aylmer, Minoo Daver, Katharine Cornell, Roger Dann, Ben Astar
Top: Katharine Cornell

Gig Young, Betsy Von Furstenberg
Larry Blyden

Gig Young

Franchot Tone, Betsy Von Furstenberg

Henry Sharp, Anne Jackson

Franchot Tone, Betsy Von Furstenberg, Gig Young

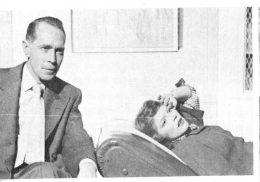

## OH, MEN! OH, WOMEN!

By Edward Chodorov; Directed by Edward Chodorov; Settings by William and Jean Eckart; Costumes Supervised by Paul du Pont.

### Cast

| | |
|---|---|
| Miss Tacher | Joan Gray |
| Alan Coles | Franchot Tone |
| Grant Cobbler | Larry Blyden |
| Myra Hagerman | Betsy Von Furstenberg |
| Dr. Krauss | Henry Sharp |
| Mildred Turner | Anne Jackson†[1] |
| Arthur Turner | Gig Young†[2] |
| Steward | Paul Andor |

A Comedy in three acts. The action takes place in Dr. Cole's Office, Myra's Apartment, and in a Suite on the S.S. Miramar.

*General Manager:* SAMUEL H. SCHWARTZ
*Press:* BEN WASHER
*Stage Managers:* JOSEPH SULLIVAN, AL WEST

† Replaced on May 29 by: 1. Barbara Baxley, 2. Tony Randall.

PHOTOS BY TALBOT

Franchot Tone, Betsy Von Furstenberg
Left Center: Franchot Tone, Anne Jackson

Lloyd Bridges, Joan Lorring, James Gregory

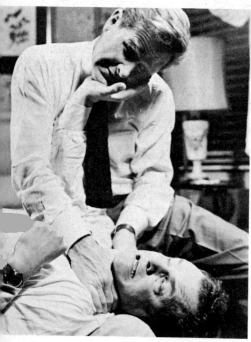

## DEAD PIGEON

By Lenard Kantor; Staged by Harald Bromley;
Setting by William and Jean Eckart.

### Cast

Lieutenant Monahan ..................... James Gregory
Sherry Parker ........................................ Joan Lorring
Detective Ernest Brady ................... Lloyd Bridges

A Drama in three acts and five scenes. The action
takes place in a room in a resort hotel near the
ocean in a suburb of a large American city, at the
present time.

*General Manager:* BEN A. BOYAR
*Press:* SAMUEL J. FRIEDMAN
*Stage Manager:* JAMES HAGERMAN
* Closed January 9, 1954. (15 performances)

James Gregory, Lloyd Bridges
**56** Right: Lloyd Bridges, Joan Lorring

Michael Sheehan, Eileen Ryan

**ROYALE THEATRE**
Opened Monday, December 28, 1953.*
Dorothy Natter presents:

## SING TILL TOMORROW

By Jean Lowenthal; Directed by Basil Langton;
Scenery and Lighting by Ralph Alswang.

### Cast

| | |
|---|---|
| Evie | Eileen Ryan |
| Hank | John Marley |
| A. J. Alexander | Raymond Bailey |
| Dan | Michael Sheehan |
| Fred Lyon | Edward Cary |
| Nick Di Giorgio | Ted Campbell |
| George Faulkner | Maurice Brenner |
| John Lowery | Arthur Oshlag |
| Sue Alexander | Virginia Bradley |
| Jake Levin | Wolfe Barzell |

The entire action of the play takes place within 24 hours. The time is the present.

*Company Manager:* JOE MOSS
*Press:* BERNARD SIMON, REUBEN RABINOVITCH
*Stage Managers:* MORGAN JAMES,
VIRGINIA BRADLEY, MAURICE BRENNER
* Closed January 2, 1954. ( 8 performances)

TALBOT PHOTOS

n Marley, Eileen Ryan, Michael Sheehan

Judith Anderson, Mildred Dunnock, Elizabeth Ross

Jean Stapleton, Mildred Dunnock

Logan Ramsey, Elizabeth Ross

Judith Anderson, Mildred Dunnock

## THE PLAYHOUSE

Opened Tuesday, December 29, 1953.*
Oliver Smith and The Playwrights' Company
present:

# IN THE SUMMER HOUSE

By Jane Bowles; Directed by Jose Quintero;
Music by Paul Bowles; Scenery by Oliver Smith;
Costumes by Noel Taylor; Lighting by Peggy Clark;
Associate Producer, Lyn Austin.

### Cast

| | |
|---|---|
| Gertrude Eastman-Cuevas | Judith Anderson |
| Molly | Elizabeth Ross |
| Mr. Solares | Don Mayo |
| Mrs. Lopez | Marita Reid |
| Frederica | Miriam Colon |
| Esperanza | Isabel Morel |
| Alta Gracia | Marjorie Eaton |
| Quintina | Phoebe MacKay |
| Lionel | Logan Ramsey |
| A Figure-Bearer | Paul Bertelsen |
| Another Figure-Bearer | George Spelvin |
| Vivian Constable | Muriel Berkson |
| Chauffeur | Daniel Morales |
| Mrs. Constable | Mildred Dunnock |
| Inez | Jean Stapleton |

A Drama in two acts and five scenes. The action
takes place at the present time in Gertrude Eastman-
Cuevas' Garden on the coast of Southern California,
on the beach, and in The Lobster Bowl.

*Company Manager:* GEORGE OSHRIN
*Press:* RICHARD MANEY, FRANK GOODMAN
*Stage Managers:* ELLIOTT MARTIN, PAUL BERTELSEN

* Closed February 13, 1954. (55 performances)

GRAPHIC HOUSE PHOTOS

Judith Anderson, Elizabeth Ross,
Mildred Dunnock

Una Merkel, Roger Stevens, Phyllis Love, Children, Burgess Meredith,
Martha Scott, Michael Wager, Glenn Anders

Glenn Anders, Thomas Chalmers, Martha Scott
Center (L-R) : Phyllis Love, Michael Wager;
Una Merkel, Martha Scott

Burgess Meredith

## CORONET THEATRE

Opened Wednesday, December 30, 1953.
Robert Whitehead and Roger L. Stevens present:

# THE REMARKABLE
# MR. PENNYPACKER

By Liam O'Brien; Directed by Alan Schneider;
Setting and Costumes by Ben Edwards. A Producers'
Theatre Production.

### Cast

| | |
|---|---|
| Laurie Pennypacker | Nancy Devlin |
| 1st Pupil | Betty Lou Keim |
| 2nd Pupil | Kathleen Gately |
| Ben Pennypacker | Billy Quinn |
| David Pennypacker | Lewis Scholle |
| Edward Pennypacker | Jackie Scholle |
| Elizabeth Pennypacker | Roni Dengel |
| Aunt Jane Pennypacker | Una Merkel |
| Wilbur Fifield | Michael Wager |
| Kate Pennypacker | Phyllis Love |
| Ma Pennypacker | Martha Scott |
| Henry Pennypacker | John Reese |
| Teddie Pennypacker | Joel Crothers |
| Grampa Pennypacker | Thomas Chalmers |
| Quinlan | William Lanteau |
| A Young Man | Roger Stevens |
| Dr. Fifield | Glenn Anders |
| Sheriff | Howard Fischer |
| Pa Pennypacker | Burgess Meredith |
| Policeman | James Holden |

A Comedy in three acts and four scenes. The
action takes place in 1890 in the Pennypacker home
in Wilmington, Delaware.

Company Manager: Oscar E. Olesen
Press: Barry Hyams, Martin Shwartz
Stage Managers: Frederic de Wilde,
     Howard Fischer

PHOTOS BY JOHN ERWIN

Una Merkel, Roger Stevens, Children, Burgess Meredith, Martha Scott
Top Right: Burgess Meredith, Martha Scott

61

Frank Silvera, William Windom, Edna Best,
Julie Harris, Mikhail Rasumny, Edna Preston,
Eli Wallach Top: Julie Harris, William
Windom

Eli Wallach, Julie Harris

LONGACRE THEATRE
Opened Wednesday, January 6, 1954.*
Robert L. Joseph and Jay Julien present:

## MADEMOISELLE COLOMBE

By Jean Anouilh; Adapted by Louis Kronen-
berger; Directed by Harold Clurman; Production
Designed by Boris Aronson; Costumes by Motley;
Production Associate, Shirley Bernstein.

### Cast

| | |
|---|---|
| Colombe | Julie Harris |
| Julien | Eli Wallach |
| Mme. Georges. | Edna Preston |
| Mme. Alexandra | Edna Best |
| Chiropodist | Edward Julien |
| Manicurist | Joanne Taylor |
| Hairdresser | Nehemiah Persoff |
| Gourette | Sam Jaffe |
| Edouard | William Windom |
| Deschamps | Frank Silvera |
| Poet-Mine-Own | Mikhail Rasumny |
| Gaulois | Harry Bannister |
| Dancers | Lee Phillips, Jeanne Jerrems |
| Stagehand | Gregory Robins |

A Drama in two acts, four scenes and an epilogue.
The action takes place in a Paris theatre around
1900.

*General Manager:* MAX ALLENTUCK
*Press:* KARL BERNSTEIN, HARVEY SABINSON,
ROBERT GANSHAW
*Stage Managers:* JAMES GELB,
EDWARD JULIEN, JOANNE TAYLOR

* Closed February 27, 1954 (61 performances)

GRAPHIC HOUSE PHOTOS

Julie Harris, Edna Best

Julie Harris, Eli Wallach

Robert Preston, Celeste Holm

**FORTY-EIGHTH STREET THEATRE**
Opened Thursday, January 7, 1954.*
Albert Selden and Morton Gottlieb present:

# HIS AND HERS

By Fay and Michael Kanin; Directed by Michael Gordon; Settings by Charles Elson; Costumes by Frank Thompson; Miss Holm's clothes by Oleg Cassini.

### Cast

| | |
|---|---|
| Jean | Helen Harrelson |
| Avis | Elizabeth Patterson |
| Maggie Palmer | Celeste Holm |
| The Super | Lou Gilbert |
| Lydia | Perry Wilson |
| George | Herbert Nelson |
| Dr. Carl Halek | George Voskovec |
| Mike Foster | Howard St. John |
| Clem Scott | Robert Preston |
| The Judge | Donald McKee |
| Her Lawyer | Heywood Hale Broun |
| His Lawyer | Harry Mehaffey |
| Bunty | Roy Monsell |

A Romantic Comedy in three acts and six scenes. The action takes place in Maggie Palmer's apartment in New York City, and in the Supreme Court of the State of New York in New York City.

*Press:* ARTHUR CANTOR
*Stage Manager:* JAMES AWE

* Closed March 13, 1954. (77 performances)

Celeste Holm, Elizabeth Patterson

Herbert Nelson, Celeste Holm, Perry W
Center: Heywood Hale Broun, Celeste F

ROYALE THEATRE
Opened Wednesday, January 13, 1954.*
John C. Wilson, Messrs. Shubert and S. S.
Krellberg present:

## THE STARCROSS STORY

By Diana Morgan; Staged by John C. Wilson;
Setting by Watson Barratt.

### Cast

| | |
|---|---|
| James Trenchard | Anthony Ross |
| Chloe Gwynn | Marta Linden |
| George Phillips | Christopher Plummer |
| Christine Starcross | Lynn Bailey |
| Ellen | Una O'Connor |
| Lady Starcross | Eva Le Gallienne |
| Alice Venning | Margaret Bannerman |
| Laura Shipman | Philippa Bevans |
| Jean Benson (Halliday) | Doris Patston |
| Anne Meredith | Mary Astor |

A Drama in three acts.

*Company Manager:* EDDIE WOODS
*Press:* BILL DOLL, ROBERT ULLMAN
*Stage Manager:* WARD BISHOP

* Closed January 13, 1954 (1 performance)

Eva Le Gallienne, Mary Astor

Eva Le Gallienne, Phillipa Bevans, Una
O'Connor, Margaret Bannerman, Doris Patston,
Lynn Bailey, Mary Astor

65

George Reich

Center: Colette Marchand in "Carmen"

Leslie Caron

**BROADWAY THEATRE**
Opened Tuesday, January 19, 1954. *
S. Hurok and the Messrs. Shubert present:

## LES BALLETS DE PARIS

with

| | |
|---|---|
| Roland Petit | Serge Perrault |
| Claire Sombert | Edmee Redoin |
| Monica Schellino | Monique Vence |
| Mosha Lazre | Colette Marchand |
| George Reich | Liliane Montevecchi |
| Andre Parizy | Claudine Barbini |
| Berti Ekkart | Fritz Hess |
| Violette Verdy | Jose Ferran |
| Francesco Varcasia | Nadine Metge |
| Jamie Bauer | Ivan Dragadze |

and guest artists

Leslie Caron    Nora Kovach    Istvan Rabovsky
Orchestra Directed by ...................... Jacques Bazire
Associate Conductor ............................ Arthur Lief

### Program

1. "Le Loup" (The Wolf). Ballet by Jean Anouilh and Georges Neveux; Music by Henri Dutilleux; Decor and Costumes by Carzou; Choreography by Roland Petit. Danced by Violette Verdy, Claire Sombert, Jose Ferran, George Reich, Serge Perrault.

2. "Deuil En 24 Heures" (The Beautiful Widow). Ballet by Roland Petit; Original music and arrangements of the "Valse Bleue" and "Mattchiche" by Thiriet; Decor and Costumes by Antoni Clave; Choreography by Roland Petit. Danced by Leslie Caron, Serge Perrault, Jose Ferran, Violette Verdy, George Reich.

3. "Grand Pas De Deux" from "Don Quixote." Music by Leon Minkus; Choreography by Guszev after Marius Petipa; Costumes by Karinska. Danced by Nora Kovach and Istvan Rabovsky.

4. "Carmen". Ballet by Roland Petit; Inspired by the Opera by Meilhac and Halevy; Music by Georges Bizet; Decor and Costumes by Antoni Clave; Choreography by Roland Petit. Danced by Colette Marchand, Roland Petit, Serge Perrault, Liliane Montevecchi, Berti Ekkart, Francesco Varcasia.

*Company Manager:* George Perper
*Press:* Martin Feinstein, Mary Ward
*Stage Manager:* Pierre Bezard

Violette Verdy, Roland Petit in "La Loup"

66

* Closed February 28, 1954. (48 performances.)

Lloyd Nolan, Henry Fonda, John Hodiak
in
"The Caine Mutiny Court Martial"

Robert Gist, Jim Bumgarner, Charles Nolte, Henry Fonda, John Hodiak.
Center: John Hodiak, Lloyd Nolan, Henry Fonda

Ainslie Pryor, Charles Nolte

John Hodiak, Ainslie Pryor

## THE CAINE MUTINY
## COURT MARTIAL

By Herman Wouk; Adapted from his Novel, "The Caine Mutiny"; Directed by Charles Laughton.

### Cast

| | |
|---|---|
| Stenographer | John Huffman |
| Orderly | Greg Roman |
| Lt. Greenwald | Henry Fonda† |
| Lt. Stephen Maryk | John Hodiak |
| Lt. Cdr. John Challee | Ainslie Pryor |
| Capt. Blakely | Russell Hicks |
| Lt. Cdr. Philip Francis Queeg | Lloyd Nolan |
| Lt. Thomas Keefer | Robert Gist |
| Signalman Junius Urban | Eddie Firestone |
| Lt. (jg) Willis Seward Keith | Charles Nolte |
| Capt. Randolph Southard | Paul Birch |
| Dr. Forrest Lundeen | Stephen Chase |
| Dr. Bird | Herbert Anderson |

Members of the Court: Larry Barton, Jim Bumgarner, T. H. Jourdan, Richard Farmer, Richard Norris, Pat Waltz

A Drama in two acts. The action takes place in the General Court Martial Room of the 12th Naval District, San Francisco; and in a private dining-room of the Hotel Fairmount, San Francisco, in February of 1945.

*Company Manager:* BERT LANG
*Press:* KARL BERNSTEIN, HARVEY SABINSON
JULIAN OLNEY
*Stage Managers:* LEN SMITH, JR., JOHN CRAWFORD
† Replaced on May 29 by Barry Sullivan.

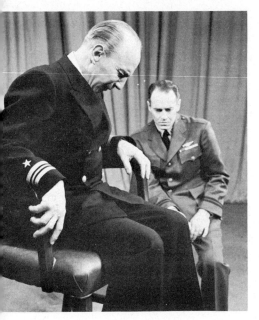

Lloyd Nolan, Henry Fonda

**GRAPHIC HOUSE PHOTOS**

Mary Boland

Kay Medford, Jack Warden

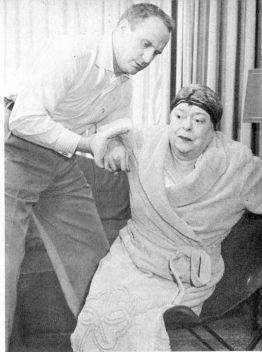

Jack Warden, Mary Boland

**LYCEUM THEATRE**
Opened Wednesday, February 3, 1954. *
Jerome Mayer and Irl Mowery present:

## LULLABY

By Don Appell; Directed by Jerome Mayer; Settings and Lighting by Ben Edwards.

### Cast

Bellhop ................................................. Al Ramsen
Johnny ............................................. Jack Warden
Eadie ................................................. Kay Medford
The Mother ....................................... Mary Boland

A Comedy in two acts and four scenes.

*Business Manager:* MICHAEL GOLDREYER
*Press:* JAMES D. PROCTOR
*Stage Managers:* ROBERT DOWNING, EARL ROWE

* Closed March 13, 1954 (45 performances)

PHOTOS BY TALBOT

Left Center: Jack Warden, Mary Boland, Kay Medford

Al Ramsen, Mary Boland, Kay Medford, Jack Warden.

71

Geraldine Page, Louis Jourdan

David J. Stewart, Louis Jourdan

James Dean,
Louis Jourdan

Louis Jourdan, Charles Ding

Geraldine Page, James Dean          Geraldine Page, Adelaide Klein

Geraldine Page

ROYALE THEATRE
   Opened Monday, February 8, 1954. *
Billy Rose presents:

## THE IMMORALIST

   By Ruth and Augustus Goetz; Adapted from book
by Andre Gide; Directed by Daniel Mann; Settings by George Jenkins; Costumes by Motley; Lighting by Abe Feder.

### Cast

Marcelline ...................................... Geraldine Page
Dr. Robert ................................. John Heldabrand
Bocage ........................................... Charles Dingle
Michel .............................................. Louis Jourdan
Bachir ............................................... James Dean†
Dr. Garrin .......................................... Paul Huber
Sidma .......................................... Adelaide Klein
Moktir ........................................ David J. Stewart
Dolit .................................................... Bill Gunn

   A Drama in three acts and eight scenes. The
action takes place in 1900 in Normandy, France,
and in Biskra, North Africa.

*Manager:* IRVING COOPER
*Press:* BILL DOLL, ROBERT ULLMAN
*Stage Managers:* LUCIA VICTOR, RICHARD GRAYSON,
VIVIAN MATALON

† Replaced by Phillip Pine
* Closed May 1, 1954 (104 performances) A
week of paid previews were presented from Feb.
1st to Feb. 7, 1954.

FRANK DONATO PHOTOS

Geraldine Page, Louis Jourdan
in
"The Immoralist"

FRANK DONATO PHOTO

Ina Claire
in
"The Confidential Clerk"

75

Ina Claire, Newton Blick, Douglas Watson, Joan Greenwood, Claude Rains
Top (Left): Newton Blick, Ina Claire, Claude Rains
(Right) Richard Newton, Joan Greenwood, Ina Claire, Claude Rains

Douglas Watson, Joan Greenwood

Ina Claire, Claude Rains

## MOROSCO THEATRE

Opened Thursday, February 11, 1954.*

Henry Sherek and The Producers' Theatre present:

## THE CONFIDENTIAL CLERK

By T. S. Eliot; Directed by E. Martin Browne; Settings, Costumes and Lighting by Paul Morrison.

### Cast

| | |
|---|---|
| Sir Claude Mulhammer | Claude Rains |
| Eggerson | Newton Blick |
| Colby Simpkins | Douglas Watson |
| B. Kaghan | Richard Newton |
| Lucasta Angel | Joan Greenwood |
| Lady Elizabeth Mulhammer | Ina Claire |
| Mrs. Guzzard | Aline MacMahon |

A Comedy in three acts. The action takes place in the study of Sir Claude's West End house and in a flat in the mews, in London.

*Company Manager:* Thomas Bodkin
*Press:* Barry Hyams, Martin Shwartz
*Stage Managers:* Del Hughes, Stuart Vaughan
* Closed May 22, 1954. (116 performances)

PHOTOS BY JOHN ERWIN

Claude Rains
Center: Aline Mac Mahon,
Douglas Watson

Joan Greenwood
Center: Ina Claire

Joan Tetzel, Phillip Pruneau, Jane Buchanan, Charles Cooper, Lothar Rewalt

THE PLAYHOUSE
Opened Wednesday, February 17, 1954. *
The Playwrights' Company presents:

## THE WINNER

By Elmer Rice; Staged by Elmer Rice; Settings by Lester Polakov.

### Cast

| | |
|---|---|
| Eva Harold | Joan Tetzel |
| Martin Carew | Tom Helmore |
| David Browning | Whitfield Connor |
| Newscaster | P. Jay Sidney |
| Arnold Mahler | Lothar Rewalt |
| Irma Mahler | Jane Buchanan |
| Haggerty | Phillip Pruneau |
| Dr. Clinton Ward | Charles Cooper |
| Miss Dodd | Lily Bretano |
| Stenographer | David Balfour |
| Judge Samuel Addison | Frederick O'Neal |
| Hilde Kranzbeck | Vilma Kurer |

A Comedy in two acts and four scenes. The action takes place in Eva's New York Apartment and in Judge Addison's chambers in Bridgeport, Connecticut.

Company Manager: GEORGE OSHRIN
Press: JOHN L. TOOHEY, WALTER ALFORD, WILLIAM FIELDS
Stage Managers: DAVID CLIVE, PHILLIP PRUNEAU
* Closed March 13, 1954. (30 performances)

Joan Tetzel, Whitfield Connor.
Center: Joan Tetzel, Whitfield Connor, Tom Helmore

Frederick O'Neal
Center: David Balfour, Vilma Kurer, Tom Helmore

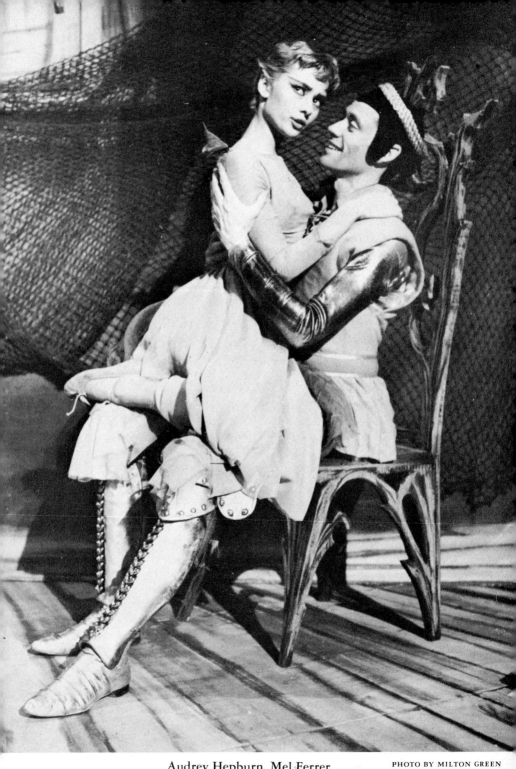

**Audrey Hepburn, Mel Ferrer**
in
"Ondine"

Audrey Hepburn, William Podmore. Top: Alan Hewitt, Audrey Hepburn, Peter Brandon

Mel Ferrer, Audrey Hepburn. Top: Edith King, John Alexander, Mel Ferrer

## FORTY-SIXTH STREET THEATRE
Opened Thursday, February 18, 1954.
The Playwrights' Company presents:

# ONDINE

By Jean Giraudoux; Adapted by Maurice Valency; Directed by Alfred Lunt; Settings by Peter Larkin; Costumes by Richard Whorf; Lighting by Jean Rosenthal; Music by Virgil Thomson; Miss Hepburn's gowns by Valentina.

### Cast

| | |
|---|---|
| Auguste | John Alexander |
| Eugenie | Edith King |
| Ritter Hans | Mel Ferrer |
| Ondine | Audrey Hepburn |
| The Ondines: Dran Seitz, Tani Seitz, Sonia Torgeson | |
| The Old One | Robert Middleton |
| The Lord Chamberlain | Alan Hewitt |
| Superintendent of the Theatre | Lloyd Gough |
| Trainer of Seals | James Lanphier |
| Bertha | Marian Seldes |
| Bertram | Peter Brandon |
| Violante | Anne Meacham |
| Angelique | Gaye Jordan |
| Venus | Jan Sherwood |
| Matho | Barry O'Hara |
| Salammbo | Lily Paget |
| A Lord | William Le Massena |
| A Lady | Stacy Graham |
| The Illusionist | Robert Middleton |
| The King | William Podmore |
| A Servant | James Lanphier |
| 1st Fisherman | Lloyd Gough |
| 2nd Fisherman | Robert Middleton |
| 1st Judge | Alan Hewitt |
| 2nd Judge | William Le Massena |
| The Executioner | Robert Crawley |
| Kitchen Maid | Stacy Graham |

A Romance in three acts. The action takes place during the Middle Ages in a fisherman's cottage, a hall in the King's palace and in a courtyard in the Castle of the Wittenstein.

*Company Manager:* LAWRENCE FARRELL
*Press:* WILLIAM FIELDS, WALTER ALFORD
*Stage Managers:* WILLIAM CHAMBERS, ROBERT CRAWLEY

PHOTOS BY MILTON GREEN

Audrey Hepburn. Top: Peter Brandon, Audrey Hepburn. Top left: Marian Seldes, Mel Ferrer

81

## NEW CENTURY THEATRE
Opened Monday, February 22, 1954.*
S. Hurok with the cooperation of H.I.H.
Prince Takamatsu and the Japanese Ministry of
Foreign Affairs presents:

## THE AZUMA KABUKI DANCERS AND MUSICIANS

Choreographer, Masaya Fujima; Decor by Kisaku Ito; Costumes by Seison Maeda and Kiyokata Kaburagi; English Narrator, Michi Okamoto.

Dancers: Kikunojo Onoe, Tokuho Azuma, Masaya Fujima, Yukiko Azuma, Haruyo Azuma, Harukiyo Azuma, Isami Hanayagi, Kitsusaburo Bando, Wakana Hanayagi, Kikusume Onoe.

Musicians: Katsutoji Kineya, Rosen Tosha, Katsumaru Kineya, Shozaburo Matsushima, Katsuyoshiro Kineya, Tomisaburo Wakayama, Umetaro Kiyomoto, Koshen Tosha, Rosshu Tosha, Tatsuichiro Mochizuki.

### Program For First Two Weeks
Kojo (Greetings), Sambaso (Offering to the Gods), Shakkyo (Lion Dance), Dojoji (Dancing Girl at the Dojoji Temple), Minzoku Buyo (Folk Dances), Nagare (Water Images), Tsuchigumo (Dance of the Spider), Ninin-Wankyu (Memories), O-Matsuribayashi (Festival Music by the Orchestra), O-Matsuri No Hi (Festival Day).

### Program For Second Two Weeks
(March 9-21)
Cha-No-Yu (Tea Ceremony), Hashi-Benkei (Sword Dance), Ocho (Ancient Court Days), Fukitori-Tsuma (The Would-Be Flute Player Seeks a Wife), Nagare (Water Images), Tsuchigumo (Dance of The Spider), Ninin-Wankyu (Memories), Koten Kabuki (Kabuki Sketches).

*Company Manager:* EDWARD HAAS
*Press:* MARTIN FEINSTEIN
*Stage Manager:* DALE WASSERMAN

* Closed March 21, 1954. (32 performances)

Kikunojo Onoe (also above). Top: Masa
Fujima in "Tsuchigumo"
Top left: Azuma IV

**LONGACRE THEATRE**   GRAPHIC HOUSE PHOTOS
Opened Thursday, March 4, 1954. *
The Theatre Guild and John C. Wilson present:

# THE BURNING GLASS

By Charles Morgan; Staged by Luther Kennett;
Setting by Oliver Smith; Costumes by Noel Taylor;
Lighting by John Davis; Miss Riva's Dresses by
Valentina.

### Cast

| | |
|---|---|
| Christopher Terriford | Scott Forbes |
| Lady Terriford | Isobel Elsom |
| Mary Terriford | Maria Riva |
| Tony Lack | Walter Matthau |
| Gerry Hardlip | William Roerick |
| Lord Henry Strait | Ralph Clanton |
| Montagu Winthrop | Cedric Hardwicke |
| Inspector Wigg | Basil Howes |

A Melodrama in three acts and four scenes. The
action takes place in the near future in the South
Room at Terriford House, sixty miles from London.

*Company Manager:* JAMES MILLER
*Press:* NAT AND IRVIN DORFMAN
*Stage Managers:* KARL NIELSEN, RHODERICK WALKER

\* Closed March 27, 1954 (28 performances)

Cedric Hardwicke, Maria Riva, Walter
Matthau. Left: Maria Riva, Isobel Elsom,
Scott Forbes. Top: Maria Riva, Cedric Hardwicke, Scott Forbes, Ralph Clanton,
Isobel Elsom

Jeanmaire (also above)

MARK HELLINGER THEATRE
Opened Friday, March 5, 1954.
Shepard Traube (in association with Anthony
B. Farrell) presents:

# THE GIRL IN PINK TIGHTS

Book by Jerome Chodorov and Joseph Fields;
Music by Sigmund Romberg; Lyrics by Leo Robin;
Music Developed and Orchestrated by Don Walker;
Entire Production Directed by Shepard Traube;
Scenery and Lighting by Eldon Elder; Costumes by
Miles White; Musical Direction by Sylvan Levin;
Ballet Music Arranged by Trude Rittman; Dances
and Musical Numbers Staged by Agnes De Mille.

## Cast

| | |
|---|---|
| Boris | Joshua Shelley |
| Volodya Kuzentsov | Alexandre Kalioujny |
| Lisette Gervais | Jeanmaire |
| Maestro Gallo | Charles Goldner |
| Lotta Leslie | Brenda Lewis |
| Clyde Hallam | David Atkinson |
| Eddington | David Aiken |
| Hattie Hopkins | Dania Krupska |
| Van Beuren | Robert Smith |
| British Tars | Tom Rieder, John Taliaferro |
| Policeman | John Stamford |
| Newspaper Boy | Maurice Hines |
| Shoe Shine Boy | Gregory Hines |
| Mike | Kalem Kermoyan |
| Bruce | John Stamford |
| Nellie | Lydia Fredericks |
| Hollister | Ray Mason |
| Simone | Katia Geleznova |
| Mimi | Eva Rubinstein |
| Lucette | Lynne Marcus |
| Odette | Nancy King |
| Gisele | Lila Popper |
| Paulette | Mickey Gunnersen |
| Fire Chiefs | Ted Thurston, John Taliaferro |
| Jenny | Jenny Workman |
| Blanchette | Beryl Towbin |
| Emile | Ted Thurston |
| Sommelier | John Taliaferro |
| Gypsy Violinist | Douglas Rideout |

**Singers:** Lydia Fredericks, Jane House, Deedy Irwin,
Peggy Kinard, Marni Nixon, Michelle Reiner,
Joanne Spiller, Beverly Weston, David Aiken, Herbert Banke, Robert Driscoll, Kalem Kermoyan, Ray
Mason, Stas Pajenski, Douglas Rideout, Tom Rieder,
James Schlader, John Stamford, John Taliaferro,
Ted Thurston.

**Dancers:** Meredith Baylis, Joan Bowman, Katia
Geleznova, Mickey Gunnerson, Mary Haywood,
Rhoda Kerns, Nancy King, Lynne Marcus, Julie
Marlowe, Ellen Matthews, Lila Popper, Eva Rubinstein, Dorothy Scott, Beverly Simms, Beryl Towbin,
Diana Turner, Jenny Workman, Harry Asmus,
Louis Kosman, Paul Olson, Edward Stinnett, William Weslow.

**Understudies:** Lisette, Dania Krupska; Gallo, Ted
Thurston; Lotta, Michelle Reiner; Clyde, Ray
Mason; Volodya, William Weslow; Van Beuren
and Mike, Tom Rieder; Hattie, Marni Nixon; Boris,
Perry Bruskin; Eddington, Douglas Rideout; Blanchette, Rhoda Kerns; Hollister, James Schlader; Emile,
John Stamford; Violinist, Robert Driscoll; Policeman, Herbert Banke.

**Musical Numbers:** "Ballet Class," "That Naughty
Show From Gay Paree," "Lost In Loveliness,"
"I Promised Their Mothers," "Up In The Elevated
Railway," "In Paris and In Love," "You've Got
To Be A Little Crazy," "When I Am Free To
Love," "Pas de Deux," "Out Of The Way," "Roll
Out The Hose, Boys," "My Heart Won't Say
Goodbye," "We're All In The Same Boat," "Bachanale," "Love Is The Funniest Thing," "The
Cardinal's Guard Are We," "Grand Imperial
Ballet."

A Musical Extravaganza in two acts and seventeen scenes. The action takes place immediately
following the Civil War in the theatrical district
of New York.

*General Manager:* J. H. DEL BONDIO
*Press:* GEORGE ROSS, MADELIN BLITZSTEIN
*Stage Managers:* BILL ROSS, BRUCE SAVAN,
PERRY BRUSKIN

PHOTOS BY TALBOT

Charles Goldner, Brenda Lewis. Center: Brenda Lewis, Charles Goldner, Jeanmaire, David Atkinson

Jeanmaire, Alexandre Kalioujny

David Atkinson, Jeanmaire

Patchwork Peggy, Jackie Cooper, Cloris Leachman, Rex Thompson

Rex Thompson, Donald Cook,
Darryl Richard

Donald Cook, Cloris Leachman,
William Sharon

Donald Cook, Jackie Cooper, Patchwork Peggy, Rex Thompson, David Lewis,
Cloris Leachman, Hilda Haynes

## LYCEUM THEATRE
Opened Thursday, April 1, 1954.
Elaine Perry presents:

# KING OF HEARTS

By Jean Kerr and Eleanor Brooke; Directed by
Walter F. Kerr; Designed and Lighted by Frederick
Fox.

### Cast

| | |
|---|---|
| Dunreath Henry | Cloris Leachman |
| Larry Larkin | Donald Cook |
| Jeniella | Hilda Haynes |
| Mike | John Drew Devereaux |
| Francis X. Dignan | Jackie Cooper |
| Joe Wickes | David Lewis |
| Norman Taylor | Rex Thompson |
| Mr. Hobart | Carl Low |
| Billy | Darryl Richard |
| Happy | Patchwork Peggy |
| Policeman | William Sharon |

A Comedy in three acts. The action takes place
in Larry Larkin's studio in New York City at the
present time.

Company Manager: GEORGE BANYAI
Press: BILL DOLL, ROBERT ULLMAN
Stage Managers: BEN KRANZ, JOHN DREW DEVEREAUX
PHOTOS BY TALBOT

Donald Cook, Cloris Leachman, Jackie
Cooper. Center: Donald Cook, Jackie Cooper

Betty Miller, Leo Penn, Emilie Stevens

Felice Orlandi, Betty Miller

Leo Penn, Betty Miller

Felice Orlandi, Betty Miller

Betty Miller, Leo Penn, Thomas Barbour, Emilie Stevens, Carl Harms

FORTY-EIGHTH STREET THEATRE
Opened Thursday, April 1, 1954. *
Circle In The Square presents:

## THE GIRL ON THE VIA FLAMINIA

By Alfred Hayes; Setting and Costumes Designed by Keith Cuerden; Lighting by Noah Kalkut; Directed by Jose Quintero.

### Cast

| | |
|---|---|
| English Sergeant | James Greene |
| American G. I. | Andy Milligan |
| Adele Pulcini | Lola D'Annunzio |
| Mimi | Emilie Stevens |
| Nina | Sylvia Daneel |
| Lisa | Betty Miller |
| Ugo Pulcini | Carl Harms |
| Robert | Leo Penn |
| Antonio | Felice Orlandi |
| Bologinini | Louis Guss |
| Carabiniere | Jason Wingreen |

A Drama in three acts and four scenes. The action takes place in the dining-room and one bedroom in the apartment of the Pulcini family in newly liberated Rome, 1944.

Press: DAVID LIPSKY, JAY RUSSELL
Stage Managers: RICHARD SPAHN, LAURA MALIN

* Opened Tuesday, Feb. 9, 1954, at the Circle In The Square where it played until moved to the 48th Street Theatre. Closed May 29, 1954, after 111 performances.

IMPACT PHOTOS

Leo Penn

Macdonald Carey, Jean Carson, Andrew Duggan, Kitty Carlisle

**BROADHURST THEATRE**
Opened Wednesday, April 7, 1954.
Joseph M. Hyman and Bernard Hart present:

# ANNIVERSARY WALTZ

By Jerome Chodorov and Joseph Fields; Directed by Moss Hart; Setting and Lighting by Frederick Fox; Costumes by Robert Macintosh.

### Cast

| | |
|---|---|
| Millie | Pauline Myers |
| Okkie Walters | Warren Berlinger |
| Alice Walters | Kitty Carlisle |
| Debbie Walters | Mary Lee Dearring |
| Bud Walters | Macdonald Carey |
| Chris Steelman | Andrew Duggan |
| Janice Revere | Jean Carson |
| Harry | Don Grusso |
| Sam | Donald Hylan |
| Mr. Gans | Howard Smith |
| Mrs. Gans | Phyllis Povah |
| Handyman | Terry Little |

A Comedy in three acts and six scenes. The action takes place in the living-room of the Walters' apartment in New York City at the present time.

*General Manager:* AL GOLDIN
*Press:* NAT AND IRVIN DORFMAN

*Stage Managers:* DONALD HERSHEY, TERRY LITTLE

**GRAPHIC HOUSE PHOTOS**

Howard Smith, Phyllis Povah

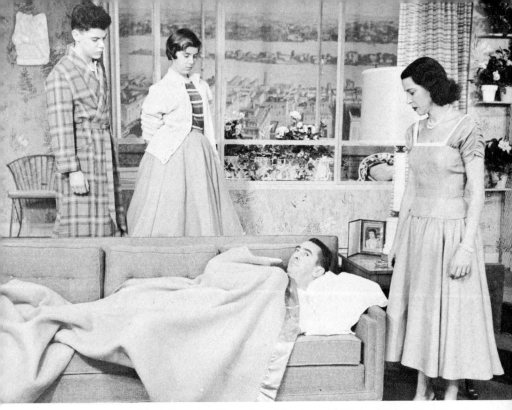

Warren Berlinger, Mary Lee Dearring, Macdonald Carey, Kitty Carlisle

Mary Lee Dearring, Macdonald
Carey, Warren Berlinger

Andrew Duggan,
Jean Carson

Kitty Carlisle, Macdonald Carey,

MAJESTIC THEATRE
Opened Thursday, April 8, 1954.
Robert Fryer and Lawrence Carr present:

# BY THE BEAUTIFUL SEA

Book by Herbert and Dorothy Fields; Music by Arthur Schwartz; Lyrics by Dorothy Fields; Setting and Lighting by Jo Mielziner; Costumes by Irene Sharaff; Musical Direction by Jay Blackton; Orchestrations by Robert Russell Bennett; Production Associate, Simon P. Herman; Choreography by Helen Tamiris; Directed by Marshall Jamison.

## Cast

Quartet: John Dennis, Reid Shelton, Ray Hyson, Larry Laurence

| | |
|---|---|
| Acrobats | Ray Kirchner, Rex Cooper |
| Cora Belmont | Mary Harmon |
| Molly Belmont | Cindy Robbins |
| Lillian Belmont | Gloria Smith |
| Ruby Monk | Mae Barnes |
| Mrs. Koch | Edith True Case |
| Carl Gibson | Cameron Prud'Homme |
| Lottie Gibson | Shirley Booth |
| Half-Note | Robert Jennings |
| Diabolo | Thomas Gleason |
| Baby Betsy Busch | Carol Leigh |
| Mickey Powers | Richard France |
| Dennis Emery | Wilbur Evans |
| Flora Busch | Anne Francine |
| Willie Slater | Warde Donovan |
| Lenny | Larry Howard |
| Sidney | Eddie Roll |
| Mr. Curtis | Paul Reed |
| Burt Mayer | Larry Laurence |
| Viola | Gaby Monet |

**Dancers:** Cathryn Damon, Dorothy Donau, Lillian Donau, Pat Ferrier, Sigyn, Mona Tritsch, Rex Cooper, Larry Howard, Bob Haddad, Ray Kirchner, Victor Reilly, Eddie Roll, Arthur Partington,

**Singers:** Suzanne Easter, Lola Fisher, Colleen O'Connor, Pat Roe, Jean Sincere, Libi Staiger, John Dennis, Warde Donovan, Thomas Gleason, Ray Hyson, Franklin Kennedy, Larry Laurence, George Lenz, Reid Shelton.

**Understudies:** Lottie, Jean Sincere; Dennis, Warde Donovan; Betsy, Cindy Robbins; Carl, Paul Reed; Ruby, Miriam Burton; Mickey, Larry Howard; Half-Note, Vincent McLeod; Principal Dancer, Lillian Donau; Mr. Curtis, Thomas Gleason; Mrs. Koch, Lola Fisher; Flora, Libi Staiger.

**Musical Numbers:** "Mona From Arizona," "The Sea Song," "Old Enough To Love," "Coney Island Boat," "Alone Too Long," "Happy Habit," "Good Time Charlie," "I'd Rather Wake Up By Myself," "Hooray For George The Third," "Hang Up," "More Love Than Your Love," "Vaudeville," "Lottie Gibson Specialty," "Throw The Anchor Away," Finale.

A Musical in two acts and fifteen scenes. The action takes place in Coney Island during the early 1900's.

*General Manager:* Jack Schlissel
*Press:* Marian Byram, Phyllis Perlman, David Powers
*Stage Managers:* Samuel Liff, Len Bedsow, Charles Millang

Anne Francine, Wilbur Evans, Carol Leigh.
Center: Shirley Booth

Wilbur Evans

Robert Jennings, Shirley Booth

Mae Barnes

Cameron Prud 'Homme, Shirley Booth,
Mae Barnes

Richard France, Carol Leigh

**Shirley Booth, Wilbur Evans**
in
"By the Beautiful Sea"

Lee Bowman, Robert Preston, Charles Taylor, Uta Hagen

## BOOTH THEATRE

Opened Friday, April 9, 1954.*

Alexander H. Cohen and Ralph Alswang present:

## THE MAGIC AND THE LOSS

By Julian Funt; Directed by Michael Gordon; Setting by Ralph Alswang; Clothes by Jocelyn; Production Assistant, Mary Ellen Hecht.

### Cast

| | |
|---|---|
| Nicki Wilson | Charles Taylor |
| Al Massio | Danny Dennis |
| Grace Wilson | Uta Hagen |
| Anita Harmon | Edith Meiser† |
| Larry Graves | Lee Bowman |
| George Wilson | Robert Preston |

A Drama in three acts and five scenes. The action takes place in the living-room of Grace Wilson's apartment near Washington Square, New York City.

*General Manager:* PHILIP ADLER
*Press:* BEN WASHER, FRANK GOODMAN
*Stage Manager:* JOHN BARRY RYAN

† Replaced by Mary Finney.
* Closed May 1, 1954. (27 performances)

GRAPHIC HOUSE PHOTOS

Robert Preston, Edith Meiser, Uta Hagen

Bibi Osterwald, Portia Nelson, Priscilla Gillette, Kaye Ballard

ALVIN THEATRE
Opened Tuesday, April 20, 1954. *
Alfred De Liagre, Jr. and Roger L. Stevens
in association with T. Edward Hambleton and
Norris Houghton present:

# THE GOLDEN APPLE

Written by John Latouche; Music by Jerome
Moross; Choreography and Musical Numbers
Staged by Hanya Holm; Directed by Norman
Lloyd; Settings by William and Jean Eckart; Light-
ing by Klaus Holm; Costumes by Alvin Colt;
Musical Director, Hugh Ross; Orchestral Arrange-
ments by Jerome Moross and Hershey Kaye.

## Cast

| | |
|---|---|
| Helen | Kaye Ballard |
| Lovey Mars | Bibi Osterwald |
| Mrs. Juniper | Shannon Bolin |
| Miss Minerva Oliver | Portia Nelson |
| Mother Hare | Martha Larrimore |
| Penelope | Priscilla Gillette |
| Menelaus | Dean Michener |

The Heroes:

| | |
|---|---|
| Captain Mars | Frank Seabolt |
| Ajax | Marten Sameth |
| Agamemnon | Crandall Diehl |
| Nestor | Maurice Edwards |
| Bluey | Murray Gitlin |
| Thirsty | Don Redlich |
| Silas | Peter De Mayo |
| Homer | Barton Mumaw |
| Diomede | Robert Flavelle |
| Achilles | Julian Patrick |
| Patroclus | Martin Keane |
| Doc MacCahan | Gary Gordon |
| Ulysses | Stephen Douglass |
| Theron | David Hooks |
| Mayor Juniper | Jerry Stiller |
| Paris | Jonathan Lucas |
| Hector Charybdis | Jack Whiting |

**Local Girls:** Sara Bettis, Dorothy Etheridge, Nelle
Fisher, Dee Harless, Janet Hayes, Lois McCauley,
Ann Needham, Joli Roberts, Jere Stevens, Tao
Strong, Helen Ahola.

**Local Boys:** Santo Anselmo, Bob Gay, Ed Grace,
Bill Nuss, Charles Post, Arthur Schoep.

**Musical Numbers:** "Nothing Ever Happens In
Angel's Roost," "Mother Hare's Seance," "My Love
Is On The Way," "The Heroes Come Home," "It
Was A Glad Adventure," "Come Along, Boys,"
"It's The Going Home Together," "Mother Hare's
Prophecy," "Helen Is Always Willing," "The
Church Social," "Introducin' Mr. Paris," "The
Judgment of Paris," "Lazy Afternoon," "The De-
parture For Rhododendron," "My Picture In The
Papers," "The Taking of Rhododendron," "Hector's
Song," "Windflowers," "Store-Bought Suit,"
"Calypso," "Scylla and Charybdis," "Goona-
Goona," "Doomed, Doomed, Doomed," "Circe,
Circe," "Ulysses' Soliloquy," "The Sewing Bee,"
"The Tirade," Finale.

**Understudies:** Kaye Ballard, Bibi Osterwald and
Shannon Bolin, Geraldine Viti; Priscilla Gillette,
Janet Hayes; Stephen Douglass, Julian Patrick; Jack
Whiting, Crandall Diehl; Jonathan Lucas, Barton
Mumaw; Portia Nelson, Helen Ahola; Martha
Larrimore, Sara Bettis; Dean Michener, Arthur
Schoen; Ann Needham, Tao Strong.

A Musical in two acts and ten scenes. The entire action takes place in the State of Washington
between 1900 and 1910 in the township of Angel's
Roost on the edge of Mt. Olympus and in the sea-
port of Rhododendron.

*General Manager:* C. EDWIN KNILL
*Press:* SAMUEL J. FRIEDMAN
*Stage Managers:* THELMA CHANDLER,
DAN BRENNAN, DAVID HOOKS

* Opened at the Phoenix Theatre, Thursday,
March 11, 1954, where it played until it moved
to the Alvin.

PHOTOS BY VANDAMM

Jonathan Lucas, Kaye Ballard.    Stephen Douglass  Jack Whiting,
Jonathan Lucas

Top: Jonathan Lucas, Kaye Ballard, Priscilla Gillette,
Stephen Douglass

**BROADWAY THEATRE**
Opened Monday, April 26, 1954. *
Charles E. Green Consolidated Concerts Corp.
presents:

## JOSE GRECO
## AND HIS COMPANY OF
## SPANISH DANCERS

with

| | |
|---|---|
| Nila Amparo | Lola deRonda |
| Luis Olivares    Juanele Maya | Salome de Cordoba |
| Tina Velez      Malena Vargas | Julio Torres |
| Angel Soler    Antonio Jimenez | Jose Mancilla |
| Margarita Zurita    Ricardo Blasco | Miguel Garcia |
| (Guitarist) | (Guitarist) |

Chinin De Triana (Flamenco Singer)
Pablo Miquel (Pianist)

### Program

Conceived, Choreographed and Directed by Jose Greco.

1. Juerga, 2. Rumores De La Caleta, 3. Tientos Y Variaciones Por Cana, 4. Malaguena, 5. Danza Extremena, 6. Cadiz Flamenca, 7. Jota De Alcaniz, 8. Mujeres De Aragon, 9. Recuerdo A Granada and La Petenera, 10. Bulerias De Burla, 11. Bolero, 12. Old Madrid, 13. Guitar Variations, 14. La Venta, 15. Danza Castellana, 16. Seguiriyas Gitanas, 17. Cordoba, 18. El Cortijo, 19. Rincon Flamenco.

*Company Manager:* BILL WILSON
*Press:* ISADORA BENNETT
*Stage Manager:* WILLIAM MARLATT

* Closed May 8, 1954, after a limited engagement of 16 performances.

**NATIONAL THEATRE**
Opened Wednesday, November 11, 1953.
(Moved to Royale, May 17, 1954)
The Playwrights' Company presents:

Nila Amparo, Jose Greco.
Top: Jose Greco

Center: Jose Greco and Company

98

Janis Paige

John Raitt

in
"The Pajama Game"

Buzz Miller, Carol Haney, Peter Gennaro

**ST. JAMES THEATRE**
Opened Thursday, May 13, 1954.
Frederick Brisson, Robert E. Griffith and Harold S. Prince present:

## THE PAJAMA GAME

Book by George Abbott and Richard Bissell; Based on Novel "7½ Cents" by Richard Bissell; Music and Lyrics by Richard Adler and Jerry Ross; Scenery and Costumes by Lemuel Ayers; Choreography by Bob Fosse; Musical Director, Hal Hastings; Orchestrations by Don Walker; Dance Music Arrangements by Roger Adams; Production Directed by George Abbott and Jerome Robbins.

### Cast

| | |
|---|---|
| Hines | Eddie Foy, Jr. |
| Prez | Stanley Prager |
| Joe | Ralph Farnworth |
| Hasler | Ralph Dunn |
| Gladys | Carol Haney |
| Sid Sorokin | John Raitt |
| Mabel | Reta Shaw |
| 1st Helper | Jack Drummond |
| 2nd Helper | Buzz Miller |
| Charlie | Ralph Chambers |
| Babe Williams | Janis Paige |
| Mae | Thelma Pelish |
| Brenda | Marion Colby |
| Poopsie | Rae Allen |
| Salesman | Jack Waldron |
| Eddie | Jim Hutchison |
| Pop | William David |
| Worker | Peter Gennaro |

**Dancers:** Carmen Alvarez, Marilyn Gennaro, Lida Koehring, Shirley MacLaine, Marsha Reynolds, Ann Wallace, Robert Evans, Eric Kristen, Jim Hutchison, Dale Moreda, Augustin Rodriguez, Ben Vargas.
**Singers:** Rae Allen, Sara Dillon, Mara Landi, Virginia Martin, Mary Roche, Mary Stanton, Rudy Adamo, Bob Dixon, Jack Drummond, Ralph Farnsworth, John Ford, Gordon Woodburn.
**Musical Numbers:** "The Pajama Game," "Racing With The Clock," "A New Town Is A Blue Town," "I'm Not At All In Love," "I'll Never Be Jealous Again," "Hey There," "Her Is," "Sleep-Tite," "Once A Year Day," "Small Talk," "There Once Was A Man," "Steam Heat," "The World Around Us," "Think Of The Time I Save," "Hernando's Hideaway," "Jealousy Ballet," "7½ Cents," Finale.

A Musical Comedy in two acts. The action takes place at the present time in a small town in the Middle West.

*Company Manager:* RICHARD HORNER
*Press:* REUBEN RABINOVITCH
*Stage Manager:* JEAN BARRERE

Janis Paige, John Raitt, Carol Haney
PHOTOS BY TALBOT

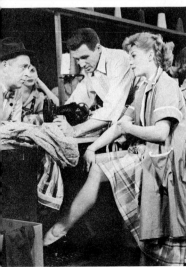

Eddie Foy, Jr., John Raitt,       Eddie Foy, Jr.       Eddie Foy, Jr., Reta Shaw
Janis Paige.       Center: Carol Haney
Top: John Raitt, Janis Paige, Marion Colby, Thelma Pelish, Buzz Miller.

Rodgers and Hammerstein present:

## OKLAHOMA!*

Based on "Green Grow The Lilacs" by Lynn Riggs; Music by Richard Rodgers; Book and Lyrics by Oscar Hammerstein 2nd; Directed by Rouben Mamoulian; Dances by Agnes de Mille; Settings by Lemuel Ayers; Costumes by Miles White; Staged by Jerome Whyte; Orchestrations by Robert Russell Bennett; Orchestra Directed by Peter Laurini; Dances Reproduced by Betty Gour. Opened Monday, Aug. 31, 1953, and closed Oct. 3, 1953, after 40 performances.

### Cast

| | |
|---|---|
| Aunt Eller | Mary Marlo |
| Curly | Ridge Bond |
| Laurey | Florence Henderson |
| Cord Elam | Charles Hart |
| Fred | Charles Scott |
| Slim | Charles Rule |
| Will Parker | Harris Hawkins |
| Jud Fry | Alfred Cibelli, Jr. |
| Ado Annie Carnes | Barbara Cook |
| Ali Hakim | David Le Grant |
| Gertie Cummings | Judy Rawlings |
| Ellen | Maggi Nelson |
| Kate | Barbara Reisman |
| Silvie | Patti Parsons |
| Armina | Lynne Broadbent |
| Aggie | Cathy Conklin |
| Andrew Carnes | Owen Martin |
| Chalmers | George Lawrence |
| Mike | Bob Lord |

Singers: Lenore Arnold, Lois Barrodin, Marylin Hardy, Frances Irby, Heidi Palmer, Barbara Reisman, Jeanne Shea, William Ambler, Dino Dante, James Fox, Christopher Golden, Bob Lord, Charles Rule, Charles Scott.

Dancers: Lynne Broadbent, Bette Burton, Cathy Conklin, Betty Koerber, Gayle Parmelee, Patti Parsons, Cynthia Price, Georganne Shaw, Louellen Sibley, Marguerite Stewart, Payne Converse, Nick Dana, Jack Ketcham, Ronnie Landry, John Pero, Jr., Tom Pickler, Joe Ribeau.

Company Manager: HARRY SHAPIRO
Press: MICHAEL MOK, GEORGE A. FLORIDA, PEGGY PHILLIPS
Stage Managers: DAVID SIDNEY WEINSTEIN, PHILIP JOHNSON, CHARLES SCOTT

David Le Grant, Barbara Cook

PHOTOS BY VANDAMM

The New York City Theatre Company presents:

# CYRANO DE BERGERAC*

The Brian Hooker version of the Edmond Rostand play; Jean Dalrymple in charge of production; Directed by José Ferrer; Assistant Director, Jess Kimmel; Settings by Richard Whorf; Costumes by Emeline Roche; Technical Scenic Director, Paul Morrison; Incidental Music by Paul Bowles. Opened Wednesday, November 11, 1953, and closed Sunday, November 22, 1953. (16 performances)

## Cast

| | |
|---|---|
| Porter | Benedict MacQuarrie |
| A Cavalier | Peter Brandon |
| A Musketeer | Carl Albertson |
| A Lackey | Richard Cowdery |
| Another Lackey | Tom Tryon |
| A Guardsman | Charles Summers |
| Flower Girl | Carmen Alvarez |
| A Citizen | Wallace Widdecombe |
| His Son | Sandy Campbell |
| A Cut Purse | Peter Buchan |
| Orange Girl | Lori March |
| A Marquis | Jack Fletcher |
| Brissaille | Albert Whitley |
| Ligniere | Gordon Nelson |
| Christian De Neuvillette | Douglas Watson |
| Ragueneau | Jacques Aubuchon |
| Le Bret | Philip Huston |
| Roxane | Arlene Dahl |
| Her Duenna | Paula Laurence |
| Comte De Guiche | Ralph Clanton |
| Vicomte de Valvert | Dean Cetrulo |
| Montfleury | Leopold Badia |
| Cyrano De Bergerac | José Ferrer |
| Bellerose | Stanley Carlson |
| Jodelet | Robinson Stone |
| A Meddler | Bill Butler |
| A Soubrette | Tamar Cooper |
| A Comedienne | Jill Kraft |
| Pasty Cooks: Sandy Campbell, Philip Prindle, Peter Buchan | |
| Lise | Betty Bartley |
| Carbon De Castel-Jaloux | G. Wood |
| A Poet | Vincent Donahue |
| Another Poet | John Glennon |
| Third Poet | Benedict MacQuarrie |
| A Capuchin | Robinson Stone |
| Sister Marthe | Jarmila Daubek |
| Mother Marguerite | Viola Roache |
| Sister Claire | Linda Berlin |
| A Nun | Ann Chisholm |
| Another Nun | Marijane Maricle |

Cadets of Gascoyne: Peter Harris, Arthur Walsh, Lee Danna, Garry Cowen, Toby Allen, Robert Lansing
Court Ladies, Nuns, etc.: Louise de la Parra, Honey Waldman, Muriel Dooley, Lily Lodge, Jill McAnney, Eva Rubinstein, Roberta MacDonald

*Company Manager:* GILMAN HASKELL
*Press:* REGINALD DENENHOLZ
*Stage Managers:* JESS KIMMEL, LUCIA VICTOR, BUFORD ARMITAGE, LUCIA VICTOR, T. J. KING

\* Last revival of this play was in 1946 at the Alvin Theatre with Jose Ferrer, Frances Reid, Ernest Graves and Ralph Clanton. (See THEATRE WORLD, Vol. III) It played 195 performances.

PHOTOS BY TALBOT

ouglas Watson, Arlene Dahl, Ralph Clanton. Top (L & R): Arlene Dahl, Jose Ferrer. Center: Paula Laurence, Jose Ferrer

Jose Ferrer, Kendall Clark       Jose Ferrer, Judith Evelyn

Judith Evelyn, Jose Ferrer

The New York City Theatre Company presents:

## THE SHRIKE*

By Joseph Kramm; Directed by Joseph Kramm and José Ferrer; Setting and Lighting by Howard Bay; Costumes by Emeline Roche; Jean Dalrymple in Charge of Production. Opened Wednesday, November 25, 1953, and closed Sunday, December 6, 1953. (15 performances)

### Cast

| | |
|---|---|
| Miss Cardell | Rica Martens |
| Fleming | Tom F. Reynolds |
| Miss Hansen | Jane Buchanan |
| Dr. Kramer | Leonard Patrick |
| Perkins | Ellsworth Wright |
| Grossberg | William Bush |
| Dr. Barrow | Isabel Bonner |
| Patient | Vincent Donahue |
| Ann Downs | Judith Evelyn |
| Jim Downs | José Ferrer |
| Dr. Schlesinger | Somer Alberg |
| Don Gregory | Philip Huston |
| Sam Tager | Arny Freeman |
| George O'Brien | Martin Newman |
| Joe Major | Van Prince |
| John Ankoritis | Jacques Aubuchon |
| Frank Carlisle | Leigh Whipper |
| William Schloss | Billy M. Greene |
| Dr. Bellman | Kendall Clark |
| Miss Wingate | Mary Bell |
| Harry Downs | Carl Frank |
| Tom Blair | Donald Foster |
| Attendants | T. J. King, Addison Powell |

Visitors: Margaret Ropp, Antoinette Griffith, James Clark, Kenneth Sleeper

*Company Manager:* GILMAN HASKELL
*Press:* REGINALD DENENHOLZ
*Stage Managers:* HERMAN SHAPIRO,
BUFORD ARMITAGE, LUCIA VICTOR, T. J. KING,

* First presented Jan. 15, 1952, at the Cort Theatre where it played 161 performances with Jose Ferrer and Judith Evelyn. (See THEATRE WORLD, Vol. VIII)

PHOTOS BY ALFREDO VALENTE

Jose Ferrer
as
Richard III

The New York City Theatre Company presents:

# RICHARD III*

By William Shakespeare; Staged by Margaret Webster; Music Composed and Conducted by Alex North; Costume Director, Emeline Roche; Production Designed by Richard Whorf; Jean Dalrymple in Charge of Production. Opened Wednesday, December 9, 1953, and closed Sunday, December 20, 1953, after 15 performances.

### Cast

| | |
|---|---|
| Richard, Duke of Gloucester, Later Richard III | José Ferrer |
| George, Duke of Clarence | Staats Cotsworth |
| Brackenbury | Paul Ballantyne |
| Lord Hastings | William Post, Jr. |
| Anne | Maureen Stapleton |
| Tressel | Tom Tryon |
| Berkeley | Benedict MacQuarrie |
| A Priest | G. Wood |
| Queen Elizabeth | Jessie Royce Landis |
| Earl Rivers | Philip Huston |
| Lord Grey | Bert Whitley |
| Duke of Buckingham | Vincent Price |
| Lord Stanley | John Straub |
| Marquis of Dorset | Robert Lansing |
| Queen Margaret | Florence Reed |
| Catesby | Eugene Stuckmann |
| 1st Murderer | Martin Kingsley |
| 2nd Murderer | Jack Bittner |
| Edward IV | Norman Roland |
| Young Clarence | John Glennon |
| Dowager Duchess of York | Margaret Wycherly |
| 1st Citizen | Stanley Carlson |
| 2nd Citizen | Jack Fletcher |
| 3rd Citizen | Will Davis |
| Richard, Duke of York | Charles Taylor |
| Edward, Prince of Wales | John Connoughton |
| The Lord Mayor of London | Leopold Badia |
| Bishop of Ely | James Arenton |
| Another Bishop | Wallace Widdecombe |
| A Messenger | Dehl Berti |
| Duke of Norfolk | Charles Summers |
| Sir Richard Ratcliff | Jay Barney |
| Lord Lovel | Robinson Stone |
| A Scrivener | Bill Butler |
| A Page | Sandy Campbell |
| Sir James Tyrell | Kendall Clark |
| 1st Messenger | Peter Harris |
| 2nd Messenger | Richard Cowdery |
| 3rd Messenger | Robert Ludlum |
| Henry, Earl of Richmond | Douglas Watson |
| Sir James Blunt | Bill Butler |
| Sir William Brandon | Vincent Donahue |
| Earl of Oxford | John Glennon |

Citizens, Soldiers, Monks, Priests, Nobles, etc.: Jack Betts, Dehl Berti, Jack Bittner, Marc Breaux, Peter Buchan, Bill Butler, David Post, Sandy Campbell, Stanley Carlson, Wyatt Cooper, Garry Cowen, Will Davis, John Devoe, Vincent Donahue, Jack Fletcher, John Glennon, Martin Kingsley, Walter Lawrence, Benedict MacQuarrie, Ray MacDonnel, Phil Prindle, Ray Rizzo, Kenneth Sleeper, Stanley Tannen, Tom Tryon, Bruce Webster, Bert Whitley, G. Wood, David Wright, Stefan Olsen.

Company Manager: GILMAN HASKELL
Press: REGINALD DENENHOLZ
Stage Managers: BUFORD ARMITAGE, JESS KIMMEL, LUCIA VICTOR

* Last revival was Feb. 8, 1949, at the Booth Theatre with Richard Whorf, Frances Reid and Philip Bourneuf. Played 23 performances. (See THEATRE WORLD, Vol. V)

Top left: Jessie Royce Landis, Philip Huston, Jose Ferrer. Center: Jose Ferrer, Vincent Price

Rehearsal shot with Vincent Price, Jose Ferrer, Margaret Wycherly, Florence Reed, Jessie Royce Landis, Maureen Stapleton

106

Jose Ferrer, Douglas Watson.
Top (center): Vincent Price, Jose Ferrer.    Center: Robert Lansing, Jessie Royce Landis,
Philip Huston, Jose Ferrer, Vincent Price, William Post, Jr.

Robert Lansing, Jose Ferrer,
Terrance Kilburn

Jose Ferrer, Jacques Aubuchon

Lori March, Jose Ferrer, Sarah Marshall,
Kent Smith, Jacques Aubuchon
Robert Lansing, Terrance Kilburn

Patricia Wheel, Jose Ferrer, Peggy Wood
Kent Smith

The New York City Theatre Company presents:

## CHARLEY'S AUNT*

By Brandon Thomas; Directed by José Ferrer;
Assistant Director, Jess Kimmel. Designed by Raoul
Pene Du Bois; Costume Director, Emeline Roche;
Jean Dalrymple in Charge of Production. Opened
Wednesday, Dec. 23, 1953, and closed Sunday,
January 3, 1954. (15 performances)

### Cast

| | |
|---|---|
| Brassett | Rex O'Malley |
| Jack Chesney | Robert Lansing |
| Charles Wykeham | Terence Kilburn |
| Lord Fancourt Babberley | José Ferrer |
| Kitty Verdun | Lori March |
| Amy Spettigue | Sarah Marshall |
| Col. Sir Francis Chesney | Kent Smith |
| Stephen Spettigue | Jacques Aubuchon |
| Farmer | Richard Cowdery |
| Donna Lucia D'Alvadorez | Peggy Wood |
| Ela Delahay | Patricia Wheel |
| Maud | Beverly Dennis |

A Comedy in three acts. The time is 1892 and
the action takes place at Oxford during Commemoration Week, and at Mr. Spettigue's house.

Company Manager: GILMAN HASKELL
Press: REGINALD DENENHOLZ
Stage Managers: BUFORD ARMITAGE,
HERMAN SHAPIRO, T. J. KING

* Last revived Oct. 17, 1940, at the Cort Theatre
where it ran for 233 performances. The cast included José Ferrer, Phyllis Avery, Nedda Harrigan
and Arthur Margetson.

Jose Ferrer, Peggy Wood

FRED FEHL PHOTOS

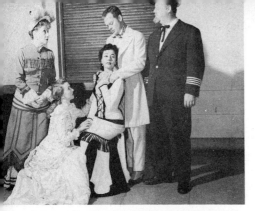

Marjorie Gateson, Laurel Hurley, Helena
Bliss, Robert Gallagher, Burl Ives

Marjorie Gateson, Laurel Hurley

Laurel Hurley, Burl Ives, Robert Rounseville

The New York City Light Opera Company presents:

# SHOW BOAT

Music by Jerome Kern; Book and Lyrics by Oscar Hammerstein 2nd; Based on Novel by Edna Ferber; Staged by William Hammerstein; Conductor, Julius Rudel; Settings by Howard Bay; Costumes by John Boyt; Lighting by Jean Rosenthal; Assistant Director, Michael Shurtleff. Opened Wednesday, May 5, 1954, and closed Sunday, May 16, 1954. (15 performances)

## Cast

| | |
|---|---|
| Windy McLain | Arthur Newman |
| Steve | Robert Gallagher |
| Pete | Boris Aplon |
| Queenie | Helen Phillips |
| Parthy Ann Hawks | Marjorie Gateson |
| Captain Andy | Burl Ives |
| Ellie | Diana Drake |
| Frank | Donn Driver |
| Rubberface | Thomas R. Powell |
| Julie | Helena Bliss |
| Gaylord Ravenal | Robert Rounseville |
| Vallon | Lawrence Haynes |
| Magnolia | Laurel Hurley |
| Joe | Lawrence Winters |
| Backwoodsman | Arthur Newman |
| Jeb | Lawrence Haynes |
| Barker | Thomas R. Powell |
| Fatima | Ann Barry |
| 2nd Barker | Charles Kuestner |
| Sport | Roland Miles |
| Strong Woman | Meri Miller |
| Landlady | Sara Floyd |
| Ethel | Gloria Wynder |
| Jake | Milton Lyon |
| Jim | Boris Aplon |
| Man With Guitar | Charles Kuestner |
| Doorman At Trocadero | Bill Smith |
| Mother Superior | Ellen Gleason |
| Nun | Barbara Ford |
| Kim (as a child) | Adele Newton |
| Drunk | Charles Kuestner |
| Lottie | Marilyn Bladd |
| Dolly | Dorothy Mirr |
| Sally | Gloria Sacks |
| Old Lady On Levee | Sara Floyd |
| Kim (in her Twenties) | Greta Thormsen |

**Congress of Beauties:** Joanne Budill, DeAnn Mears, Peg Shirley, Barbara Sohmers.

**Children:** Ginger Brooks, Georgianna Catal, Claudia Crawford, Dale Dennard, Leonard Grinnage, Joan Nickel, Bonnie Sawyer.

**Singing Ensemble:** Benjamin Bajorek, Marilyn Bladd, Adelaide Boatner, Eugene S. Brice, Doryce Brown, Walter P. Brown, Joseph E. Crawford, Dawin Emanuel, Rina Falcone, John Fleming, Barbara Ford, Mareda Gaither, Ellen Gleason, Russell Goodwin, Louise Hawthorne, Ida Frances Johnson, Charles Kuestner, Sheila Mathews, James Martindale, William McDaniel, Roland Miles, Dorothy Mirr, John Neilsen, Benjamin Plotkin, Madeline Porter, William W. Reynolds, Gloria Sacks, Christine Spencer, William Starling, Joseph Tanner, Frederick L. Thomas, Greta Thormsen, DeLoyd Tibbs, Rodester Timmons, Clyde S. Turner, Rose Virga, Gloria Wynder.

**Understudies:** Julie, Rina Falcone; Fatima and Ellie, Meri Miller; Windy and Vallon, Russell Goodwin; Pete, Barker and Jim, Roland Miles; Rubberface, Backwoodsman and Jeb, Benjamin Plotkin; Magnolia, Sheila Mathews; Ethel, Louise Hawthorne; Man With Guitar and Drunk, Benjamin Bajorek.

*Company Manager:* GILMAN HASKELL
*Press:* JOHN L. TOOHEY
*Stage Managers:* LUCIA VICTOR,
HANS SONDHEIMER, LEE WILLIAMS

PHOTOS BY TALBOT

The New York City Center Light Opera Company presents:

# FLEDERMAUS

Music by Johann Strauss; Libretto by C. Haffner and Richard Genee; English Book and Lyrics by Ruth and Thomas Martin; Conductor, Thomas Martin; Choreography by Robert Pagent; Costumes by John Boyt; Lighting by Jean Rosenthal; Production Assistant, Michael Shurtleff. Opened Wednesday, May 19, and closed June 6, 1954. (15 performances)

## Cast

| | |
|---|---|
| Alfredo | Lloyd Thomas Leech |
| | Harold R. Brown† |
| Adele | Adelaide Bishop |
| Rosalinda | Gloria Lind |
| | Guen Omeron† |
| Gabriel Von Eisenstein | Jack Russell |
| | Lloyd Thomas Leech† |
| Blind | Carl Nicholas |
| Dr. Falke | John Tyers |
| Frank | Stanley Carlson |
| Sally | Lidija Franklin |
| Prince Orlofsky | Donald Gramm |
| Ivan | Thomas R. Powell |
| Boris | Robert Pagent |
| Frosch | Colee Worth |

**Servants:** Stanley Bakis, Hill Eller, Alan James, Don Ratka, James Spicer, George Tucker

**Guests:** Marilyn Bladd, Rina Falcone, Barbara Ford, Ellen Gleason, Sheila Mathews, Dorothy Mirr, Gloria Sacks, Greta Thormsen, Rose Virga, Benjamin Bajorek, Dawin Emanuel, Russell Goodwin, Charles Kuestner, James Martindale, Roland Miles, Benjamin Plotkin, William W. Reynolds, Joseph Tanner.

*Company Manager:* GILMAN HASKELL
*Press:* JOHN L. TOOHEY
*Stage Managers:* LUCIA VICTOR,
HANS SONDHEIMER, LEE WILLIAMS

† Alternate sang role Saturday and Sunday matinees and Saturday evenings.

John Tyers, Guen Omeron

PHOTOS BY TALBO[T]

Top Right: John Tyers, Guen Omeron, Lidija Franklin, Donald Gramm

# SOLO PERFORMERS

FORTY-EIGHTH STREET THEATRE
Opened Tuesday, September 22, 1953. *
Charles Bowden and Richard Barr present:

## AT HOME WITH ETHEL WATERS

Reginald Beane at the Piano; Staged by Richard Barr; Setting by Oliver Smith; Costumes by Robert Mackintosh. Standby for Mr. Beane, Norene Tate.

### Program

Miss Waters
"I Ain't Gonna Sin No More," "Sleepy Time Down South," "Throw Dirt," "Am I Blue," "Half of Me," "Washtub Rubsudy"
Miss Waters and Mr. Beane
"Bread and Gravy"
Mr. Beane
Moods from his own "Jazzantasy Suite"
    Blues, Syncopation, Boogie
"Love For Sale"
Miss Waters
"Dinah," "Go Back Where You Stayed Last Night," "My Man," "St. Louis Blues," "Suppertime"

*Intermission*

Miss Waters
"Dance Hall Hostess"
Mr. Beane
"Odd Moments," Jerome Kern Medley
Miss Waters
"Takin' A Chance On Love," "Somethin' Told Me Not To Trust That Man," "Happiness Is Jes' A Thing Called Joe," "Lady Be Good," "Stormy Weather," "Mammy," "Motherless Chile," "Crucifixion," "Cabin In The Sky."

*General Manager:* PHIL ADLER
*Press:* RICHARD MANEY, FRANK GOODMAN
*Stage Manager:* ELLIOT MARTIN

* Closed October 10, 1953. (23 performances)

Ethel Waters

Ethel Waters

JOHN GOLDEN THEATRE
Opened Friday, October 2, 1953.
Harry D. Squires presents:

**VICTOR BORGE**
in
**COMEDY IN MUSIC**

A Solo performance by Mr. Borge presented in two acts.

*Manager:* IRVING SQUIRES
*Press:* KARL BERNSTEIN, HARVEY SABINSON, ALAN EDELSON
*Stage Manager:* LESTER HAMILTON

Victor Borge

Ruth Draper

**LONGACRE THEATRE**
Opened Monday, April 19, 1954.*

## MILBOURNE CHRISTOPHER
### and his magic show
### "NOW YOU SEE IT"
**Program**
ACT I

The Wizard's Welcome, Sorcery at Six, It Happened In Paris, Science Outdone, Chinese Problem, Invisible Passage, What's Cooking?, A Trip To Mexico, Chapeaugraphy, How It's Done, Further Explanation?, Party Tip, It's In The Bag.

ACT II

Stretching The Imagination, Turn To The Right, No Tobacco, Bang, The Closer You Watch, Three Invisible Cards, Testing, Sawing A Spectator, Knotty Necromancy, Unity, Easy Come, Easy Go, Horticultural Hocus Pocus.

ACT III

Bosco's Bell, Coincidence, Thought Control, Concentrate!, Remote Control, Solving The Crime, Inside The Cabinet, Imagination.

*Company Manager:* HAL OLVER
*Press:* NAT AND IRVIN DORFMAN

* Closed Saturday, April 24, 1954. (8 performances)

Right: Milbourne Christopher

**VANDERBILT THEATRE**
Opened Monday, January 25, 1954.*
Charles Bowden and Richard Barr present:

## RUTH DRAPER
### and
### Her Company of Characters
**Program**

(Monday and Tuesday Evenings and Wednesday Afternoon)
    The Italian Lesson
    A Dalmatian Peasant In The Hall of A New York Hospital
    Doctors and Diets
    On The Porch In A Maine Coast Village
    In A Church In Italy
(Wednesday, Thursday and Friday Evenings)
    Opening A Bazaar
    In County Kerry — 1919
    At An Art Exhibition In Boston
    Three Women and Mr. Clifford
    A Scottish Immigrant At Ellis Island
(Saturday Afternoon and Saturday and Sunday Evenings)
    A Children's Party In Philadelphia
    Three Generations In The Court of Domestic Relations
    Showing The Garden
    A Class In Greek Poise
    A Debutante At A Dance
    "Vive La France" — 1940
(Following Week Alternates)
    Three Breakfasts
    In A Railway Station On The Western Plains
    An English Houseparty
    The Actress

*Company Manager:* BEN BOYAR
*Press:* PHILLIP BLOOM, REUBEN RABINOVITCH
*Stage Manager:* GERRY O'BRIEN

* Closed March 13, 1954, after limited engagement of 56 performances.

Ruth Draper

# PLAYS OPENING IN PAST SEASONS THAT CLOSED DURING THIS SEASON

| Play | Performances | Opened | Closed |
|------|-------------|--------|--------|
| "South Pacific" | 1925 | April 7, 1949 | Jan. 16, 1954 |
| "The King and I" | 1246 | March 29, 1951 | March 20, 1954 |
| "Guys and Dolls" | 1200 | Nov. 24, 1950 | Nov. 28, 1953 |
| "Wish You Were Here" | 597 | June 25, 1952 | Nov. 28, 1953 |
| "Dial 'M' For Murder" | 552 | Oct. 29, 1952 | Feb. 27, 1954 |
| "Picnic" | 485 | Feb. 19, 1953 | April 10, 1954 |
| "Me and Juliet" | 358 | May 28, 1953 | April 3, 1954 |
| "My Three Angels" | 342 | March 11, 1953 | Jan. 2, 1954 |
| "Porgy and Bess" | 312 | March 10, 1953 | Nov. 28, 1953 |
| "Time Out For Ginger" | 238 | Nov. 26, 1952 | June 27, 1953 |
| "The Crucible" | 197 | Jan. 22, 1953 | July 11, 1953 |
| "Hazel Flagg" | 190 | Feb. 11, 1953 | Sept. 19, 1953 |
| "Misalliance" | 147 | Feb. 18, 1953 | June 27, 1953 |

# VAUDEVILLE

**RKO PALACE THEATRE**
Opened Wednesday, October 14, 1953.
Closed November 10, 1953.

### BETTY HUTTON
and her
### ALL-STAR INTERNATIONAL SHOW
**Program**

Overture — RKO Palace Orchestra
Jo Lombardi, Conductor
1. The Shyrettos
2. Bil and Cora Baird and their Marionettes with Franz Fazakas and Frank Sullivan
3. Trio Charlivel
4. Dick Shawn
5. Los Chavales De Espana with Trini Reyes
6. Betty Hutton
Featuring The Skylarks
Produced and directed by Charles O'Curran; Costumes by Kay Nelson; Original Songs by Jay Livingston and Ray Evans; Musical Arrangement by Nelson Riddle; Lou Bring, Conductor; Jack Latimer, Pianist; Remo Belli, Percussionist; Milton Starr, Production Supervisor and Stage Manager; Staging and Lighting by David Bines.

Betty Hutton

FULTON THEATRE
Opened Thursday, November 20, 1952. *
Courtney Burr and Elliott Nugent present:

## THE SEVEN YEAR ITCH

By George Axelrod; Directed by John Gerstad; Designed and Lighted by Frederick Fox; Incidental Music Composed and Arranged by Dana Suesse; Production Supervised by Elliott Nugent.

### Cast

| | |
|---|---|
| Richard Sherman | Tom Ewell†1 |
| Helen Sherman | Neva Patterson |
| Ricky | Johnny Klein |
| Miss Morris | Marilyn Clark†2 |
| Elaine | Joan Donovan |
| Marie What-Ever-Her-Name-Was | Irene Moore†3 |
| The Girl | Vanessa Brown |
| Dr. Brubaker | Robert Emhardt |
| Tom Mackenzie | George Keane |
| Voice of Richard's Conscience | George Ives |
| Voice of The Girl's Conscience | Pat Fowler |

A Comedy in three acts and four scenes. The action takes place in the apartment of the Richard Shermans, in the Gramercy Park section of New York City, at the present time.

Company Manager: JOHN H. POTTER†4
Press: MARIAN BYRAM, PHYLLIS PERLMAN
Stage Managers: CHARLES DURAND, PAT FOWLER, JAMES LEE

* For the original cast see THEATRE WORLD, Vol. IX.

† Replaced by: 1. Eddie Albert for December, 1953, during Mr. Ewell's vacation. 2. Pat Fowler, 3. Paulette Girard, 4. Richard E. French

PHOTO BY TALBOT
Left: Tom Ewell, Vanessa Brown

CORT THEATRE
Opened Friday, January 23, 1953. *
George Kondolf presents:

## THE FIFTH SEASON

By Sylvia Regan; Directed by Gregory Ratoff; Scenery by Sam Leve; Costume Supervision by Edythe Gilfond; Produced by George Kondolf and Sherman S. Krellberg.

### Cast

| | |
|---|---|
| Ruby D. Prince | John Kullers |
| Shelly | Nita Talbot |
| Lorraine McKay | Phyllis Hill |
| Ferelli | Norman Rose |
| Max Pincus | Menasha Skulnik |
| Johnny Goodwin | Richard Whorf |
| Frances Goodwin | Augusta Roeland |
| Miriam Goodwin | Lois Wheeler |
| Dolores | Dorian Leigh†1 |
| Redhaired Model | Midge Ware†2 |
| Brunette Model | Carolyn Block†3 |
| Miles Lewis | John Griggs |
| Marty Goodwin | Dick Kallman†4 |

Understudies: David Kurlan, John Boruff, Gedda Petry, Helen Alexander, Midge Ware, Richard Wendley.

A Comedy in three acts and five scenes. The action passes in the office of Goodwin-Pincus, on Seventh Avenue in New York, at the present time.

Business Manager: JESSE LONG
Press: BERNARD SIMON
Stage Managers: NICHOLAS SAUNDERS, RICHARD WENDLEY, JOHN CASSAVETES

* For original cast see THEATRE WORLD, Vol. IX.

† Replaced by: 1. Midge Ware, 2. Teddy Tavenner, 3. Helen Alexander, 4. Bill Penn

Menasha Skulnik, Richard Whorf, Bill Penn

Carol Channing
in
"Wonderful Town"

117

## WINTER GARDEN
Opened Wednesday, February 25, 1953.*
Robert Fryer presents:

# WONDERFUL TOWN

Book by Joseph Fields and Jerome Chodorov; Music by Leonard Bernstein; Lyrics by Betty Comden and Adolph Green; Dances and Musical Numbers Staged by Donald Saddler; Sets and Costumes by Raoul Pene duBois; Lighting by Peggy Clark; Miss Russell's clothes by Main Bocher; Musical Direction and Vocal Arrangements by Lehman Engel; Orchestrations by Don Walker; Based on Play, "My Sister Eileen," and the stories by Ruth McKenney; Directed by George Abbott.

## Cast

| | |
|---|---|
| Hermit | Don Barton |
| Guide | Warren Galjour |
| Appopoulous | Henry Lascoe |
| Lonigan | Walter Kelvin |
| Wreck | Jordan Bentley |
| Helen | Michele Burke†1 |
| Violet | Dody Goodman |
| Valenti | Ted Beniades |
| Eileen | Edith Adams |
| Ruth | Rosalind Russell†2 |
| Strange Man | Nathaniel Frey |
| Drunks | Lee Papell, Delbert Anderson |
| Robert Baker | George Gaynes |
| Associate Editors | Warren Galjour, Albert Linville |
| Mrs. Wade | Isabella Hoopes |
| Frank Lippencott | Cris Alexander |
| Chef | Nathaniel Frey |
| Waiter | Delbert Anderson |
| Delivery Boy | Alvin Beam |
| Chick Clark | Dort Clark |
| Shore Patrolman | Lee Pappell |
| 1st Cadet | David Lober |
| 2nd Cadet | Ray Dorian |

Policemen: Lee Papell, Albert Linville, Delbert Anderson, Chris Robinson, Nathaniel Frey, Warren Galjour, Michael Mason
Ruth's Escort .................. Chris Robinson
Greenwich Villagers: Jean Eliot, Marta Becket, Maxine Berke, Carol Cole, Geraldine Delaney, Babs Heath, Betty Gillette, Dody Goodman, Virginia Poe, Doris Wright, Hugh Lambert, Alvin Beam, Ray Dorian, Edward Heim, David Neuman, Paul Lyday, David Lober, Walter Rinner, Marion Lauer, Evelyn Page, Helen Rice, Patty Wilkes, Delbert Anderson, Warren Galjour, Michael Mason, Lee Papell, Chris Robinson, Don Barton

**Understudies:** Ruth, Patricia Wilkes; Eileen, Betty Gillette; Appopolous, Lee Papell; Baker, Chris Robinson; Wreck, Michael Mason; Lippencott, Hal Prince; Mrs. Wade, Helen Rice; Helen, Geraldine Delaney; Chic, Delbert Anderson; Valenti, Warren Galjour.

*General Manager:* CHARLES HARRIS
*Press:* PHYLLIS PERLMAN, MARIAN BYRAM
*Stage Managers:* JOHN EFFRAT, WALTER RINNER, ED BALIN

* For original New York production see THEATRE WORLD, Vol. IX.

† Replaced by: 1. Diana Herbert, 2. Carol Channing

Carol Channing, George Gaynes, Albert Linville, Warren Galjour.
Center: Edith Adams, Carol Channing

PHOTOS BY VANDAMM

## SAM S. SHUBERT THEATRE

Opened Thursday, May 7, 1953.*
Feuer and Martin present:

# CAN-CAN

Music and Lyrics by Cole Porter; Book and Direction by Abe Burrows; Dances and Musical Numbers Staged by Michael Kidd; Settings and Lighting by Jo Mielziner; Costumes by Motley; Musical Direction by Milton Rosenstock; Orchestrations by Philip J. Lang; Dance Music Arranged by Genevieve Pitot.

## Cast

| | |
|---|---|
| Bailiff | David Collyer |
| Registrar | Michael Cavallaro |
| Policemen: Joe Cusanelli, Jon Silo, Arthur Rubin, Ralph Beaumont, Michael DeMarco, Socrates Birsky | |
| Judge Paul Barriere | C. K. Alexander |
| Court President, Henri Marceaux | David Thomas |
| Judge Aristide Forestier | Peter Cookson |
| Claudine | Gwen Verdon |
| Gabrielle | Mary Anne Cohan†1 |
| Marie | Beverly Purvin†2 |
| Celestine | Jean Kraemer |
| Hilaire Jussac | Erik Rhodes |
| Boris Adzinidzinadze | Hans Conried |
| Hercule | Robert Penn |
| Theophile | Phil Leeds |
| Etienne | Richard Purdy |
| Waiter | Clarence Hoffman |
| La Mome Pistache | Lilo |
| 2nd Waiter | Ferdinand Hilt |
| Cafe Waiter | Jon Silo |
| Cafe Customer | Joe Cusanelli |
| Jailer | Deedee Wood |
| Model | Pat Turner†3 |
| Mimi | Dania Krupska†4 |
| Customers | Sheila Arnold,†5 David Thomas, Ferdinand Hilt |
| Doctor | Michael Cavallaro |
| Second | Arthur Rubin |
| Prosecutor | Ferdinand Hilt |

**Dancers:** Mary Jane Doerr, Marcella Dodge, Shelah Hackett, Ina Hahn, Ann Sparkman, Beverly Tassoni, Eleonore Treiber, Ruth Vernon, Deedee Wood, Ralph Beaumont, Socrates Birsky, Michael DeMarco, Al Lanti, Bert May, Tom Panko, Duncan Noble, Eddie Phillips, Michael Scittorale.

**Understudies:** Pistache, Guylaine Guy; Forestier, Ferdinand Hilt; Claudine, Shelah Hackett and Ina Hahn; Boris, Phil Leeds; Jussac, Ferdinand Hilt; Theophile, Jon Silo; Barriere, David Collyer; Etienne, Michael Cavallaro; Hercule, Clarence Hoffman; Model, Marcella Dodge.

*Company Manager:* JOSEPH HARRIS
*Press:* KARL BERNSTEIN, HARVEY SABINSON
*Stage Managers:* HENRI CAUBISENS, HERMAN MAGIDSON, DAVID COLLYER

* For original cast see THEATRE WORLD, Vol. IX.

† Replaced by: 1. Ruth Schoeni, 2. Basha Regis, 3. Ruth Vernon, 4. Ann Sparkman, 5. Beverly Tassoni

Peter Cookson, Lilo. Center: Gwen Verdon, Erik Rhodes

**BARBIZON-PLAZA THEATRE**
Opened Friday, May 1, 1953. *
Howard Da Silva and Arnold Perl present:

## THE WORLD OF
## SHOLOM ALEICHEM

Dramatized by Arnold Perl; Directed by Howard Da Silva; Music by Serge Hovey and Robert De Cormier; Costumes by Aline Bernstein; Lighting by Bernard Gersten.

### Cast

"A Tale of Chelm" ...................... Folk Story

| | |
|---|---|
| The Melamed | Will Lee |
| Rifkele | Phoebe Brand |
| Rabbi David | Gilbert Green[1] |
| The Angel Rochele | Marjorie Nelson[2] |
| Stranger | Jack Banning |
| Rifkele's Friend | Warren Logan[3] |
| Dodi | Vincent Beck |
| The Goatseller | Sarah Cunningham |

"Bontche Schweig" ................ by I. L. Peretz

| | |
|---|---|
| 1st Angel | Jack Banning |
| 2nd Angel | Marjorie Nelson[2] |
| 3rd Angel | Phoebe Brand |
| 4th Angel | Warren Logan[3] |
| 5th Angel | Vincent Beck |
| 6th Angel | Sarah Cunningham |
| Father Abraham | Will Lee |
| Bontche Schweig | Jack Gilford |
| Presiding Angel | Morris Carnovsky |
| Defending Angel | Ruby Dee |
| Prosecuting Angel | Gilbert Green[1] |

Intermission

"The High School"..Story by Sholom Aleichem

| | |
|---|---|
| Aaron Katz | Morris Carnovsky |
| Hannah | Sarah Cunningham |
| Moishe | Jack Banning |
| Man at the list | Jack Gilford |
| The Tutor | Vincent Beck |
| Woman at the list | Marjorie Nelson[2] |
| The Principal | Gilbert Green[1] |
| Uncle Maxl | Will Lee |
| Aunt Reba | Phoebe Brand |
| Kholyava | Warren Logan[3] |
| Mendele | Howard Da Silva[4] |

**General Understudies:** Herschell Bernardi, Osna Palmer

*General Manager:* BERNARD GERSTEN
*Press:* MERLE DEBUSKEY
*Stage Manager:* OSSIE DAVIS

* Closed May 23, 1954. (305 performances) A Chicago Company opened at the Eleventh Street Theatre, Feb. 13, 1954, and Closed on April 11, 1954, after 67 performances.

† Replaced by: 1. Elliott Sullivan, 2. Ellie Pine, 3. Rick Fredericks, 4. Herschell Bernardi.

Warren Logan, Jack Banning, Sarah Cunningham, Morris Carnovsky.

Center: Jack Gilford, Morris Carnovsky. Top (L – R): Sarah Cunningham, Morris Carnovsky; Phoebe Brand, Gilbert Green, Will Lee; Howard Da Silva

PHOTOS BY TALBOT

Nora Dunfee, Donald Draper, Jessica Tandy, Robert Emmett

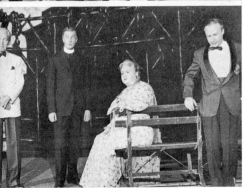

PHOENIX THEATRE
> Opened Tuesday, December 1, 1953. *
> T. Edward Hambleton and Norris Houghton present:

## MADAM, WILL YOU WALK

By Sidney Howard; Staged by Hume Cronyn and Norman Lloyd; Settings and Lighting by Donald Oenslager; Dances by Anna Sokolow; Costumes by Alvin Colt; Incidental Music by Max Marlin.

### Cast

| | |
|---|---|
| Mrs. Broderick | Madeleine King |
| Broderick | Arthur Jarrett |
| Officer Mallon | John Randolph |
| Mrs. Fanaghy | Susan Steell |
| Father Christy | William Roerick |
| Judge Moskowitz | Edwin Jerome |
| Miss Auchincloss | Dorrit Kelton |
| Mr. Dockwiler | Norman Lloyd |
| Mary Doyle | Jessica Tandy |
| Dr. Brightlee | Hume Cronyn |
| Scupper | Robert Emmett |
| Alderman Doyle | David Clarke |
| Magistrate | Leon Janney |
| Court Clerk | David Hooks |
| Marshal | Buff Shurr |

Assorted Citizens of New York City: Nora Dunfee, Jill Andre, Donald Draper, Dan Hogan, Elizabeth Johnstone, Mavis Mitchell, Fred Smith

A Drama in three acts and five scenes. The action takes place at the present time in the Doyle residence on Fifth Avenue, New York; behind the bandstand on the Mall in Central Park; the 72nd Street Lake in Central Park; in Night Court.

> *General Manager:* CARL FISHER
> *Press:* SOL JACOBSON, LEWIS HARMON
> *Stage Managers:* PAUL A. FOLEY, ROBERT WOODS

* Closed January 10, 1954, after limited six-week run. (48 performances)

FRED FEHL PHOTOS

Edwin Jerome, William Roerick, Susan Steell, Norman Lloyd.
Center: Hume Cronyn, Jessica Tandy

Alan Napier, Will Geer,
Joseph Holland

Robert Ryan

Right: Lori March, Mildred Natwick

Lori March, Paula Laurence, Mildred Natwick. Center: Robert Ryan, John Emery

**PHOENIX THEATRE**
Opened Tuesday, January 19, 1954.*
T. Edward Hambleton and Norris Houghton present:

# CORIOLANUS†

By William Shakespeare; Production by John Houseman; Settings by Donald Oenslager; Costumes by Alvin Colt; Music by Alex North.

## Cast

| | |
|---|---|
| 1st Citizen | Frederick Rolf |
| 2nd Citizen | David Clarke |
| 3rd Citizen | Jack Bittner |
| 4th Citizen | Carl Jacobs |
| 5th Citizen | Jerry Stiller |
| 6th Citizen | Jack Klugman |
| 7th Citizen | Gene Saks |
| Menenius Agrippa | Alan Napier |
| Caius Martius Coriolanus | Robert Ryan |
| Senatorial Messenger | Michael Tolan |
| Titus Lartius | Lou Polan |
| 1st Senator | Joseph Macaulay |
| 2nd Senator | George Fells |
| Cominius | Joseph Holland |
| 1st Aedile | Jamie Smith |
| 2nd Aedile | Carl Jacobs |
| Junius Brutus | John Randolph |
| Sicinius | Will Geer |
| Volumnia | Mildred Natwick |
| Virgilia | Lori March |
| Gentlewoman | Nora Dunfee |
| Valeria | Paula Laurence |
| Tullus Aufidius | John Emery |
| Lieutenant to Aufidius | Jamie Smith |
| 1st Volscian Servant | Gene Saks |
| 2nd Volscian Servant | Jack Klugman |
| 3rd Volscian Servant | Jerry Stiller |
| 1st Sentinel | Michael Tolan |
| 2nd Sentinel | Carl Jacobs |
| Son to Coriolanus | Terry Nardin |
| 1st Conspirator | Carl Jacobs |
| 1st Lord | Lou Polan |

Senators, Soldiers, Citizens, etc.: Norman Beim, Peter Benzoni, Peter Buchan, Nat Burns, Donald Draper, Mel Fillini, Jack Friend, Joseph Elic, Erle Hall, Richard Lederer, Frank Lucas, Paul Lukather, Richard Marr, Hugh Mosher, Joseph Nathan, Jim Oyster, Richard Shull, Tim Squires, Laurence Vide.

Presented in two acts. The action takes place in Rome and in Antium and Corioles, two cities of the Volsces.

*General Manager:* CARL FISHER
*Press:* SOL JACOBSON, LEWIS HARMON, DEWEY EBBIN
*Stage Managers:* ROBERT WOODS, GEORGE QUICK

* Closed February 28, 1954, after limited six-week run. (48 performances)

† Last presented in repertory in 1938 at the Maxine Elliott Theatre by Charles Hopkins for the WPA New York State Federal Theatre Project.

Mildred Natwick, Robert Ryan, John Emery

Robert Ryan, Alan Napier

Judith Evelyn

Montgomery Clift,
Mira Rostova

Maureen Stapleton

Kevin McCarth

Montgomery Clift

Sam Jaffe, Montgomery Clift
Center: George Voskovec, Mira Rostova,
Judith Evelyn, Sam Jaffe, John Fiedler

Mira Rostova

PHOENIX THEATRE
Opened Tuesday, May 11, 1954.*
T. Edward Hambleton and Norris Houghton
present:

## THE SEA GULL†

By Anton Chekhov; Directed by Norris Houghton; Settings by Duane McKinney; Costumes by
Alvin Colt; Lighting by Klaus Holm; Music Arranged by Max Marlin; Adaptation of the play for
this production was prepared by Mira Rostova,
Kevin McCarthy and Montgomery Clift; Make-up
by Ernest Adler.

### Cast

| | |
|---|---|
| Madame Irina Arkadina | Judith Evelyn |
| Constantin Treplev | Montgomery Clift |
| Peter Sorin | Sam Jaffe |
| Nina Zarechnaya | Mira Rostova |
| Shamrayev | Will Geer |
| Paulina | June Walker |
| Masha | Maureen Stapleton |
| Boris Trigorin | Kevin McCarthy |
| Dr. Dorn | George Voskovec |
| Medvedenko | John Fiedler |
| Yakov | Karl Light |
| Cook | Lou Polan |
| Housemaid | Sarah Marshall |

*General Manager:* CARL FISHER
*Press:* SAMUEL J. FRIEDMAN, MAX GENDEL
*Stage Managers:* ROBERT WOODS, JOHN CORNELL,
KARL LIGHT

† Last Broadway presentation, March 28, 1938,
by the Theatre Guild at the Shubert Theatre, for 41
performances, with Alfred Lunt, Lynn Fontanne,
Uta Hagen, Sydney Greenstreet, Richard Whorf and
Margaret Webster.

PHOTOS BY

WALTER LATWAITE, AVERY WILLARD AND VANDAMM

op: Mira Rostova, Montgomery Clift, Sam
ffe, Kevin McCarthy, Judith Evelyn,
eorge Voskovec, John Fiedler, Maureen
Stapleton, Will Geer, June Walker

Will Geer, Judith Evelyn, Sam Jaffe

125

John Heldabrand, Martin Ritt, Helen Craig

THEATER DE LYS
Opened Tuesday, June 9, 1953.
Terese Hayden in association with Liska March
presents a series of four plays:

## MAYA

By Simon Gantillon; Directed by Roger Kay;
Production Designed by William and Jean Eckart;
Theme Music by Roger Kay. Opened June 9th and
closed June 14, 1953. (7 performances)

### Cast

| | |
|---|---|
| Sailor | John Randolph |
| Bella | Helen Craig |
| Celeste | Kay Medford |
| Albert | John Pavelko |
| Phonsine | Rebecca Darke |
| Fifine | Susan Strasberg |
| Laundress | Florence Anglin |
| Ida | Sono Osato |
| Fruit Woman | Doris Blair |
| Dockyard Worker | Milton Carney |
| Mama | Joanna Roos |
| The Interpreter | Tom Russino |
| A Man | Vivian Matalon |
| Valentin | Stefan Gierasch |
| The Norwegian | Leo Penn |
| Ernest | Martin Ritt |
| The Painter | John Heldabrand |
| Coal Stoker | Mark Rydell |
| Quartermaster | Salem Ludwig |
| Sidi | Stefan Gierasch |
| Wharf Hand | Milton Carney |
| The East Indian | James O'Rear |
| Guitar Player | John Randolph |
| Accordionist | Matt King |

Stage Managers: AUDREY HILLIARD, DORIS BLUM,
KEN LEEDOM

ALIX JEFFRY PHOTOS

Susan Strasberg, Helen Craig

Douglas Watson, Eli Wallach, Nora Dunfee, Leo Penn, Anne Jackson,
Milton Carney

## THEATER DE LYS
### THE SCARECROW

By Percy MacKaye; Directed by Frank Corsaro;
Designed by William and Jean Eckart; Music Composed by Joseph Liebling; Costumes Supervised by
Ruth Morley. Presented June 16-21, 1953. (7 performances)

### Cast

| | |
|---|---|
| Goody Rickby | Patricia Neal |
| Dickon | Eli Wallach |
| Rachel Merton | Anne Jackson |
| Ebenezer | Milton Carney |
| Richard Talbot | Bradford Dillman |
| Justice Gilead Merton | Milton Selzer |
| Lord Ravensbane | Douglas Watson |
| Mistress Cynthia Merton | Mary Bell |
| Capt. Bugby | Albert Salmi |
| Minister Dodge | Alan MacAteer |
| Mistress Dodge | Zita Rieth |
| Sir Charles Reddington | Harold Preston |
| Mistress Reddington | Sybil Baker |
| Amelia Reddington | Eavan O'Connor |
| Rev. Master Rand | Milton Carney |
| Rev. Master Todd | Ed Williams |
| Micah | Stefan Gierasch |

*Stage Managers:* Edgar Kaufman, Patricia Fay

ALIX JEFFRY PHOTOS

Anne Jackson, Eli Wallach, Douglas Watson

**127**

Patricia Neal, David Stewart, Eva Stern, Sara Seegar, Leo Lucker, Joanna Roos, Leon Janney

## THEATER DE LYS
### SCHOOL FOR SCANDAL

By Richard Brinsley Sheridan; Directed by Terese Hayden; Designed by William and Jean Eckart; Costumes Supervised by Frances Malek. Presented June 23-28, 1953. (7 performances)

### Cast

| | |
|---|---|
| Lady Sneerwell | Sara Seegar |
| Snake | Sidney Armus |
| Joseph Surface | David Stewart |
| Maria | Eva Stern |
| Mrs. Candour | Joanna Roos |
| Crabtree | Leo Lucker |
| Sir Benjamin Backbite | Leon Janney |
| Sir Peter Teazle | John Heldabrand |
| Rowley | Richard Poston |
| Lady Teazle's Servant | Melissa Weston |
| Lady Teazle | Patricia Neal |
| Sir Oliver Surface | Howard Caine |
| Moses | William Myers |
| Trip | Vivian Matalon |
| Charles Surface | Leo Penn |
| Careless | Orson Bean |
| Sir Harry Bumper | Robert Di Martino |
| Joseph's Servant | Milton Carney |

*Stage Managers:* JOHN DEVOE, BETH GARDE

ALIX JEFFRY PHOTOS

Howard Caine, Leo Penn. Center Left: John Heldabrand, Patricia Neal. Center Right Leo Lucker, Leon Janney, Sara Seegar

Stefan Gierasch, John Bemis, Dennis Duggan, Ed Williams, Alan MacAteer,
Sy Travers

## THEATER DE LYS
### THE LITTLE CLAY CART

By King Shudraka; Translated by Arthur William
Ryder; Directed by Edward G. Greer; Designed by
William and Jean Eckart; Music Composed by
Lester Trimble; Costumes by Ruth Morley and
Dale Clement. Presented June 30th to July 5th,
1953. (7 performances)

#### Cast

| | |
|---|---|
| The Courtier | Leo Lucker |
| Maitreya | Will Hare |
| Charudatta | Richard Waring |
| Radanika | Ruth Volner |
| Vasantasena | Sono Osato |
| Madanika | Susan Willis |
| Sanathanaka | Stefan Gierasch |
| The Shampooer | Vivian Matalon |
| Mathura | Sy Travers |
| Another Gambler | Fred Vogel |
| Daruraka | Arthur La Rol |
| Sharvilaka | Phillip Pine |
| Charudatta's Wife | Kay Medford |
| Another Maid | Rebecca Darke |
| Rohasena | Joe Kinego |
| Vardhanaka | Ed Williams |
| Sthavaraka | Fred Vogel |
| Aryaka | Tom Raynor |
| Viraka | Strowen Robertson |
| Chandanaka | Milton Carney |
| The Beadle | Ed Williams |
| The Judge | Alan MacAteer |
| The Clerk | Sy Travers |
| Vasantasena's Mother | Ruth Volner |
| Goha, A Headsman | Milton Carney |

*Stage Managers:* DORIS BLUM, IRVING BUCHMAN
Staff For Play Series:
*General Manager:* JULIAN BERCOVICI
*Stage Manager:* AUDREY HILLIARD
*Press:* MAX EISEN, ROBERT GANSHAW,
MERLE DEBUSKEY

ALIX JEFFRY PHOTOS

Richard Waring, Sono Osato

THEATRE DE LYS
Opened Tuesday, January 12, 1954.*
Modern American Theatre presents:

# BULLFIGHT

By Leslie Stevens; Directed and Staged by Joseph Anthony; Technical Advisor, Sloan Simpson; Setting and Lighting by Kim Swados; Music Composed and Arranged by Rolando Valdes-Blain; Executive Producer, Stanley S. Kostner.

## Cast

| | |
|---|---|
| Guitarist | Rolando Valdes-Blain |
| Esteban De La Cruz Salamanca | Mario Alcalde |
| Josefina Tecos | Vivian Nathan |
| Pilar Tecos | Loretta Leversee |
| Hernan Tecos | Milton Selzer |
| Domingo Del Cristobal Salamanca | Hurd Hatfield |
| Lucho | Ronald Lopez |
| La Bruja | Tamara Daykarhanova |
| Jesus Flores | Edward Rutzisky |
| Pedro Flores | Robert Jacquin |

Villagers: Felipe Lanza, Flori Waren, Barbara Burris, Jan Henry, Catherine Holst, Nona Medici, Marie Stuccio, William Lennard, Robert Loggia, Ed Setrakian, Alex Tartaglia, Irving Winter

*General Manager:* GAYLE STINE
*Press:* MAX EISEN, MARIAN GRAHAM
*Stage Managers:* HELEN DAYTON, JOSEPHINE GRIFFITH
* Closed Feb. 28, 1954. (56 performances)

**Left: Hurd Hatfield, Loretta Leversee.**

**Top: Loretta Leversee, Tamara Daykarhanova, Vivian Nathan**

Vivian Nathan, Mario Alcalde

Vivian Nathan, Mario Alcalde, Hurd Hatfield

Mario Alcalde, Hurd Hatfield

Beatrice Arthur    Gerald Price    Charlotte Rae    Scott Merrill,    Jo Sullivan

Scott Merrill   Jo Sullivan

132

THEATRE DE LYS
Opened Wednesday, March 10, 1954. *
Carmen Capalbo and Stanley Chase present:

# THE THREEPENNY OPERA

English adaptation of book and lyrics by Marc Blitzstein; Music by Kurt Weill; Original text by Bert Brecht; Settings by William Pitkin; Costumes by Bolasni; Musical Director, Samuel Matlowsky; Original Orchestration by Kurt Weill; Staged by Carmen Capalbo.

## Cast

| | |
|---|---|
| Streetsinger | Gerald Price |
| Jenny | Lotte Lenya |
| Mr. J. J. Peachum | Leon Lishner†[1] |
| Mrs. Peachum | Charlotte Rae†[2] |
| Filch | William Duell |
| MacHeath (Mack The Knife) | Scott Merrill |
| Polly Peachum | Jo Sullivan†[3] |
| Readymoney Matt | John Astin |
| Crookfinger Jake | Joseph Beruh |
| Bob The Saw | Bernard Bogin |
| Walt Dreary | Paul Dooley |
| Rev. Kimball | Donald Elson |
| Tiger Brown | George Tyne |
| Betty | Marcella Markham |
| Molly | Marion Selee |
| Dolly | Gerrianne Raphael |
| Coaxer | Gloria Sokol |
| Smith | Chuck Smith |
| Lucy Brown | Beatrice Arthur |
| 1st Constable | Stan Schneider |
| 2nd Constable | Miles Dickson |
| Messenger | William Duell |

A Musical in three acts and ten scenes. The action takes place in 19th Century London.

*General Manager:* ZELDA DORFMAN
*Press:* ARTHUR CANTOR, REGINAL DENENHOLZ
*Stage Managers:* GENE PERLOWIN, CHARLES BELLIN
* Closed May 30, 1954. (95 performances)
† Replaced by: 1. Martin Wolfson, 2. Mildred Cook, 3. Gerrianne Raphael.

Jo Sullivan, Scott Merrill
(also at top)

Lotte Lenya

Charlotte Rae, Leon Lishner

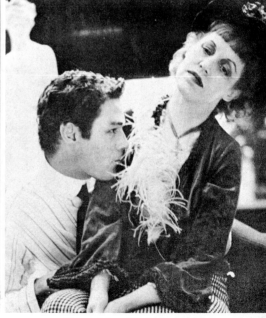

Beatrice Arthur, Scott Merrill, Jo Sullivan

Scott Merrill, Lotte Lenya

Tani Seitz, Cavada Humphrey in "Moon In Capricorn"

Norma Winters, Robert Emmett in "The Knight Of The Burning Pestle"

**134**

THEATER DE LYS
Opened Friday, October 23, 1953.
D'Ancona-Hilliard Productions present:

## THE KNIGHT
## OF THE BURNING PESTLE

By Francis Beaumont; Directed by Robert Laning; Designed and Lighted by Richard Burns; Costumes by Ruth Morley; Incidental Music by Joseph Liebling. Presented Oct. 23-25, 1953.

### Cast

| | |
|---|---|
| Speaker of The Prologue | Vivian Matalon |
| Venturewell | Lee Hauptman |
| Merrythought | Raymond Johnson |
| Jasper | Ric Lavin |
| Michael | Vivian Matalon |
| Humphrey | Paul Stevens |
| Tim | Del Parker |
| George | John Robertson |
| Luce | Jo Gilberg |
| Mistress Merrythought | Norma Winters |
| A Citizen | Dana Elcar |
| His Wife | Gertrude Kinnell |
| Ralph | Robert Emmett |

*Stage Managers:* JEFFERY LONGE, DEL PARKER

THEATER DE LYS
Opened Friday, October 23, 1953.
D'Ancona-Hilliard Productions present:

## MOON IN CAPRICORN

By James Leo Herlihy; Directed by Miranda d'Ancona; Sets and Costumes by John Blankenchip; Incidental Music by Joseph Liebling. Presented Oct. 27, 28, 29, 1953.

### Cast

| | |
|---|---|
| Si | Del Parker |
| Mrs. Wilkes | Norma Winters |
| Jeanne Wilkes | Tani Seitz |
| Darryl Lang | Paul Stevens |
| Madame Zoe | Cavada Humphrey |
| Bill Walker | Bradford Hoyt |
| Madame Zepetrini | Gertrude Kinnell |
| Policeman | Dana Elcar |
| Sailor | Lee Hauptman |
| His Girl | Jo Gilberg |
| 2nd Sailor | Vivian Matalon |

*Stage Managers:* DORIS BLUM, LEE HAUPTMAN
*Press:* MAX EISEN, ROBERT GANSHAW

Clarice Blackburn, Richard Woods

Jean Stapleton, Clarice Blackburn,
Emilie Stevens

CIRCLE IN THE SQUARE
    Opened Tuesday, November 10, 1953.*
Emilie Stevens, Theodore Mann, José Quintero
and Jason Wingreen present:

## AMERICAN GOTHIC

By Martin Wolfson; Directed by José Quintero;
Setting, Costumes and Lighting by Warwick Brown.

### Cast

| | |
|---|---|
| Ed Moody | Jason Robards, Jr. |
| Elwood | James Greene |
| Earl | William Major |
| Sheb Moody | Fred Herrick |
| Mrs. Paine | Mabel Cochran |
| Mr. Paine | Dwight Marfield |
| Mrs. Adams | Jean Stapleton |
| Halsey Curtis | Richard Woods |
| Addie | Clarice Blackburn |
| Jenny | Emilie Stevens |
| Mrs. Dorey | Charis Bain |
| Mr. Willis | Sidney Kaplan |
| Berta | Gloria Scott Backe |
| Mrs. Doane | Mildred Cook |
| Mr. Doane | Stuart Lyons |

Townspeople: Arleen McCarthy, Roxy Horen, Barbara Macon

*Press:* DAVID LIPSKY
*Stage Managers:* RICHARD SPAHN, ARLEEN MCCARTHY
* Closed January 24, 1954. (77 performances)

PHOTOS BY TALBOT

Clarice Blackburn, Jason Robards, Jr.

PRESIDENT THEATRE
Opened Tuesday, March 23, 1954. *
The Gilbert and Sullivan Festival Theatre, Inc.
presents:

# THE AMERICAN SAVOYARDS GILBERT AND SULLIVAN REPERTOIRE

Produced and Directed by Dorothy Raedler; Libretto by Sir W. S. Gilbert; Music by Sir Arthur Sullivan; Conducted by Lucille Burnham; Organist, Keith Verhey.

## THE MIKADO

Presented March 23-28, and May 11-16, 1954. (16 performances)

### Cast

| | |
|---|---|
| The Mikado | Ronald Bush |
| Nanki-Poo | Norman Paige |
| Ko-Ko | Rue Knapp |
| Pooh-Bah | Francis Barnard |
| Pish-Tush | John Bridson |
| Go-To | Henry Fitzgibbon |
| Yum-Yum | Sally Knapp |
| Pitti-Sing | Joan Brower |
| Peep-Bo | Virginia Bower |
| Katisha | Mary-Ellen Thompson |

School-Girls and Nobles: Raymond Allen, Virginia Carroll, Kenneth Doubrava, Georgia Lyke, Herbert Moore, Lore Reckel, Marilyn Sofia, Eunice Wilcox, Glenn Wilder, Henry Fitzgibbon.

## THE PIRATES OF PENZANCE

Presented March 30 — April 4, 1954. (8 performances)

### Cast

| | |
|---|---|
| Major-General Stanley | Rue Knapp |
| The Pirate King | Ronald Rush |
| Samuel | John Bridson |
| Frederic | Norman Paige |
| Sergeant of Police | Francis Barnard |
| Mabel | Sally Knapp |
| Edith | Lore Reckel |
| Kate | Joan Brower |
| Isabel | Virginia Carroll |
| Ruth | Mary-Ellen Thompson |

Pirates, Police, and General's Daughters: Raymond Allen, Joe Baylon, Virginia Bower, Kenneth Doubrava, Henry Fitzgibbon, Georgia Lyke, Herbert Moore, Marilyn Sofia, Eunice Wilcox, Glenn Wilder.

## PATIENCE

Presented April 6-11, 1954. (8 performances)

### Cast

| | |
|---|---|
| Colonel Calverley | Ronald Bush |
| Major Murgatroyd | Raymond Allen |
| Lt. Duke of Dunstable | Norman Paige |
| Reginald Bunthorne | Rue Knapp |
| Archibald Grosvenor | John Bridson |
| Mr. Bunthorne's Solicitor | Joe Baylon |
| Lady Angela | Marilyn Sofia |
| Lady Saphir | Lore Reckel |
| Lady Ella | Virginia Bower |
| Lady Jane | Mary-Ellen Thompson |
| Patience | Sally Knapp |

Rapturous Maidens and Officers of Dragoon Guards: Francis Barnard, Joan Brower, Virginia Carroll, Kenneth Doubrava, Henry Fitzgibbon, Georgia Lyke, Herbert Moore, Eunice Wilcox, Glenn Wilder.

Norman Paige, Sally Knapp in "The Mikado"

Ronald Bush, Rue Knapp, John Bridson in "The Pirates of Penzance"

## THE GONDOLIERS

Presented April 13-18, 1954. (8 performances)

### Cast

Duke of Plaza-Toro .......................... Rue Knapp
Luiz ................................................ Raymond Allen
Don Alhambra Del Bolero ............... Ronald Bush
Marco Palmieri .............................. Norman Paige
Giuseppe Palmieri ........................ Francis Barnard
Antonio ......................................... John Bridson
Francesco ..................................... Herbert Moore
Giorgio .......................................... Glenn Wilder
Annibale ................................. Henry Fitzgibbon
Duchess of Plaza-Toro ....... Mary-Ellen Thompson
Casilda ........................................... Sally Knapp
Gianetta ...................................... Virginia Bower
Tessa ............................................ Joan Brower
Fiametta .......................................... Lore Reckel
Vittoria ........................................... Marilyn Sofia
Giulia ........................................ Virginia Carroll
Inez ............................................. Georgia Lyke

Gondoliers, Contadine and Courtiers: Joe Baylon,
Virginia Carroll, Kenneth Doubrava, Henry Fitz-
gibbon, Georgia Lyke, Herbert Moore, Lore Reckel,
Marilyn Sofia, Eunice Wilcox, Glenn Wilder.

## RUDDIGORE

Presented April 20-25, 1954. (8 performances)

### Cast

Sir Ruthven Murgatroyd ...................... Rue Knapp
Richard Dauntless ........................... Norman Paige
Sir Despard Murgatroyd ................... Ronald Bush
Old Adam Goodheart ................. Francis Barnard
Rose Maybud ................................... Sally Knapp
Mad Margaret ............................... Marilyn Sofia
Dame Hannah .................... Mary-Ellen Thompson
Zorah ......................................... Virginia Bower
Ruth ........................................... Virginia Carroll
Sir Rupert Murgatroyd ............. Kenneth Doubrava
Sir Jasper Murgatroyd ........................ Joe Baylon
Sir Lionel Murgatroyd ................... Herbert Moore
Sir Conrad Murgatroyd ............... Raymond Allen
Sir Desmond Murgatroyd .......... Henry Fitzgibbon
Sir Mervyn Murgatroyd ................... Glenn Wilder
Sir Roderic Murgatroyd ................... John Bridson

Officers, Ancestors, Professional Bridesmaids: Raymond Allen, Joe Baylon, Joan Brower, Kenneth
Doubrava, Henry Fitzgibbon, Georgia Lyke, Herbert Moore, Lore Reckel, Eunice Wilcox, Glenn
Wilder.

## IOLANTHE

Presented April 27 - May 2, 1954. (8 performances)

### Cast

The Lord Chancellor ........................... Rue Knapp
Lord Mountararat ........................... Ronald Bush
Lord Tolloller ............................... Norman Paige
Private Willis ................................. John Bridson
Strephon ..................................... Herbert Moore
Queen of The Fairies ......... Mary-Ellen Thompson
Iolanthe ......................................... Joan Brower
Celia ........................................... Virginia Carroll
Leila ............................................... Lore Reckel
Fleta ............................................ Virginia Bower
Phyllis ........................................... Sally Knapp

Dukes, Marquises, Earls, Viscounts, Barons and
Fairies: Raymond Allen, Francis Barnard, Virginia
Bower, Virginia Carroll, Kenneth Doubrava,
Henry Fitzgibbon, Georgia Lyke, Lore Reckel,
Marilyn Sofia, Eunice Wilcox, Glenn Wilder.

KERR PHOTOS

## THE YEOMAN OF THE GUARD

Presented May 4-9, 1954. (8 performances)

### Cast

Sir Richard Cholmondeley .............. John Bridson
Colonel Fairfax ............................. Norman Paige
Sergeant Meryll ........................... Francis Barnard
Leonard Meryll ............................ Raymond Allen
Jack Point ......................................... Rue Knapp
Wilfred Shadbolt ............................ Ronald Bush
1st Yeoman .................................. Herbert Moore
2nd Yeoman ................................. Glenn Wilder
1st Citizen ....................................... Joe Baylon
Elsie Maynard ................................. Sally Knapp
Phoebe Meryll ................................ Joan Brower
Dame Carruthers ............... Mary-Ellen Thompson
Kate ........................................... Virginia Carroll

Yeoman of the Guard, Gentlemen and Citizens:
Virginia Bower, Joe Baylon, Kenneth Doubrava,
Henry Fitzgibbon, Jack Frymire, Georgia Lyke,
Herbert Moore, Lore Reckel, Marilyn Sofia, Eunice
Wilcox, Glenn Wilder.

Marilyn Sofia, Ronald Bush in "Ruddigore".
Top: Francis Barnard, Mary-Ellen Thompson in "The Yeoman of The Guard"

## H.M.S. PINAFORE

Presented May 18-23, 1954. (8 performances)

### Cast

Rt. Hon. Sir Joseph Porter ................ Rue Knapp
Captain Corcoran ............................. John Bridson
Ralph Rackstraw ........................... Norman Paige
Dick Deadeye ................................. Ronald Bush
Bill Bobstay ............................... Francis Barnard
Bob Becket ..................................... Glenn Wilder
Josephine .................................... Sally Knapp
Cousin Hebe ............................... Marilyn Sofia
Little Buttercup .................. Mary-Ellen Thompson

First Lord's Sisters, Cousins, Aunts and Sailors:
Raymond Allen, Virginia Bower, Joan Brower,
Virginia Carroll, Kenneth Doubrava, Henry Fitz-
gibbon, Georgia Lyke, Herbert Moore, Lore Reckel,
Eunice Wilcox, Glenn Wilder.

## THE SORCERER

Presented May 25-30, 1954. (8 performances)

### Cast

Sir Marmaduke Pointdextre ............... Ronald Rush
Alexis .......................................... Norman Paige
Dr. Daly ...................................... Herbert Moore
Notary ........................................ John Bridson
John Wellington Wells ..................... Rue Knapp
Lady Sangazure .................. Mary-Ellen Thompson
Aline ............................................. Sally Knapp
Mrs. Partlet .................................. Marilyn Sofia
Constance ....................................... Lore Reckel

Chorus of Villagers: Raymond Allen, Francis Barnard, Joe Baylon, Virginia Bower, Joan Brower,
Virginia Carroll, Kenneth Doubrava, Henry Fitzgibbon, Georgia Lyke, Eunice Wilcox, Glenn
Wilder.

*Company Manager:* Oscar Green
*Press:* Max Eisen
*Stage Manager:* Joe Baylon

\* Closed May 30, 1954. (80 performances)

Right: Raymond Allen, Norman Paige,
Mary-Ellen Thompson, Marilyn Sofia, Ron-
ald Bush in "Patience". Top right: Norman
Paige, Joan Brower, Virginia Bower, Francis
Barnard

Don Gordon, Rusty Lane, Murray Hamilton
in "Stockade"

138

## PRESIDENT THEATRE

Opened Thursday, February 4, 1954. \*
Diana Green and Paul Butler present:

## STOCKADE

By Mark J. Applemam; Based on Novel "From
Here To Eternity" by James Jones; Directed by
Robert H. Gordon; Settings and Lighting by Albert
Johnson; Music Composed by Jay Chernis; Pro-
duction Associate, Chryst Marvel.

### Cast

Pfc. Hanson .................................... Norman Keats
Pvt. Turnipseed ................................. Tom Poston
Robert E. Lee Prewitt ............... Murray Hamilton
Major Thompson ................................. Jay Barney
S/Sgt. Judson ................................ Gerald Milton
Angelo Maggio ................................ Don Gordon
Jack Malloy .......................................... Rusty Lane
Blues Berry ......................................... Ted Jordan
Francis Murdock ............................. Stephen Pluta
Lt. Culpepper .................................. George Hall
Stonewall Jackson .............................. Barnet Biro
A Soldier .................................. Cam Applegate
Sgt. Dixon ............................... William Thourlby
Cpl. Oliver ................................... Tige Andrews

A Drama in three acts and nine scenes.

*Company Manager:* Oscar Green
*Press:* Max Eisen, Marian Graham
*Stage Managers:* William Johnson, Cam Applegate

\* Closed February 6, 1954. (4 performances)

**BROADWAY TABERNACLE CHURCH**
Opened Sunday, April 4, 1954. *
The Broadway Chapel Players present:

## THE BOY WITH A CART

By Christopher Fry; Directed by Richard Barr;
Costumes Designed by Helen Alexander.

### Cast

| | |
|---|---|
| Narrator | Florida Friebus |
| | (Olive Dunbar on May 9th) |
| Cuthman | Bill Penn |
| Bess | Sylvia Davis |
| Mildred | Elsa Pohl |
| Matt | Charles Aidman |
| Neighbors: Helen Alexander, Ward Asquith, Alex | |
| | Berko |
| Cuthman's Mother | Cynthia Latham |
| Tawm | Robinson Stone |
| Tawm's Daughter | Helen Alexander |
| Mrs. Fipps | Sylvia Davis |
| Alfred | Ward Asquith |
| Demiwulf | Alex Berko |
| Villager | Charles Aidman |
| Soloist | June Ericson |

*Technical Assistant:* CARLEEN ANDERSON
*Press:* TED KRAUS

* Presented on Sundays only at 5:30 P.M. for
9 performances

### Right: Bill Penn

Florida Friebus, Helen Alexander, Robinson
Stone, Cynthia Latham, Bill Penn

**Earle Hyman as Othello**

**JAN HUS AUDITORIUM**
Opened Thursday, October 29, 1953.*
The Shakespeare Guild Festival Company presents:

## OTHELLO

By William Shakespeare; Staged by Luis Martinez; Settings, Costumes and Lighting by Donald Goldman; Original Music by Coleridge-Taylor Perkinson; Producer, William Thornton.

### Cast

| | |
|---|---|
| Duke of Venice | Charles MacCawley |
| Brabantio | William Myers |
| Gratiano | Erle Hall |
| Othello | Earle Hyman |
| Cassio | Forrest Compton |
| Iago | William Thornton |
| Roderigo | James O'Brien |
| Montano | Charles MacCawley |
| Ludovico | William Myers |
| Desdemona | Blanche Cholet |
| Emilia | Jacqueline Brookes |
| Bianca | Elaine Limpert |
| Lady-in-Waiting | Margarita Borrows |

*General Manager:* GEORGE DENHAM FORD
*Press:* HILARY MASTERS
*Stage Manager:* CHARLES OLSEN

* Closed January 31, 1954. (72 performances)

## HAMLET

By William Shakespeare; Directed by Herbert Kramer; Sets Designed by Herb Raynaud; Costumes by Herb Raynaud and Wyman Kane.

### Cast

| | |
|---|---|
| Francisco | Alfred Muscari |
| Bernardo | Joseph Peeples |
| Marcellus | Carl Shelton |
| Horatio | James O'Brien |
| Ghost | Peter Dearing |
| King | Donald Mork |
| Queen | Maurine Gray |
| Laertes | Robert Baines |
| Polonius | Raymond Johnson |
| Hamlet | William Thornton |
| Ophelia | Elena Moore |
| Rosencrantz | Wyman E. Kane |
| Guildenstern | Alfred Muscari |
| 1st Player (King) | Peter Dearing |
| 2nd Player (Queen) | Wally White |
| 3rd Player (Lucianus) | Gordon Matthews |
| 4th Player (Prologue) | Janet Conway |
| 1st Grave Digger | John Monk |
| 2nd Grave Digger | John Brinkley |
| Priest | Warren Gogan |
| Osric | Wally White |

Courtiers: Diane Rocklin, Linda Harris, Bess Welch. William Damon, Thor Nielson, Ronald Bell, Joyce Orwig, Lee Meier.

*Press:* ROBERT GANSHAW, ELEANOR BEESON
*Stage Managers:* ROBERT MILLER, JOHN BRINKLEY, GORDON MATTHEWS

Closed May 30, 1954. (25 performances)

Jacqueline Brooks, Blanche Cholet.
Left: William Thornton, Earle Hyman

William Thornton, James O'Brien

## CLUB THEATRE, INC.

Opened Friday, March 5, 1954. *
Club Theatre, Inc. presents:

## THE INFERNAL MACHINE

By Jean Cocteau; Directed by Iza Itkin; Designed by John Boyt; Music by Cecil Bentz; Costumes Executed by Chris Mahan and Walt Watson.

### Cast

| | |
|---|---|
| Young Soldier | David Gard |
| The Soldier | Morgan Holden |
| The Chief | William Adler |
| Jocasta | Lesley Woods |
| Tiresias | Roland von Weber |
| The Sphinx | Louise Troy |
| Anubis | Calvin Holt |
| Theban Matron | Susan Roy |
| Oedipus | Alan Shayne |
| Creon | Charles Grunwell†¹ |
| Messenger | Arthur Walsh†² |
| Shepherd | Ross Anderson |
| Antigone | Lee Graham |

*Managing Director:* ED STRUM
*Press:* BETTY ANN WELCH

*Stage Managers:* ROSS ANDERSON, ALEK DENOFF

\* Closed March 28, 1954. (16 performances — weekends only)

† Replaced by: 1. Kenneth Paine, 2. Tom Woods.

PHOTOS BY JOHN ERWIN

Right: Alan Shayne, Lesley Woods.
Top right: Louise Troy, Calvin Holt

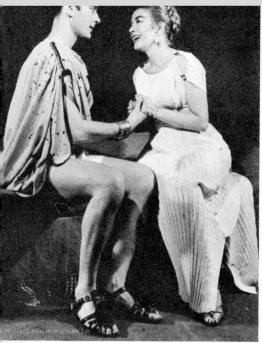

Alan Shayne, Lesley Woods

Alan Shayne

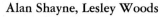

142

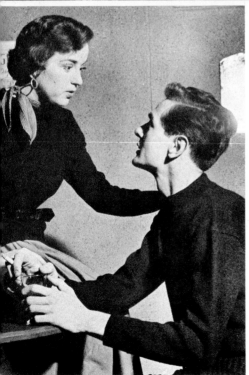

**ORIGINALS ONLY PLAYHOUSE**
Opened Wednesday, July 1, 1953.*
Originals Only present:

## ONE FOOT TO THE SEA

By Harold Levitt; Directed by Tom Hill; Setting by Robert Williams; Lighting by Ed Corley; Songs and Music by Fran Ziffer, Gordon Burdge, Hardy Weider and J. Russel Robinson.

### Cast
(including alternates)

| | |
|---|---|
| Allen Gode | Gene Remington |
| | Bob Boucher |
| Steve Montvidas | Donald Stuart |
| | Joe Ecktman |
| Beth | Pat Crawford |
| | Muriel Dorne |
| Delachaux | Jim Dukas |
| | Henry Miller |
| Volkening | Rolfe Tandberg |
| | Steve Kenton |
| Tony Cima | Tom Shields |
| | Billy Leydon |
| Christie | Raoul G. Reardon |
| | A. Rhu Taylor |
| John Beggs | Paul Brown |
| | Bill Ellis |
| Paddy | Steve Kenton |
| | Jamo Blake |

* Closed April 11, 1954. (249 performances)

**ALIX JEFFRY PHOTOS**

Pat Crawford, Gene Remington.
Top: Tom Shields, Gene Remington

## HENRY STREET PLAYHOUSE

Opened Sunday, April 18, 1954. *
Playhouse Actors Company presents:

# ELECTRA

Translated by Winifred Smith from Jean Giraudoux; Directed by Archie Smith; Sets and Lighting by David Lemmon; Costumes by Jeanne Button; Music by Vittorio Rieti; Produced by Betty Young.

### Cast

Gardener ............................ Gerald E. McGonagill
The Little Eumenides: Patricia Goldstein, Sylvia Levine, Susan Weissman
Orestes ................................................ Tom Troupe
President ........................................ Joel Friedman
Agatha .............................................. Carolyn Coates
Aegisthus ............................................ James Noble
Servant ........................................ Mitchell Erickson
Beggar ................................................ Leonardo Cimino
Electra ............................................ Barbara Lester
Clytemnestra .................................... Sylvia Gassel
Young Man ........................................ Val Dufour
The Eumenides: Betty Lou Robinson, Sylvia Burnell, Barbara Van Ornam
Captain ................................................ Luke Bragg
Narses' Wife .................................... Ruth Volner

*Production Manager:* WILLIS GOULD
*Stage Managers:* LEONARD SOLOWAY,
CHARLOTTE FALKENBURG, ALICE KENNER

* Closed Sunday, April 25, 1954. (8 performances)

Luke Bragg, Carolyn Coates, Joel Friedman, James Noble, Sylvia Gassel, Barbara Lester, Leonardo Cimino. Top (L-R): Val Dufour; Carolyn Coates, Val Dufour; James Noble. Center (Left): Sylvia Gassel, (right) Tom Troupe, Barbara Lester

Standing: Jonathan York, Ruth Newton, Nancy Templeton, Rick Fredericks,
William Blenk, Jr., Ellen Klein. Kneeling: Gerald Metcalfe, Mamie Jones,
Charles Gordon

## CURRENT STAGES

Opened October 6, 1953. *
Current Stages present:

## THE CLIMATE OF EDEN

By Moss Hart; Directed by Joseph Leberman;
Designed by Murray Sherman; Incidental Music
Composed by Matt Mathews.

### Cast

| | |
|---|---|
| Mrs. Harmston | Adelle Bradley, Ruth Newton |
| Olivia | Ellen Klein, Eva Stern |
| Berton | William Blenk, Jr., John Connoughton |
| Rev. Harmston | George Ebeling, Jonathan York |
| Ellen | Mamie Jones, Vi Mazzei |
| Mabel | Sheila Keddy, Moya Diana Moynahan, Nancy Templeton |
| Garvey | Rick Fredericks, Curt Paul |
| Gregory | James Paul, Robert McQueeney, Gerald Metcalfe |
| Logan | Charles Gordon |
| Robert | Jack Gordon |

*General Manager:* Robert Kamlot
*Press:* Esther Benson
*Stage Manager:* Henry Mavis

* Closed Sunday, March 14, 1954. (138 performances)

MURRAY SHERMAN PHOTOS

145

George Ebeling, Robert McQueeney. Center
(L−R): Ellen Klein, Nancy Templeton;
William Blenk, Jr., Mamie Jones, Ellen Klein

## OKLAHOMA*

Music by Richard Rodgers; Book and Lyrics by
Oscar Hammerstein 2nd; Based on "Green Grow
The Lilacs" by Lynn Riggs; Directed by Rouben
Mamoulian; Reproduced by Jerome Whyte; Dances
by Agnes De Mille; Recreated by Betty Gour; Set-
tings by Lemuel Ayers; Costumes by Miles White;
Orchestrations by Robert Russell Bennett; Presented
by Rodgers and Hammerstein. Closed at the Shubert,
Philadelphia, Pa., May 8, 1954.

### Cast

| | |
|---|---|
| Aunt Eller | Mary Marlo |
| Curly | Ridge Bond |
| Laurey | Florence Henderson |
| Cord Elam | Charles Hart |
| Fred | Charles Scott |
| Slim | Charles Rule |
| Will Parker | Harris Hawkins |
| Jud Fry | Alfred Cibelli, Jr. |
| Ado Annie Carnes | Barbara Cook |
| Ali Hakim | David Le Grant |
| Gertie Cummings | Judy Rawlings |
| Ellen | Maggi Nelson |
| Kate | Frances Irby |
| Silvie | Patti Parsons |
| Armina | Lynne Broadbent |
| Aggie | Cathy Conklin |
| Andrew Carnes | Owen Martin |
| Chalmers | George Lawrence |
| Mike | Bob Lord |

**Dancers:** Lynn Broadbent, Bette Burton, Cathy Conk-
lin, Betty Koerber, Gayle Parmelee, Patti Parsons,
Cynthia Price, Georganne Shaw, Louellen Sibley,
Marguerite Stewart, Payne Converse, Nick Dana,
Jack Ketcham, Ronnie Landry, John Pero, Jr., Tom
Pickler, Joe Ribeau.

**Singers:** Lenore Arnold, Lois Barrodin, Marylin
Hardy, Frances Irby, Heidi Palmer, Barbara Reis-
man, Jeanne Shea, William Ambler, Dino Dante,
James Fox, Christopher Golden, Bob Lord, Charles
Rule, Charles Scott.

Company Manager: HARRY SHAPIRO
Press: MICHEL MOK, GEORGE A. FLORIDA
Stage Managers: DAVID SIDNEY WEINSTEIN,
PHILIP JOHNSON, CHARLES SCOTT

* THEATRE WORLD, Vols. I-IX.

Ridge Bond. Top (L – R): Florence Henderson, Alfred Cibelli, Jr.; Barbara Cook
Judy Rawlings, David Le Grant

## SOUTH PACIFIC*

Music by Richard Rodgers; Lyrics by Oscar Hammerstein 2nd and Joshua Logan; Adapted from "Tales of The South Pacific" by James A. Michener; Book and Musical Numbers Staged by Joshua Logan; Scenery and Lighting by Jo Mielziner; Costumes by Motley; Musical Director, Phil Ingalls; Orchestrations by Robert Russell Bennett; Produced by Richard Rodgers and Oscar Hammerstein 2nd in association with Leland Hayward and Joshua Logan. Opened at the Shubert Theatre, Chicago, Nov. 14, 1950.

### Cast

| | |
|---|---|
| Ngana | Elsie or Frances Rodriguez |
| Jerome | Orlando Rodriguez |
| Henry | Arsenio Trinidad |
| Ensign Nellie Forbush | Janet Blair†1 |
| Emile de Becque | Webb Tilton |
| Bloody Mary | Dorothy Franklin |
| Bloody Mary's Assistant | Jeanette Migenes |
| Abner | Clifton Gray |
| Stewpot | John Ferry |
| Luther Billis | Benny Baker |
| Professor | Earl Drebing |
| Lt. Joseph Cable | Stanley Grover |
| Capt. George Brackett | Robert Emmett Keane†2 |
| Cmdr. William Harbison | Alan Baxter |
| Yeoman Herbert Quale | Patrick Tolson†3 |
| Sgt. Kenneth Johnson | Vincent McMahon†4 |
| Seabee Richard West | Evans Thornton |
| Seabee Morton Wise | Don Wortman |
| Seaman Tom O'Brien | David Daniels†5 |
| Radio Operator Bob McCaffrey | LeRoy Busch†6 |
| Cpl. Hamilton Steeves | Gordon Ewing |
| Pvt. Sven Larsen | Don Swenson†7 |
| Lt. Genevieve Marshall | Jane Haskell†8 |
| Seaman James Hayes | Jay MacKenzie |
| Ens. Dinah Murphy | Edith Lane |
| Ens. Janet MacGregor | Bernice Massi†9 |
| Ens. Sue Yaeger | Priscilla Mullins†10 |
| Ens. Lisa Minelli | Mildred Slavin†11 |
| Ens. Connie Walewska | Betty Graeber |
| Ens. Bessie Noonan | Genie Balmer |
| Ens. Cora MacRae | Nancy Bramlage |
| Ens. Peggy Olsen | Rosemary O'Shea |
| Liat | Norma Calderon†12 |
| Marcel | William McKenna |
| Lt. Buzz Adams | Warren Brown |
| Liwana | Jeanette Migenes |
| Chin Yu | Mari Young†13 |

*Company Manager:* HAROLD GOLDBERG
*Press:* AL BUTLER
*Stage Managers:* ROSS BOWMAN, LEROY BUSCH, ROBERT DeCOST

† Replaced by: 1. Jeanne Bal, 2. Russ Brown, 3. Vincent McMahon, 4. Tom Legate, 5. David Ferris, 6. Gordon Hanson who was replaced by Patrick Tolson, 7. Sam Kirkham, 8. Ann Richards, 9. Priscilla Mullins, 10. Genevieve Crovo, 11. Christy Palmer, 12. Mari Young, 13. Rosemarie Cardinoza.

* For original New York production see THEATRE WORLD, Vol. V.

Jeanne Bal, Orlando and Elsie Rodriguez, Webb Tilton. Center (L — R): Benny Baker, Dorothy Franklin, Webb Tilton

## NEW FACES OF 1952*

Words and Music by Ronny Graham, Arthur Siegel, June Carroll, Sheldon Harnick, Michael Brown; Sketches by Ronny Graham and Melvin Brooks, Entire Production Devised and Staged by John Murray Anderson; Choreography and Musical Numbers Staged by Richard Barstow; Sketches Directed by John Beal; Costumes by Thomas Becher; Scenery by Raoul Pene duBois; Musical Director, Anton Coppola; Orchestral Arrangements by Ted Royal; Produced, Compiled, Assembled and Supervised by Leonard Sillman; Presented by Walter P. Chrysler, Jr. Opened at the Shubert Theatre, Boston, April 6, 1953, and closed at the Cass, Detroit, Mich., April 10, 1954.

### Cast

| | |
|---|---|
| Virginia Bosler | Carol Lawrence |
| June Carroll | Paul Lynde |
| Robert Clary | Bill Mullikin |
| Allen Conroy | Rosemary O'Reilly |
| Virginia de Luce†1 | Jimmy Russell |
| Alice Ghostley†2 | James Shelton |
| Ronny Graham | George Smiley |
| Eartha Kitt | Dinnie Smith |
| Johnny Laverty | Polly Ward |

*General Manager:* Leon Spachner
*Press:* Herb Carlin
*Stage Managers:* Clark Ranger, Leonard Auerbach

† Replaced by: 1. Lee Perkins, 2. Jenny Lou Law

* For original New York production see THEATRE WORLD, VOL. VIII.

148

Robert Clary, Eartha Kitt. Center: (L — R): Ronny Graham, Paul Lynde, Alice Ghostley, June Carroll, Bill Mullikin

## PAL JOEY*

Music by Richard Rodgers; Lyrics by Lorenz Hart; Book by John O'Hara; Dances and Musical Numbers Staged by Robert Alton; Settings by Oliver Smith; Costumes by Miles White; Lighting by Peggy Clark; Special Orchestrations by Don Walker; Production Associate, Emil Katzke; Musical Director, Jacques Rabiroff; Book Directed by David Alexander; Entire Production Supervised by Robert Alton. Presented by Jule Styne and Leonard Key in association with Anthony B. Farrell. Opened at the Shubert, Washington, D.C., April 20, 1953, and closed at the Nixon in Pittsburgh, Nov. 28, 1953.

### Cast

| | |
|---|---|
| Mike | Jack Waldron |
| Joey | Harold Lang |
| Kid | Dorothy Love |
| Gladys | Beverley Bozeman |
| Agnes | Elaine Pallie |
| Dottie | Lyda Koehring |
| Adele | Mable Rea |
| Waiter | Hank Brunjes |
| Amarilla | Eloise Milton |
| Francine | Doris Light |
| Dolores | Gloria Slater |
| Linda | Pat Johnson |
| Vera | Carol Bruce |
| Valerie | Barbara Nichols |
| Ernest | Gordon Peters |
| Victor | Ward Ellis |
| Stage Manager | T. J. Halligan |
| Louis | Lewis Bolyard |
| Melba | Libi Staiger |
| Ludlow Lowell | Lionel Stander |
| Doorman | Gordon Peters |
| O'Brien | T. J. Halligan |

**Dancers:** Jean Acheson, Vivian Joyce, Charlene Hargrove, Mabin Hewes, Cherie Faye, Doris Light, Doris Lorenz, Eloise Milton, Elaine Pallie, Claire Patrick, June Stern, Mable Rea, Gloria Slater, Carol Stevens, Lyda Koehring, Babs Warden, Delia Weddington, Hank Brunjes, Nick Dotoratos, Athan Karras, Dick Korthaze, Bill Regan, James Ryan, Chris Scott, Terry Violino, James White.

*Company Manager:* Joseph M. Grossman
*Press:* Reuben Rabinovitch
*Stage Managers:* J. Myles Putnam, T. J. Halligan

\* For 1952 New York revival see THEATRE WORLD, Vol. VIII.

GRAPHIC HOUSE PHOTOS

Carol Bruce, Harold Lang. Center: Harold Lang, Betty O'Neil, Jack Waldron

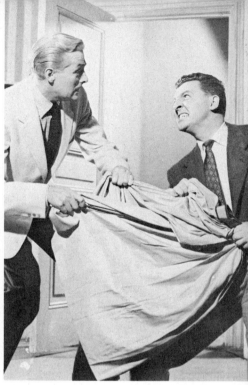

Edward Hunt, Eddie Bracken

## THE SEVEN YEAR ITCH*

By George Axelrod; Directed by John Gerstad; Designed and Lighted by Frederick Fox; Incidental Music Composed by Dana Suesse; Production Supervised by Elliott Nugent; Produced by Courtney Burr and Elliott Nugent. Opened at the Cass Theatre, Detroit, Sept. 7, 1953.

### Cast

| | |
|---|---|
| Richard Sherman | Eddie Bracken |
| Helen Sherman | Lydia Clarke |
| Ricky | Darryl Richard |
| Miss Morris | Shirley Ballard |
| Elaine | Gena Rowlands |
| Marie What-Ever-Her-Name-Was | Jo Kaiser |
| The Girl | Louise King |
| Dr. Brubaker | Howard Freeman |
| Tom Mackenzie | Edward Hunt |
| The Voice of Richard's Conscience | Joseph Leon |
| The Voice of The Girl's Conscience | Mary Warren |
| Sports Announcer | Marty Glickman |

*Company Manager:* JOHN H. POTTER
*Press:* CHARLES WASHBURN
*Stage Managers:* JOSE VEGA, ROBERT PASCHALL, MARY WARREN

* For original New York production see THEATRE WORLD, Vol. IX.

PHOTOS BY TALBOT

Eddie Bracken, Louise King.
Top: Lydia Clarke, Eddie Bracken

John Philip, Beatrice Lillie

## AN EVENING WITH
## BEATRICE LILLIE*
### with Reginald Gardiner

Directed by Edward Duryea Dowling; Settings by Rolf Gerard; Eadie and Rack at the pianos. Presented by Edward Duryea Dowling. Opened at the Shubert, Boston, Sept. 14, 1953.

ACT I

Reginald Gardiner, "A Star's First Night," "One In Three" by Reginald Gardiner, "Wind" by Beatrice Lillie, "Trains" by Reginald Gardiner, "Father and Son," "Anesthesia" by Reginald Gardiner, "References," "The Conductor" by Reginald Gardiner.

ACT II

Eadie and Rack; Reginald Gardiner; Beatrice Lillie accompanied by Rack with singer John Philip.

Miss Lillie was assisted by Xenia Bank, Shannon Dean and John Philip.

Company Manager: LOUIS EPSTEIN
Press: HARRY DAVIES
Stage Managers: MILTON STERN, ELLEN BLUME, JOHN PHILIP

* For original New York production see THEATRE WORLD, Vol. IX.

GRAPHIC HOUSE PHOTOS

Beatrice Lillie. Top: Beatrice Lillie, Reginald Gardiner

151

## THE LOVE OF FOUR COLONELS*

By Peter Ustinov; Directed by Rex Harrison; Settings and Costumes by Rolf Gerard; Production under Supervision of Lawrence Langner and Theresa Helburn. Presented by The Theatre Guild and Aldrich and Myers. Opened Oct. 2, 1953, at Community Theatre, Hershey, Pa., and closed at the National in Washington, D.C., Nov. 14, 1953.

### Cast

| | |
|---|---|
| Col. Wesley Breitenspiegel | Larry Gates†[1] |
| Col. Desmond De S. Rinder-Sparrow | Robert Coote |
| Col. Aime Frappot | George Voskovec |
| Col. Alexander Ikonenko | Stefan Schnabel |
| Mayor of Herzogenberg | Reginald Mason |
| The Man | Rex Harrison |
| Donovan | Leueen MacGrath†[2] |
| Beauty | Lilli Palmer |

*Company Manager:* PETER DAVIS
*Press:* NAT AND IRVIN DORFMAN
*Stage Managers:* KARL NIELSEN, HAIM WINANT

† Replaced by: 1. Edward Andrews, 2. Maureen Hurley
* For original New York production see THEATRE WORLD, Vol. IX.

Robert Coote, Rex Harrison, Lilli Palmer

## THE CHILDREN'S HOUR*

By Lillian Hellman; Settings by Howard Bay; Staged by Del Hughes; Costumes by Anna Hill Johnstone; Associate Producer, Peter Glenn; Presented by Kermit Bloomgarden. Opened at the Wilmington, Del., Playhouse, October 1, 1953, and closed at the Harris, Chicago, Ill., Dec. 5, 1953.

### Cast

| | |
|---|---|
| Peggy Rogers | Sandra March |
| Catherine | Nancy Plehn |
| Lois Fisher | Doreen Lane†[1] |
| Mrs. Lily Mortar | Mary Finney |
| Evelyn Munn | Mary Lee Dearring |
| Helen Burton | Carolyn Rosser |
| Rosalie Wells | Lynn Thatcher |
| Mary Tilford | Janet Parker†[2] |
| Karen Wright | Priscilla Gillette |
| Martha Dobie | Patricia Neal |
| Dr. Joseph Cardin | Theodore Newton |
| Agatha | Edna Courtleigh |
| Mrs. Amelia Tilford | Fay Bainter |
| Grocery Boy | Gordon Russell |

*Company Manager:* PAUL GROLL
*Press:* TED GOLDSMITH
*Stage Managers:* LEONARD PATRICK, EDWIN GORDON

† Replaced by: 1. Carol Sinclair, 2. Iris Mann for the Chicago run.
* For 1952 New York revival see THEATRE WORLD, Vol. IX.

GRAPHIC HOUSE PHOTOS

Fay Bainter, Janet Parker. Center (left): Fay Bainter, Theodore Newton, Priscilla Gillette, Janet Parker, Patricia Neal. Center (right): Priscilla Gillette, Patricia Neal, Gordon Russell

Mary Hartig, Nancy Malone, Edith Atwater, Melvyn Douglas,
Jacqueline Hernly

Edith Atwater, Melvyn Douglas

## TIME OUT FOR GINGER*

By Ronald Alexander; Scenery and Lighting by
Eldon Elder; Directed by Shepard Traube; Cos-
tumes by Virginia Volland. Presented by Shepard
Traube and Gordon Pollock in association with Don
Hershey. Opened at the Shubert, New Haven, Conn.,
Oct. 1, 1953.

### Cast

| | |
|---|---|
| Lizzie | Laura Pierpont |
| Agnes Carol | Edith Atwater |
| Howard Carol | Melvyn Douglas |
| Joan | Mary Hartig† |
| Jeannie | Jaqueline Hernly |
| Ginger | Nancy Malone |
| Eddie Davis | Barry Truex |
| Tommy | Steve McQueen |
| Mr. Wilson | Will Hussung |
| Ed Hoffman | Philip Loeb |

*Company Manager:* J. H. Del Bondio
*Press:* Arthur Jay Levy
*Stage Managers:* Daniel Broun, Bruce Savan

† Replaced by Marian Brown.
* For original New York production see THEA-
TRE WORLD, Vol. IX.

## JOHN BROWN'S BODY*

By Stephen Vincent Benét; Adapted and Directed by Charles Laughton; Music and Effects by Walter Schumann; On Stage Choral Director, Richard White; Presented by Paul Gregory. Opened at the Geary Theatre, San Francisco, Oct. 5, 1953, and closed at Liberty Hall, El Paso, Texas, Jan. 31, 1954.

### Cast

Tyrone Power     Ann Baxter     Raymond Massey

**Choral Group:** Joe Baker, Don Burke, Betty Benson, Keith Carver, Jack B. Dailey, Barbara Ford, Gillian Grey, Homer W. Hall, Les Helsdon, Bob Jensen, William Longmire, Donna McDaniel, John Mc Mahon, Roger Miller, Smith Russell, Jr., Lynda Stevens, Jack Vander-Laan, Robert Vaughn, Gordon B. Wood.

**Soloists:** Roger Miller, Betty Benson
**Dancers:** Donna McDaniel, Keith Carver

*Company Manager:* LES THOMAS
*Press:* KARL BERNSTEIN
*Stage Manager:* CLAY RANDOLPH

* For original New York production see THEA-TRE WORLD, Vol. IX.

Rehearsal shot with Charles Laughton, Anne Baxter, Tyrone Power, Raymond Massey

## MISALLIANCE*

By Bernard Shaw; Directed by Cyril Ritchard; Setting by John Boyt; Costumes by Robert Fletcher; Production Supervisor, Lemuel Ayers. Presented by The Theatre Guild-American Theatre Society. Opened Oct. 5, 1953, at the Locust Theatre, Philadelphia, and closed at the Erlanger, Buffalo, Feb. 10, 1954.

### Cast

Bentley Summerhays ...................... Robert Casper
Johnny Tarleton .......................... Robert Fletcher
Hypatia Tarleton ........................... Jan Farrand†¹
Mrs. Tarleton ............................ Dorothy Sands†²
Lord Summerhays .......................... George Turner
Mr. Tarleton .............................. Martyn Green
Percival ......................................... Lee Richardson
Lina ........................................ Katherine Sergava
Gunner ...................................... Hugh Thomas

*General Manager:* JOHN YORKE
*Press:* SAMUEL MACLEARY WELLER
*Stage Managers:* BURRY FREDRIK, RICHARD BALDRIDGE

† Replaced by: 1. Priscilla Morrill, 2. Isobel Elsom.

* For New York revival see THEATRE WORLD, Vol. IX.

PHOTOS BY TALBOT

Jan Farrand, Martyn Green, Robert Fletcher, Edith King. Center (L-R): Robert Fletcher, Katherine Sergava; Jan Farrand, Lee Richardson

Entire cast in "Twin Beds"

## TWIN BEDS

By Salisbury Field and Margaret Mayo; Directed by George Lipton; Presented by Manny Davis. Opened October 20, 1953, in Allentown, Pa., and closed June 5, 1954, at The Blackstone, Chicago.

### Cast

| | |
|---|---|
| Terry Howe | Kyle MacDonnell†[1] |
| Charles Monti | Iggie Wolfington†[2] |
| Bill Howe | John Tyers†[3] |
| Andy Larkin | Stuart Kerns†[4] |
| Ellen Larkin | Corinne Bissette†[5] |
| Joan Monti | Nina Olivette |
| Mabel | Marie Foster†[6] |

*Company Manager:* JOSEPH MOSS
*Press:* MAURICE TURET
*Stage Manager:* JOHN ARMSTRONG

† Replaced by: 1. Betty Bartley, 2. Jack Harrold, 3. John Shanks, 4. John Armstrong, 5. Adrienne Angel, 6. Kathleen Kerr

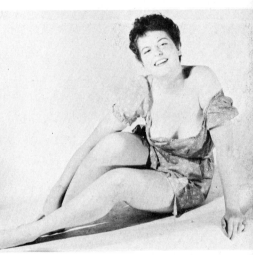

## MAID IN THE OZARKS

By Claire Parrish; Staged by Leslie Cutler; Presented by John Kenley. Opened at the American Theatre, Pittston, Penna., Oct. 27, 1952, and closed at the Nixon in Pittsburgh, Dec. 5, 1953.

### Cast

| | |
|---|---|
| Gram Calhoun | Kay Hart |
| Thad Calhoun | Francis Perkins |
| Mohawk | Leslie Cutler |
| Bart Calvert | Brad Olson |
| Lydia Tolliver | Ann Sorg |
| Temple Calhoun | David Tyrell |
| Frances Tolliver | Ann Vaughn |
| Cypress Young | Bert Wheeler |
| Amy Young | Jen Jones |
| Daisy-Belle | Janet Stack |
| Miss Bleecker | Dulcie Cooper |

*General Manager:* JOSEPH MOSS
*Press:* MAURICE TURET
*Stage Managers:* ALICE KENLEY, ROSS ANDERSON

HELEN MERRILL PHOTOS

Ann Vaughn, Bert Wheeler, Janet Stack.
Right center: Janet Stack

## PORGY AND BESS*

Music by George Gershwin; Libretto by DuBose Heyward; Lyrics by DuBose Heyward and Ira Gershwin; Based on Play "Porgy" by Dorothy and DuBose Heyward; Directed by Robert Breen; Musical Director, Alexander Smallens; Settings by Wolfgang Roth; Costumes by Jed Mace; Assistant Musical Director, William Jonson; Presented by Blevins Davis and Robert Breen. Opened Dec. 2, 1953, at the Forrest, Philadelphia, Pa.

### Cast

| | |
|---|---|
| Clara | Helen Colbert |
| Mingo | Jerry Laws |
| Sportin' Life | Cab Calloway |
| Serena | Helen Thigpen |
| Jake | Joseph James |
| Robbins | Howard Roberts |
| Jim | Sherman Sneed |
| Joe | Hugh Dilworth |
| Peter | Merritt Smith |
| Lily | Helen Dowdy |
| Maria | Georgia Burke |
| Porgy | LeVern Hutcherson or Leslie Scott or Irving Barnes |
| Crown | John McCurry |
| Annie | Catherine Ayers |
| Bess | Leontyne Price or Irene Williams or Elizabeth Foster |
| Policeman | Sam Kasakoff |
| Detective | Walter Riemer |
| Undertaker | William Veasey |
| Frazier | Moses LaMarr |
| Dancin' Ruby | Elizabeth Foster |
| Crab Man | Ray Yeates |
| Coroner | Sam Kasakoff |
| Policeman | Cecil Rutherford |
| Porgy's Goat | Jebob VI. |

**Residents of Catfish Row:** Joseph Attles, Irving Barnes, Lawson Bates, James Hawthorne Bey, Rhoda Boggs, Sibol Cain, Elsie Clarke, Charles Colman, Clarice Crawford, Helen Ferguson, Doris Galiber, Ruby Greene, Paul Harris, Lillian Hayman, Kenneth Hibbert, George A. Hill, Fredye Marshall, Joy McLean, Edna Ricks, Anabelle Ross, George A. Royston, Dolores Swan, Eva Taylor, Eloise C. Uggams, Catherine Van Buren, Barbara Ann Webb, Millard Williams, Ned Wright.

**Children:** Jacqueline Barnes, George Royston, Jr.

*General Manager:* LEONARD FIELD
*Press:* BILL DOLL, TED GOLDSMITH
*Stage Managers:* ELLA GERBER, WALTER RIEMER,
SAM KASAKOFF, CECIL RUTHERFORD,
J. C. HODGIN, JERRY LAWS

* For cast of New York revival see THEATRE WORLD, Vol. IX.

LeVern Hutcherson, Irene Williams, Cab Calloway. Center: Catherine Ayes, Helen Thigpen. Top left: Elizabeth Foster, John McCurry

# WISH YOU WERE HERE*

By Arthur Kober and Joshua Logan; Based on Mr. Kober's Play "Having Wonderful Time"; Music and Lyrics by Harold Rome; Direction and Dances by Joshua Logan; Settings and Lighting by Jo Mielziner; Costumes by Robert Mackintosh; Musical Direction by Jay Blackton; Orchestrations by Don Walker; Musical Continuity by Trude Rittman; Presented by Leland Hayward and Joshua Logan; Opened Dec. 8, 1953, at the Shubert in Chicago, and closed there Feb. 13, 1954.

## Cast

| | |
|---|---|
| Teddy Stern | Patricia Marand |
| Chick Miller | Peter Kelley |
| Fay Fromkin | Sheila Bond |
| Itchy Flexner | Frank Aletter |
| Pinky Harris | Ray Shaw |
| Harry "Muscles" Green | John Perkins |
| Lou Kandel | Sammy Smith |
| Herman Fabricant | Pat Chandler |
| Marvin | Wally Strauss |
| Sonja | Iris Burton |
| Schmutz | Robert Dixon |
| Eli | Frank Green |
| Barney | Buddy Martin |
| Sid | Lucky Kargo |
| Lenny | Skeet Guenther |
| Sam | Ben Varges |
| Monty | Tom Ayre |
| Henrietta | Barbara Cavanaugh |
| Gussie | Trudy De Luz |
| Irma | Pat Kelley |
| Shirley | Marilyn Bladd |
| Lena | Beth Park |
| Judy | Genevieve Boles |
| Miriam | Robin Oliver |
| The New Girl | Jane Hennessy |
| The Girl Diver | Patti Gillette |
| The Acrobat | Lucky Kargo |
| Eccentric Diver | Steve Wiland |
| Mel | Kelly McCormick |
| Fred | Alfred Sander |
| Morrie | Ed Johnson |
| Bill | Ray Morrissey |
| Butch | Warren Hayes |
| Joe | Reid Shelton |
| Harry | Frank Green |
| Phil | Stewart Vannerson |
| Alex | Dick Reed |
| Mac | Lowell Harris |
| Billie | Schelle Janis |
| Kitty | Virginia Hurst |
| Sarah | Stasia Olstowsky |
| Felice | Eleanore Gregory |
| Anna | Anne Wallace |
| Wilma | Carolyn Hoffman |

*Company Manager:* Carl Fisher
*Press:* Leo Freedman, Abner Klipstein
*Stage Managers:* Dan W. Sattler, Joe Calvan, Robert Griffith

\* For original New York production see THEATRE WORLD, Vol. IX.

Peter Kelley, Patricia Marand. Top (L-R): Frank Aletter; Ray Shaw, Patricia Marand; Sheila Bond, Frank Aletter, Patricia Marand. Center: Peter Kelley, Patricia Marand, Ray Shaw

# GUYS AND DOLLS*

Music and Lyrics by Frank Loesser; Book by Jo Swerling and Abe Burrows; Based on Story and Characters by Damon Runyon; Dances and Musical Numbers Staged by Michael Kidd; Settings and Lighting by Jo Mielziner; Costumes by Alvin Colt; Musical Director, Stanley Lebowsky; Orchestral Arrangements by George Bassman and Ted Royal; Vocal Arrangements and Direction by Herbert Greene; Staged by George S. Kaufman. Presented by Feuer and Martin. Opened at Ford's Theatre, Baltimore, Nov. 30, 1953.

### Cast

| | |
|---|---|
| Nicely-Nicely Johnson | Jack Prince |
| Benny Southstreet | Al Nesor |
| Rusty Charlie | Carle Erbele |
| Sarah Brown | Susan Hight |
| Arvide Abernathy | Pat Rooney |
| Mission Band: Jeanne Schlegel, Eddie Herm, Courtenay Wright | |
| Harry The Horse | Dell Markee |
| Lt. Brannigan | Tom Ahearne |
| Nathan Detroit | Julie Oshins |
| Miss Adelaide | Iva Withers |
| Sky Masterson | Norwood Smith |
| Joey Biltmore | Tony Gardell |
| Dave, The Dude | Jack Dabdoub |
| Mimi | Carol Risser |
| Gen. Matilda Cartwright | Netta Packer |
| Big Jule | B. S. Pully |
| Drunk | Carl Erbele |
| Waiter | Roy Wilson |

Dancers: Barbara Allen, Alice Clift, Jewell Diehl, Joan Hansen, Arlene McKenna, Joyce Rees, Carol Risser, Sandi Simpson, Gretchen Wyler, Bob Curran, Donn Driver, Carle Erbele, Edmund Gasper, Rudy Mattice, Bill Miller, Paul Rees, Tony Rosa, Roy Wilson.

Singers: Jeanne Schlegel, Courtenay Wright, Tom Bennett, Jack Dabdoub, Tony Gardell, Bill Jones, Paul Kane, Earle Styres.

*Company Manager:* Harold Kusell
*Press:* Joseph Shea
*Stage Managers:* Andy Anderson, Marge Ellis, Bill Jones

* For original New York production see THEATRE WORLD. Vol. VII.

**Right: Norwood Smith, Susan Hight. Top right: Julie Oshins, Norwood Smith, Iva Withers, Julie Oshins**

B. S. Pully and Chorus    GRAPHIC HOUSE PHOTOS

## THE MOON IS BLUE*

By F. Hugh Herbert; Staged by Maximilian Slater; Presented by Jody Associates. Opened at the Erlanger, Buffalo, N. Y., Dec. 24, 1953, and closed May 15, 1954, at the Shubert in Washington, D.C.

### Cast

| | |
|---|---|
| Patty O'Neill | Jacqueline Holt |
| Donald Gresham | Michael Lipton |
| David Slater | Edward Andrews |
| Michael O'Neill | Lester Mack |

*Company Manager:* TOM POWERS
*Press:* VINCE MCKNIGHT
*Stage Managers:* JOHN HOLDEN, LESTER MACK

\* For original New York production see THEATRE WORLD, Vol. VII.

Edward Andrews, Jacqueline Holt, Michael Lipton

Ray Newcomer, George Mully, Jeno Mate, Marvin Greene

Albert Dannibal

George Tobias

## STALAG 17*

By Donald Bevan and Edmund Trzcinski; Staged by Robert Shawley; Presented by Leonard Altobell and Charles Harrow. Opened Jan. 18, 1954, at the Nixon in Pittsburgh, and closed May 29, 1954, at The Great Northern, Chicago.

### Cast

| | |
|---|---|
| S.S. Guard | Charles Remington |
| Stosh | George Tobias |
| Harry Shapiro | Carmen Filpi |
| Price | Len Wayland |
| Herb Gordon | Robert Shawley† |
| Hoffman | Ray Newcomer |
| Sefton | Albert Dannibal |
| Duke | John DeMastri |
| Horney | Melvin Clay |
| Marko | Robert Getz |
| Cpl. Schultz | Robert Bernard |
| Dunbar | Marvin Greene |
| Reed | Frank Downing |
| Red Dog | Robert Cercotti |
| Peterson | William Bronder |
| German Captain | Jeno Mate |
| Geneva Man | George Mully |

*Company Manager:* LESTER AL SMITH
*Press:* LENNY TRAUBE
*Stage Manager:* GEORGE MULLY

† Replaced by Ray Stricklyn
\* For original New York production see THEATRE WORLD, Vol. VII.

Robert Shawley

Dolores Mann, Walter Slezak,
Don Covert

Walter Slezak,
Lea Penman

Peter Donat, Dolores Mann
Paul Lipson

## MY 3 ANGELS*

By Sam and Bella Spewack; Based on "La Cuisine des Anges" by Albert Husson; Directed by Sam Spewack; Setting by Boris Aronson; Costumes by Lucinda Ballard. Presented by Leland Hayward by arrangement with Saint-Subber, Rita Allan and Archie Thomson. Opened at the Playhouse, Wilmington, Del., Feb. 4, 1954, and closed May 29, 1954, at The Selwyn, Chicago.

### Cast

Felix Ducotel ................................. Byron Foulger
Emilie Ducotel ............................... Dorothy Adams
Mme. Parole .................................... Lea Penman
Marie Louise Ducotel .................... Dolores Mann
Joseph .............................................. Walter Slezak
Jules ................................................... Royal Beal
Alfred ................................................... Carl Betz
Henri Trochard .................................. Paul Lipson
Paul ..................................................... Peter Donat
Lieutenant ......................................... Don Covert
Adolphe ..................................................... Adolphe
General Understudies: Guy Arbury, Corinna Lothar, Larry Buchanan

Company Manager: EDGAR RUNKLE
Press: HOWARD NEWMAN
Stage Managers: WALTER NEAL, LARRY BUCHANAN

* For original New York production see THEATRE WORLD, Vol. IX.

PHOTOS BY TALBOT

Carl Betz, Walter Slezak, Royal Beal,
Dolores Mann

Carl Betz, Royal Beal, Walter Slezak

160

Margaret Phillips,
Francis Bethencourt

Maurice Evans, J. Pat O'Malley, Margaret Phillips,
Logan Field

## DIAL 'M' FOR MURDER*

By Frederick Knott; Staged by Reginald Denham;
Setting and Lighting by Peter Larkin; Costumes by
Noel Taylor; Associate Producer, Emmett Rogers;
Presented by James P. Sherwood. Opened March 1,
1954, at Walnut Street Theatre, Philadelphia, and
closed May 29, 1954, at the Biltmore Theatre in
Los Angeles.

### Cast

| | |
|---|---|
| Margot Wendice | Margaret Phillips |
| Max Halliday | Logan Field |
| Tony Wendice | Maurice Evans |
| Capt. Lesgate | Francis Bethencourt |
| Inspector Hubbard | J. Pat O'Malley |
| Thompson | Robert McQueeney |

Company Manager: JAMES HUGHES
Press: GERTRUDE BROMBERG
Stage Managers: BILLY MATHEWS,
ROBERT McQUEENEY, VAN WILLIAMS

* For original New York production see THEA-
TRE WORLD, Vol. IX.

GRAPHIC HOUSE PHOTOS

Margaret Phillips, Maurice Evans,
Logan Field

Margaret Phillips, Maurice Evans

161

Patricia Morison,
Barclay Hodges

Suzanne Lake,
Ken Remo

Yul Brynner, Santy Josol

Yul Brynner

## THE KING AND I*

Music by Richard Rodgers; Book and Lyrics by Oscar Hammerstein 2nd; Based on Novel "Anna and The King of Siam" by Margaret Landon; Directed by John Van Druten; Settings and Lighting by Jo Mielziner; Costumes by Irene Sharaff; Choreography by Jerome Robbins; Orchestrations by Robert Russell Bennett; Musical Director, Will Irwin. Presented by Rodgers and Hammerstein. Opened at the Community Theatre, Hershey, Pa., March 22, 1954.

### Cast

Captain Orton ............................ Charles Lawrence
Louis Leonowens ........................ Barclay Hodges
Anna Leonowens .......................... Patricia Morison
Interpreter ...................................... Charles Hulse
The Kralahome ............................ Leonard Graves
The King ...................................... Yul Brynner
Phra Alack ...................................... Duane Camp
Tuptim ........................................ Suzanne Lake
Lady Thiang .................................. Terry Saunders
Prince Chulalongkorn ...................... Santy Josol
Princess Ying Yaowalak ........... Yvette Cardinoza
Lun Tha ........................................ Ken Remo
Sir Edward Ramsay .......................... Leon Shaw

**Princes and Princesses:** Patrick Adiarte, Andrew Binaso, Vincent Binaso, Dennis Bonilla, Thomas Bonilla, Dorothy De Arco, Andrea Del Rosario, Lorraine Ibanes, Kenneth Lee, Geraldine Lorente.

**The Royal Dancers:** Purie Adiarte, Muriel Bentley, Jean Bledsoe, Hazel Chung, Betsy Cushman, Bettina Dearborn, Joan Fitzmaurice, Kupi Fraker, Wonci Lui, Michiko, Shirley Mitchell, Barbara Newman, Joan Parmer, Meryl Sargent, Prue Ward, Rosemary Zinner.

**Wives:** Jeanne Beauvais, Bonnie Elms, Corinna Manetto, Mary Louise Repult.

**Amazons:** Marian Carr, Carleen Clark, Norma Larkin, Joyce Stansell.

**Priests:** Bob Held, Hubert Bland, Duane Camp, Joseph Caruso, Vito Durante, Charles Hulse.

**Slaves:** Hubert Bland, Beau Cunningham, Vito Durante, Charles Hulse.

*Company Manager:* Harold Goldberg
*Press:* Michel Mok, Al Spink
*Stage Managers:* Duane Camp, Ruth Mitchell, Ed Preston

* For original New York production see THEATRE WORLD, Vol. VII.

PHOTOS BY VANDAMM

162

Patricia Morison, Yul Brynner

## THE FOURPOSTER*

By Jan De Hartog; Directed by Paul A. Foley; Setting by Syrjala; Costumes by Lucinda Ballard; Presented by H. Clay Blaney and Cy Metrick. Opened at the Court Square Theatre, Springfield, Mass., April 15, 1954, and closed at the Forrest, Philadelphia, May 15, 1954.

### Cast

Agnes ................................................ Carol Stone
Michael ............................................ John Beal

Company Manager: WILLIAM CROUCHER
Press: JOSEPH HEIDT
Stage Managers: PAUL A. FOLEY, MAE BLANEY

* For original New York production see THEATRE WORLD, Vol. VIII.

### Right: Carol Stone, John Beal

Isabel Bigley, Bill Hayes. Center: Joan McCracken, Robert Fortier

164

## ME AND JULIET*

Music by Richard Rodgers; Book and Lyrics by Oscar Hammerstein 2nd; Directed by George Abbott; Scenery and Lighting by Jo Mielziner; Costumes by Irene Sharaff; Vocal and Orchestral Arrangements by Don Walker; Musical Director, Salvatore Dell'Isola; Dances and Musical Numbers staged by Robert Alton; Presented by Rodgers and Hammerstein. Opened at the Shubert, Chicago, Ill., April 7, 1954, and closed there May 29, 1954.

### Cast

George ................................................ Randy Hall
Sidney ............................................ Edwin Philips
Jeanie ............................................ Isabel Bigley
Herbie .............................................. Harry Eno
Chris ............................................ Warren Meyers
Michael .......................................... John M. King
Bob .............................................. Mark Dawson
Larry ................................................ Bill Hayes
Mac .............................................. Ray Walston
Monica ............................................ Anne Waugh
Ruby ............................................... Joe Lautner
Charlie ........................................ Arthur Maxwell
Dario ......................................... George S. Irving
Lily ............................................... Shirley Jones
Jim .............................................. Bob Fortier
Susie .......................................... Svetlana McLee
Voice of Mr. Harrison .............. Henry Hamilton
Voice of Miss Davenport .............. Anne Waugh
Hilda .......................................... Sonja Lindgren
Marcia ........................................ Thelma Tadlock
Betty ........................................ Joan McCracken
Bobby ......................................... Bobby Lindgren
Frank ............................................ Frank Derbas
Miss Oxford ...................................... Sari Price
Sadie ...................................... Janyce Ann Wagner
Mildred ............................ Lorraine Havercroft
A Theatre Patron ........................... Donna Sanders
Another Patron ................................. Cherry Davis
**Dancers:** Betty Buday, Jan Lothian, Maria Harriton, Lorraine Havercroft, Lucia Lambert, Sonja Lindgren, Joan McCallum, Dana Sosa, Nina Starkey, Janyce Ann Wagner, Anne Waugh, Rosemary Williams, Thelma Tadlock, Lance Avant, Kip Carlisle, Gerry Fries, John George, Jack Konzal, Frank Derbas, Bill Sumner, Bob St. Claire, Keith Willis.
**Singers:** Peggy Acheson, Margaret Broderson, Cherry Davis, Janet Pavek, Louise Pearl, Dolores Peterson, Shari Price, Donna Sanders, Key Ayers, Henry Hamilton, Warren Kemmerling, John M. King, Jack Rains, Fred Smith, Herbert Surface, Don Swenson.

Company Manager: MAURICE WINTERS
Press: MICHEL MOK, SAM STRATTON
Stage Managers: CHARLES ATKIN, BEAU TILDEN, JAMES HAMMERSTEIN

* For original New York production see THEATRE WORLD, Vol. IX.

GRAPHIC HOUSE PHOTOS

Frances Woodbury, Daryl Grimes, Ralph Meeker, Louise Larabee, Elizabeth Wilson, Sandra Church, John C. Becher, Fred Eisley

Ralph Meeker

## PICNIC *

By William Inge; Directed by Joshua Logan; Setting and Lighting by Jo Mielziner; Costumes by Mildred Trebor. Presented by The Theatre Guild and Joshua Logan. Opened April 19, 1954, at the National, Washington, D.C.

### Cast

| | |
|---|---|
| Helen Potts | Frances Woodbury |
| Hal Carter | Ralph Meeker |
| Millie Owens | Daryl Grimes |
| Bomber | John Perkins |
| Madge Owens | Sandra Church |
| Flo Owens | Elizabeth Wilson |
| Rosemary Sidney | Louise Larabee |
| Alan Seymour | Fred Eisley |
| Irma Kronkite | Dulcie Cooper |
| Christine Schoenwalder | Kelcey Mackaye |
| Howard Bevans | John C. Becher |

*Company Manager:* JAMES S. MILLER
*Press:* ALLAN C. DALZELL
*Stage Managers:* SCOTT JACKSON, WILLIAM FORESTER

\* For original New York production see THEATRE WORLD, Vol. IX.

ZINN ARTHUR PHOTOS

## DAPHNE

A Comedy in three acts and four scenes by Thaddeus Suski; Directed by Rex O'Malley; Setting, Lighting and Costumes by John Blankenchip. Opened Sept. 14, 1953, at the Wilbur in Boston, and closed there Sept. 19, 1953.

### Cast

| | |
|---|---|
| Don | Jack Kennedy |
| Oliver | Karl Redcoff |
| Daphne | Irene Hayes |
| Robert Esmond Smith | Rex O'Malley |
| Maisie O'Donnell | Grace Valentine |
| Mr. Robert's Young Ladies: | |
| | Dee Edwards, Cynthia Ashley |

*Company Manager:* PAUL GROLL
*Press:* RICHARD MANEY, FRANK GOODMAN
*Stage Managers:* HOWARD WHITFIELD, E. E. CLIVE, JR.

## MAKE MOMMA HAPPY

A Comedy in three acts and four scenes by George Baxt. Presented by Jay Julien and Hal Zieger; Directed by Jay Julien; Settings, Lighting and Costumes by John Boyt. Opened at the New Parsons, Hartford, Conn., Nov. 19, 1953, and closed Dec. 5, 1953, at the Walnut in Philadelphia.

### Cast

| | |
|---|---|
| Norma Talmadge Greenwald | Peg Feury |
| Mrs. Greenwald | Molly Picon |
| Alfred Greenwald | Jacob Kalich |
| Jackie Coogan Greenwald | Mark Rydell |
| Becky Moscowitz | Dolores Sutton |
| Tessie Moskowitz | Dorie Warren |
| Mrs. Moskowitz | Anna Appel |
| Francis X. Bushman Greenwald | Norman Feld |
| Officer Gary Taylor | Matt Pelto |
| Laura Case | Shirley Grayson |
| Deke Clayton | Cecil Scaife |

## THE PARADISE QUESTION

A Comedy in three acts and five scenes by Walter Hart and Richard Maibaum; Presented by Elaine Perry; Staged by Walter Hart; Designed and Lighted by George Jenkins; Clothes by Virginia Volland. Opened at the Shubert, New Haven, Conn., Sept. 17, 1953, and closed at the Locust in Philadelphia, Sept. 26, 1953.

### Cast

| | |
|---|---|
| Lucille Appleton | Barbara Robbins |
| Ava Appleton | Patricia Barry |
| Cully Haskins | Russ Dearborn |
| Prof. George Appleton | Leon Ames |
| Mr. Rojek | Lothar Rewalt |
| Jack | Frank Dudley |
| Dorothy | Trudy Farmillant |
| Vivian Hapgood | Ann Lee |
| Count Stendhal | Eugene Stuckmann |
| Senor Corona | Robert Carricart |
| M. Bruneval | Stiano Braggiotti |
| Jezireh | Wood Romoff |
| Abdullah Ibn Rashid | John Vivyan |

*Company Manager:* GEORGE BANAI
*Press:* BILL DOLL, ROBERT ULLMAN, RICHARD WILLIAMS
*Stage Managers:* LUCIA VICTOR, FRANK DUDLEY, EUGENE STUCKMANN

Russ Dearborn, Patricia Barry. Top: Jac Kennedy, Grace Valentine, Irene Haye Center: Molly Picon

Todd Karns, John Kellogg.
Top: Todd Karns, Jack Lord

Stuart Carson, Harry Carey, Jr., Joe Locke,
Philip Kenneally

## LITTLE JESSE JAMES

A Musical in two acts; Presented by Alpha Productions Co. in association with Hal Olver; Book by Harlan Thompson; Music by Harry Archer; Lyrics by Gladys Shelley and Harlan Thompson; Staged by Robert C. Jarvis; Choreography by Edward Noll; Settings by A. A. Ostrander; Costumes by George Bockmann; Orchestrations by Don Walker; Orchestra Conductor, Harry Archer; Entire production Supervised by Hal Olver. Opened at the Taft Auditorium, Cincinnati, Nov. 30, 1953, and closed at Ford's in Baltimore, Dec. 19, 1953.

### Cast

| | |
|---|---|
| Tommy | Jack Mann |
| Juliet | Libby Dean |
| Mrs. Flower | Ruth Gillette |
| Geraldine | Beverly McFadden |
| Becky | Rebecca Barksdale |
| Barbara | Barbara Maye |
| Geneve | Geneve Dorn |
| Doris | Doris Driver |
| Peggy | Peggy Genders |
| Lynda | Lynda Lynch |
| Ann | Ann Dunbar |
| Joy | Joy Shoemaker |
| Paul | Mitchell Gregg |
| Cassidy | Dave Mallen |
| Mrs. Jamieson | Sara Floyd |
| Jessie Jamieson | Mimi Kelly |
| Pierce | Jack Davis |
| Gus | Alan North |

## FLAME-OUT

A Comedy Drama in three acts by Alan Mowbray; Presented by M. M. Productions; Directed by Alan Mowbray. Opened at the New Parsons, Hartford, Conn., Nov. 12, 1953, and Closed Dec. 5, 1953, at the Shubert in Washington, D.C.

### Cast

| | |
|---|---|
| Texas | Joe Locke |
| Arizona | Jack Lord |
| Beanie | Herbert Bott |
| New Yorker | Philip Kenneally |
| Draftee | Harry Carey, Jr. |
| OPS Officer | Stuart Carson |
| Brown | Todd Karns |
| Robertson | Rick Owens |
| Chicago | John Kellogg |
| Flight Surgeon | William M. Neil |
| Chaplain | Jay Tolliver |
| Native | Tafa Lee |

*General Manager:* JOHN J. GARRITY
*Press:* SAMUEL J. FRIEDMAN
*Stage Managers:* MONTY BANKS, JR., BARRY SINKOW

MAURICE SEYMOUR PHOTOS

Robert Coote, Henry Garrard, Hiram Sherman, Ruth Pratt, Oscar Karlweis, Lili Darvas, Judson Rees, Philip Reed

## DEAR CHARLES

A Comedy in three acts by Marc-Gilbert Sauvajon; Adapted by Alan Melville; Directed by Romney Brent; Setting and Lighting by Donald Oenslager; Costumes Supervised by Patton Campbell; Miss Darvas' Gowns by Hattie Carnegie; Presented by Richard Aldrich and Richard Myers with John J. Wildberg and Julius Fleischmann. Opened at the New Parsons, Hartford, Conn., Dec. 30, 1953, and closed at the Shubert, Washington, D.C., January 9, 1954.

### Cast

| | |
|---|---|
| Louise | Norah Howard |
| Walter | Henry Garrard |
| Bruno | Judson Rees |
| Edward | Hiram Sherman |
| Denise | Lili Darvas |
| Martine | Ruth Pratt |
| Sir Michael Harvey | Robert Coote |
| Jan Pienchikowski | Oscar Karlweis |
| Dominique Leclerc | Philip Reed |
| Madame Duchemin | Harriet MacGibbon |
| Jean-Pierre | Tom Raynor |
| Lucienne | Grace Raynor |

*Company Manager:* CHARLES MOONEY
*Press:* WILLIAM FIELDS, WALTER ALFORD,
PATRICIA BUTLER
*Stage Managers:* JOHN EFFRAT, TOM RAYNOR

FRED FEHL PHOTOS

Lili Darvas, Henry Garrard, Ruth Prat
Hiram Sherman, Judson Rees

William Hickey, Bryarly Lee, Stefan Gierasch

Lois Smith, Steven Hill, Robert Simon,
Ruth White

## MARDI GRAS

A Drama in two acts and four scenes by Norman Rosten; Music by Duke Ellington; Setting, Costumes and Lighting by Leo Kerz; Directed by Peter Kass; Presented by Anthony Parella. Opened Wednesday, Jan. 13, 1954, at the Locust in Philadelphia and closed there Saturday, Jan. 16, 1954. Re-opened at the Locust on Jan. 22, and closed on Jan. 23, 1954.

### Cast

| | |
|---|---|
| Drunk | Stefan Gierasch |
| Concession Man | Joseph Sullivan |
| Frankel | Albert Ottenheimer |
| Junk Man | Daniel Reed |
| Albert | Robert F. Simon |
| Jimmy | William Hickey |
| Sailor | Bernard Kates |
| Merelda | Lenore Ulric† |
| Harrington's Voice | Joseph Bernard |
| Barbara | Janet Vickers |
| Inspector | William Darrid |
| Stanley | Sidney Syden |
| College Boy | Stefan Gierasch |
| College Girl | Nancy Lee |
| Cathy | Lois Smith |
| Rajah | Gregory Morton |
| Balloon Man | Daniel Reed |
| Clown | Joseph Bernard |

Bathers: Thelma, Terron, Frida Schubert, Jean Free, Patricia Baker, Bryarly Lee

| | |
|---|---|
| Walter | Steven Hill |
| Doctor | James Maloney |

Revelers: Patricia Baker, Jean Free, Frida Schubert, Janet Vickers, Thelma Terron, Nancy Lee

| | |
|---|---|
| A Girl | Bryarly Lee |

*General Manager:* Robert A. Willey
*Press:* David Lipsky
*Stage Managers:* Peg Santvoord, Joseph Bernard
† Replaced by Ruth White.

PHOTOS BY TALBOT

Lenore Ulric, Steven Hill

## STRATFORD SHAKESPEAREAN FESTIVAL OF CANADA

Presented alternately at the Stratford Festival Theatre, Stratford, Ontario, Canada, from Monday, July 13th to Saturday, August 22, 1953. Directed by Tyrone Guthrie; Decor by Tanya Moiseiwitsch; Music Composed by Louis Applebaum; Assistant Director and Production Manager, Cecil Clarke; Fights arranged by Douglas Campbell; Miss Worth's Gowns by Valentina.

## THE TRAGEDY OF KING RICHARD III

### By William Shakespeare

#### Cast

| | |
|---|---|
| Richard III | Alec Guinness |
| George | Lloyd Bochner |
| Sir Robert Brackenbury | William Hutt |
| Lord Hastings | Douglas Campbell |
| Lady Anne | Amelia Hall |
| Tressel | Bruce Scott |
| Berkley | Neil Carson |
| Earl Rivers | Norman Roland |
| Sir Thomas Vaughan | Richard Easton |
| Lord Grey | Alex Smith |
| Marquis of Dorset | Douglas Rain |
| Elizabeth | Betty Leighton |
| Duke of Buckingham | Robert Christie |
| Earl of Derby | George Alexander |
| Margaret | Irene Worth |
| Catesby | Timothy Findley |
| 1st Murderer | William Needles |
| 2nd Murderer | Eric House |
| King Edward IV | Edward Holmes |
| Bishop of Ely | Eric Atkinson |
| Duchess of York | Eleanor Stuart |
| Richard, Duke of York | Tony Rotherham |
| Edward, Prince of Wales | Garrick Hagon |
| Lord Mayor of London | Michael Bates |
| Cardinal Bourchier | Peter Mews |
| A Messenger | Roland Bull |
| Ratcliff | Robert Robinson |
| Lovel | Donald Harron |
| Scrivener | Eric House |
| Page | Jim Colbeck |
| Tyrel | Douglas Rain |
| 1st Messenger | Roland Bull |
| 2nd Messenger | Jonathan White |
| 3rd Messenger | Harold Burke |
| 4th Messenger | Neil Carson |
| Sir Christopher Urswick | Eric House |
| Henry, Earl of Richmond | Robert Goodier |
| Sir Walter Herbert | Bruce Swerdfager |
| Earl of Exford | Peter Mews |
| Captain Blunt | William Hutt |
| Duke of Norfolk | William Needles |
| George Stanley | Neil Vipond |

Aldermen, Men at Arms, Monks and Priests: Roland Bull, Harold Burke, Neil Carson, Vincent Edward, Morris Fine, William Glen, Don Gollan, Peter Harcourt, John Hayward, John Jeffrey, Alex Jeffories, Jim Jorgensen, Eugene Jousse, Ron Knowles, Drew Lennox, Jim Manser, Newman O'Leary, Kenneth Pauli, Bruce Scott, Dan Slote, Graham Stratford, Neil Vipond, Jonathan White, Beverley Wilson.

Choir: F. P. Polley, Conductor. Robert Babensee, Glen Bain, Ronald Bart, Tom Baterman, Lyle Bender, James Brothers, Colin Currie, Brian Double, Grant Ellison, Geoffrey Green, William Harrison, Ruddell Hottot, Ernest House, Robert Hyde, Robert Kobe, Kenneth Landers, Stephen Landers, George Leinweber, Tom McNaught, William McNaught, Donald McPherson, James Miller, Robert Moorehead, Alan Mutton, Robert Mutton, Michael Ogden, Fred Overholt, Robert Phillips, Richard Reinhart, Glenn Richards, Alex Roemer, Gordon Sarll, Tim Showalter, Tony Skells, Stephen Turnbull, Alex Way, Ricky Wyatt, Rodger Wyatt, Wayne Yundt.

**PETER SMITH PHOTOS**

Alec Guinness.

Top: Alec Guinness, Neil Vipond

Alec Guinness as Richard III.

Top: Robert Goodier, Alec Guinness

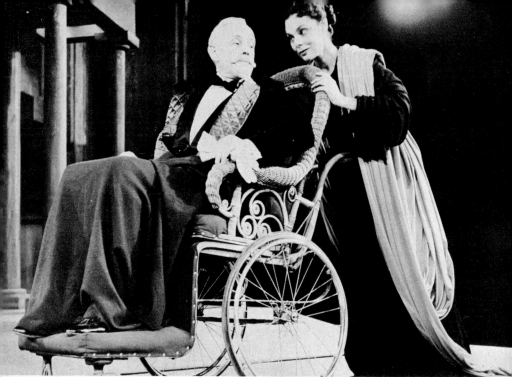

Top: Alec Guinness, Irene Worth

## ALL'S WELL THAT ENDS WELL
### By William Shakespeare
**Cast**

| | |
|---|---|
| King of France | Alec Guinness |
| Countess of Rousillion | Eleanor Stuart |
| Bertram | Donald Harron |
| Helena | Irene Worth |
| Parolles | Douglas Campbell |
| Lafeu | Michael Bates |
| Ministers of State | Robert Christie, Eric Atkinson, William Hutt, Bruce Swerdfager |
| Duke of Florence | George Alexander |
| Longaville | Lloyd Bochner |
| Dumain | Robert Goodier |
| Officers | Timothy Findley, Robert Robinson |
| Renaldo | William Needles |
| Morgan | Eric House |
| Another Soldier | Peter Mews |
| A Widow | Amelia Hall |
| Diana | Beatrice Lennard |
| Neighbors | Betty Leighton, Marionne Johnston, Ann Corke, Jo Hutchings, Leone Kastner |
| A Gentleman | Norman Roland |

Ladies, Officers, Gentlemen and Footmen: Wendy Aitken, Anne Corke, Dawn Greenhalgh, Jo Hutchings, Marionne Johnston, Shirley Jordan, Leone Kastner, Rosamund Merivale, Kathleen Roland, Norma Turner, Joan Watts, Lynn Wilson, Roland Bull, Neil Carson, Richard Easton, Vincent Edward, John Hayward, Edward Holmes, John Jeffrey, Eugene Jousse. Douglas Rain, Bruce Scott. Dan-Slote, Alex Smith, Graham Stratford, Neil Vipond.

Soldiers In The Florentine Army: Harold Burke, Morris Fine, William Glenn, Don Gollan, Peter Harcourt, Alex Jefferies, Jim Jorgensen, Ron Knowles, Drew Lennox, Jim Manser, Newman O'Leary, Kenneth Pauli, Jonathan White, Beverley Wilson.

*General Manager:* H. T. PATTERSON
*Stage Director:* ELSPETH COCHRANE
*Stage Managers:* JOHN HAYES, JACK MERIGOLD

Irene Worth

# THEATRE WORLD AWARD WINNERS
## PROMISING PERSONALITIES

### 1944-45

Judy Holliday
Bambi Linn
Betty Comden
Richard Davis

John Lund
Richard Hart
John Raitt
Charles Lang

Margaret Phillips
Donald Murphy
Nancy Noland

### 1945-46

Beatrice Pearson
Burt Lancaster
Patricia Marshall

Barbara Bel Geddes
Wendell Corey
Bill Callahan

Marlon Brando
Paul Douglas
Mary James

### 1946-47

David Wayne
Marion Bell
Peter Cookson
Ellen Hanley

Patricia Neal
James Mitchell
Dorothea MacFarland
John Jordan

Keith Andes
Ann Crowley
George Keane

### 1947-48

Meg Mundy
June Lockhart
Valerie Bettis
Patrice Wymore

Ralph Meeker
Peggy Maley
Estelle Loring
Whitfield Connor

Douglas Watson
Mark Dawson
Edward Bryce
James Whitmore

### 1948-49

Carol Channing
Gene Nelson
Tod Andrews
Cameron Mitchell

Julie Harris
Allyn McLerie
Jean Carson
Bob Scheerer

Mary McCarty
Richard Derr
Byron Palmer
Doe Avedon

### 1949-50

Charlton Heston
Priscilla Gillette
Rick Jason
Marcia Henderson

Charles Nolte
Roger Price
Lydia Clarke
Phil Arthur

Grace Kelly
Nancy Andrews
Don Hanmer
Barbara Brady

### 1950-51

Richard Burton
Maureen Stapleton
Eli Wallach
William Smithers

Walter Jack Palance
Marcia Van Dyke
James Daly
Barbara Ashley
Isabel Bigley

Pat Crowley
Martin Brooks
Cloris Leachman
Russell Nype

### 1951-52

Audrey Hepburn
Patricia Benoit
Tony Bavaar
Charles Proctor
Virginia de Luce

Kim Stanley
Ronny Graham
Helen Wood
Conrad Janis
Peter Conlow

Diana Herbert
Dick Kallman
Marian Winters
Eric Sinclair

### 1952-53

Geraldine Page
Paul Newman
Eileen Heckart
Ray Stricklyn
Gwen Verdon

John Kerr
Edith Adams
Rosemary Harris
Johnny Stewart
Sheree North

Richard Kiley
Penelope Munday
Peter Kelley
Gloria Marlowe

**Ben Gazzara**
of "End As A Man"

LOUIS MELANCON PHOTO

PORTRAITS OF PROMISING PERSONALITIES

Eva Marie Saint
of "The Trip To Bountiful"

LOUIS MELANCON PHOTO

**Harry Belafonte**
of "John Murray Anderson's Almanac"

177

**Elizabeth Montgomery**
of "Late Love"

Leo Penn
of "The Girl On The Via Flaminia"

Jonathan Lucas
of "The Golden Apple"

Joan Diener
of "Kismet"

**Carol Haney**
of "The Pajama Game"

**Scott Merrill**
of "The Threepenny Opera"

Orson Bean
of "John Murray Anderson's Almanac"

Kay Medford
of "Lullaby"

James Dean
of "The Immoralist"

Standing: Paul Newman, Publisher Jae Greenberg, Editor Daniel Blum, Ray
Stricklyn, Peter Kelley. Seated: Johnny Stewart, Eileen Heckart, Edith Adams,
Geraldine Page, Richard Kiley.

## 1952-1953 AWARD PARTY

Ralph Meeker Presents Award To
Geraldine Page

Former Award Winner, Grace Kelly,
Congratulates Peter Kelley   **187**

Jeanne Eagles in "Rain", Otis Skinner in "The Honor Of The Family", Laurette Taylor in "The Glass Menagerie", Alfred Lunt and Lynn Fontanne in "Amphitryon '38".

PORTRAIT DOLLS BY MARY GREEN, YORK ARTIST, FROM THE DANIEL BLUM COLLECTION

LOUIS MELANÇON PHOTOS

Phil Arthur       Barbara Ashley       Mario Alcalde

# BIOGRAPHIES OF BROADWAY PLAYERS

**ADAMS, EDITH.** Born in Kingston, Pa. Educated in Tenafly, N. J., public schools, Juilliard and Columbia's School of Drama. Appeared in night clubs and on T.V. before making her Broadway debut, Feb. 25, 1953, in "Wonderful Town."

**ADDY, WESLEY.** Born in 1912 in Omaha, Neb. His N. Y. appearances include Maurice Evans' productions of "Henry IV," "Hamlet," "Twelfth Night," Leslie Howard's "Hamlet," Laurence Olivier's "Romeo and Juliet," and more recently "Antigone," "Candida" (1946), "Another Part of The Forest" (replaced Leo Genn), "The Leading Lady," "The Traitor," "The Enchanted," "King Lear," "The Strong Are Lonely."

**AFTON, EFFIE.** Born in Steubenville, Ohio. Has appeared on Broadway in "Ritzy," "Sailor Beware," "My Sister Eileen," "That's Gratitude," "Carousel," "Show Boat" (revival), "Courtin' Time," "A Red Rainbow."

**AHERNE, BRIAN.** Born in Kings' Norton, Worcestershire, Eng., May 2, 1902. Educated at Malvern College. Made Broadway debut Feb. 9, 1931, in "The Barretts of Wimpole Street," and "St. Joan." Played Iago in "Othello" in 1937. From 1937 to 1945 spent most of his time in Hollywood. Returned to Broadway for revival of "The Barretts of Wimpole Street," "The French Touch," "She Stoops To Conquer," "The Constant Wife" (1951), "Escapade."

**ALBERTSON, FRANK.** Born in Fergus Falls, Minn., Feb. 2, 1909. Educated at Hollywood High School. Has appeared on Broadway in "Brother Rat," "The More The Merrier," "The Walrus and The Carpenter," "Mr. Adam," "Seventeen," "Late Love."

**ALCALDE, MARIO.** Born in Key West, Fla., Sept. 6, 1926. Educated at New York High School and trained for the stage with Theatre School of Dramatic Arts and American Theatre Wing. Made Broadway debut in City Center's revival of "Captain Brassbound's Conversion." Appeared since in "Bullfight."

**ALEXANDER, CRIS.** Born in Tulsa, Okla., in 1920. Made Broadway debut in revival of "Liliom." More recently appeared in "On The Town," "Present Laughter," "Wonderful Town."

**ALEXANDER, JOHN.** Born in Newport, Ky., Nov. 29, 1897. Studied at Helen Schuster-Martin Dramatic School, Cincinnati. Made first N. Y. appearance in 1919 in Robert B. Mantell's "The Merchant of Venice." Has more recently played in "Swing Your Lady," "Red Harvest," "The Greatest Show On Earth," "All The Living," "Kiss The Boys Goodbye," "Morning's At Seven," "Out From Under," "Arsenic and Old Lace," "Born Yesterday" (replaced Paul Douglas), "Hilda Crane," "Ondine."

**ALLEN, VERA.** Born in N.Y.C. Made N. Y. debut in 1925 in "The Grand Street Follies." More recent appearances include "At Home Abroad," "The Show Is On," "Susan and God," "A Woman's A Fool To Be Clever," "Glorious Morning," "The Philadelphia Story," "Strange Fruit," "The Ladies of The Corridor."

**ANDERS, GLENN.** Born in Los Angeles, Sept. 1, 1890. Educated at Columbia. Among his many Broadway appearances are "Just Around The Corner," "Civilian Clothes," "Scrambled Wives," "Hell-Bent Fer Heaven," "Bewitched," "They Knew What They Wanted," "The Constant Nymph," "Strange Interlude," "Farewell To Arms," "Hotel Universe," "Tomorrow and Tomorrow," "Another Language," "If This Be Treason," "The Masque of Kings," "Three Waltzes," "Call It A Day," "Skylark," "Soldier's Wife," "Light Up The Sky," "One Bright Day," "The Remarkable Mr. Pennypacker."

**ANDERSON, JUDITH.** Born in Adelaide, Australia, Feb. 10, 1898. Made N. Y. debut in 1918 with 14th St. stock company. Made Broadway bow in 1923 in "Peter Weston." Has appeared since in "Cobra," "The Dove," "Behold The Bridegroom," "Anna," "Strange Interlude," "As You Desire Me," "Firebird," "The Mask and The Face," "The Drums Begin," "Come of Age" (original and 1952 revival), "The Old Maid," "Family Portrait," Queen to Gielgud's Hamlet, Lady Macbeth to Maurice Evans' Macbeth, "Three Sisters" (Cornell revival), "Medea," "Tower Beyond Tragedy," "John Brown's Body," "In The Summer House."

**ANDREWS, TOD.** Born Nov. 10, 1920, in N.Y.C. Educated at Washington State College. Stage training at Pasadena Playhouse. Broadway plays include "Quiet Please," "My Sister Eileen," "Storm Operation," "Mrs. Kimball Presents," "Public Relations," "That Old Devil," "Summer and Smoke," "Mister Roberts" (on tour), "A Girl Can Tell," "Sabrina Fair."

**ARTHUR, PHIL.** Born in Plattsburg, N. Y., Nov. 30, 1923. Educated at Rutgers Prep School and William and Mary College. Made Broadway bow Dec. 4, 1944, in "A Bell For Adano." Has appeared since in "Bathsheba," "With A Silk Thread," "Not For Children," "Point of No Return."

**ASHLEY, BARBARA.** Born in Brooklyn, March 3rd. Educated at St. Anslems and St. Francis Xavier Academy. Worked with American Theatre Wing. Made Broadway debut May 9, 1948, in "Ballet Ballads." Has since appeared in "The Liar" and "Out of This World."

**ASTAR, BEN.** Born in Jaffa, Palestine, June 15th. Educated at Berlin Drama College. Made Broadway debut Dec. 17, 1953, in "The Prescott Proposals."

Fay Bainter    Tony Bavaar    Kaye Ballard

**AUBUCHON, JACQUES.** Born in Fitchburg, Mass., Oct. 30, 1924. Educated at Assumption College, Worcester. Trained at American Theatre Wing. Made Broadway appearances in "The Madwoman of Chaillot," "The Happy Time," "Mr. Pickwick," City Center revivals of "Charley's Aunt," "Cyrano de Bergerac" and "The Shrike."

**BAINTER, FAY.** Born in Los Angeles, Dec. 7, 1892. Made Broadway debut in 1912 in "The Rose of Panama." Other appearances include "Arms and The Girl," "The Willow Tree," "The Kiss Burglar," "East Is West," "The Lady Cristilinda," "The Dream Girl," "The Enemy," "The Two Orphans," "Fallen Angels," "The Admirable Crichton," "Lysistrata," "Jealousy," "For Services Rendered," Topsy in Players' Club revival of "Uncle Tom's Cabin," "Dodsworth," "The Next Half Hour," 'Gayden.''

**BALLANTYNE, PAUL.** Born in Moorhead, Iowa, July 18, 1909. Trained at Eva Le Gallienne's Civic Repertory Theatre. Made Broadway debut in 1933 in "Talent." Subsequently appeared in "Brown Danube," "Brother Rat," "Goodbye In The Night," "The Unconquered," "Mrs. O'Brien Entertains," "Susannah and The Elders," "St. Joan" (1952), "Love's Labour's Lost" (1953), "The Strong Are Lonely," "Richard III."

**BALLARD, KAYE.** Born in Cleveland, Ohio, Nov. 20th. Appeared in summer stock, vaudeville and night clubs before making Broadway bow in "The Golden Apple."

**BANKHEAD, TALLULAH.** Born in Huntsville, Ala., Jan. 31, 1902. Received education in Montgomery, Ala., N.Y.C. and Washington, D.C. Made Broadway debut in "Squab Farm," followed by "39 East," "Footloose," "Nice People," "Danger," "Her Temporary Husband," "The Exciters." From 1923 until 1930 appeared in England in many plays. Reappeared on Broadway in 1933 in "Forsaking All Others," followed by "Dark Victory," "Something Gay," "Reflected Glory," revivals of "Rain," "The Circle'" and "Antony and Cleopatra," "The Little Foxes," "Clash By Night," "The Skin Of Our Teeth," "The Eagle Has Two Heads," "Private Lives" (revival).

**BANNISTER, HARRY.** Born in Holland, Mich., Sept. 29, 1893. Educated at Univ. of Mich. Made Broadway bow in "The Passing Show of 1921." His many N. Y. appearances include "Strange Interlude," "Zander The Great," "Strip For Action," "Life With Father," "John Loves Mary," "Forward The Heart," "Love Me Long," "Affairs of State," "The Bat" (1952), "Mademoiselle Colombe."

**BARKER, MARGARET.** Born in Baltimore, Oct. 10, 1908. Educated at Bryn Mawr. Made first N. Y. appearance in 1928 in "The Age of Innocence." Other Broadway appearances include "The Barretts of Wimpole Street," "House of Connelly," "Men In White," "Gold Eagle Guy," "The Leading Lady," "The Member of The Wedding." "The Autumn Garden," "See The Jaguar," "The Ladies of The Corridor."

**BARNES, MAE.** Born in N.Y.C., Jan. 23rd. Made her Broadway debut in "Runnin' Wild" in 1924. Other appearances include "Lucky Sambo," "Hot Rhythm," "Rang Tang," revival of "Shuffle Along," "By The Beautiful Sea."

**BARRYMORE, DIANA.** Born March 3, 1921, in N.Y.C. Trained at American Academy and made Broadway debut in 1939 in "The Romantic Mr. Dickens," followed by "The Happy Days," "The Land Is Bright," "Rebecca," "Hidden Horizons," "Joan of Lorraine" (on tour).

**BARRYMORE, ETHEL.** Born in Philadelphia, Aug. 15, 1879. Made N.Y. debut at Empire Theatre, Jan. 25, 1894, in "The Rivals." Among the many plays in which she has appeared are "Captain Jinks of The Horse Marines." "Cousin Kate," "Alice-Sit-By-The-Fire." "Mid-Channel," "The Twelve Pound Look," "A Slice of Life," "Tante," "Our Mrs. McChesney," "The Lady of The Camellias," "The Constant Wife," "Scarlet Sister Mary," "The Kingdom of God," "The Love Duel," revivals of "The Second Mrs. Tanqueray," "School For Scandal" and "Trelawney of The Wells," "An International Incident," "Ghost of Yankee Doodle," "Whiteoaks," "Farm of Three Echoes," "The Corn Is Green," "Embezzled Heaven," "The Joyous Season" on tour.

**BARTON, JAMES.** Born in Gloucester, N. Y., Nov. 1. 1890. Spent early years in stock companies in Mid-West and South. Made Broadway debut in "The Passing Show of 1919." Has appeared since in "The Last Waltz," "Rose of Stamboul," "Dew Drop Inn," "Passing Show of 1924," "Artists and Models," "No Foolin'," "Sweet and Low," "Burlesque" on tour, "Tobacco Road," "The Iceman Cometh," "Paint Your Wagon."

**BAVAAR, TONY.** Born in Brooklyn, June 22, 1921. Appeared in night clubs and on television before making Broadway debut, Nov. 12, 1951, in "Paint Your .Wagon." Has appeared since in "Hazel Flagg," "John Murray Anderson's Almanac."

**BAXLEY, BARBARA.** Born in Porterville, Calif., Jan. 1, 1925. Graduate of College of the Pacific, Stockton, Calif. Trained at Neighborhood Playhouse. Appeared on Broadway in "Private Lives" (1948), "Out West of Eighth," "Peter Pan" (replaced Jean Arthur), "I Am A Camera" (replaced Julie Harris), "Camino Real," "The Frogs of Spring," "Oh Men! Oh, Women!"

Warren Berlinger       Edna Best       Orson Bean

**BAXTER, ALAN.** Born in East Cleveland, Ohio, Nov. 19, 1908. Educated at Williams College and Yale. Appeared on Broadway in "Lone Valley," "Men In White," "Gold Eagle Guy," "Black Pit," "Winged Victory," "The Hallams," "Home of The Brave," "The Voice of The Turtle," "Jenny Kissed Me," and is now in National Company of "South Pacific."

**BAXTER, FRANK.** Born in Bola Synwyd, Pa., Mar. 25, 1922. Received stage training at Barter Theatre and Neighborhood Playhouse. Has appeared on Broadway in "Janie," "R.U.R." (revival), and "Catherine Was Great."

**BAYNE, BEVERLY.** Born in Minneapolis, Minn., Nov. 22, 1896. Educated at Hyde Park High, Chicago. Famous star of silent films. Has appeared on Broadway in "Gala Night," "Pied Piper," "Claudia," "I Like It Here," "Loco," "The Cup of Trembling."

**BEAL, JOHN.** Born in Joplin, Mo., Aug. 13, 1909. Educated at Univ. of Penn. Studied for stage at Hedgerow Theatre. Made first N.Y. appearance in 1931 in "Give Me Yesterday." Subsequently appeared in "Wild Waves," "Another Language," "She Loves Me Not," "Russet Mantle," "Soliloquy," "Miss Swan Expects," "Liberty Jones," "The Voice of The Turtle," "Lend An Ear."

**BEAN, ORSON.** Born in Burlington, Vt., July 22, 1928. Educated at Cambridge High School. Appeared in night clubs before making Broadway debut, April 30, 1953, in "Men of Distinction." Appeared this season in "John Murray Anderson's Almanac."

**BELAFONTE, HARRY.** Born in N.Y.C., March 1, 1924. Educated at Howard Univ. Trained at American Negro Theatre and New School. Made Broadway debut Dec. 10, 1953, in "John Murray Anderson's Almanac."

**BEL GEDDES, BARBARA.** Born in N.Y.C., Oct. 31, 1923. Made Broadway debut in "Out Of The Frying Pan" in 1941. Has appeared since in "Little Darling," "Nine Girls," "Mrs. January and Mr. X," "Deep Are The Roots," "Burning Bright," "The Moon Is Blue."

**BELLAMY, RALPH.** Born in Chicago, June 17, 1904. Made Broadway debut in 1929 in "Town Boy," followed by "Roadside" which took him to Hollywood where he made films until 1943. Returned to Broadway in "Tomorrow The World," "State of The Union," "Detective Story."

**BERGHOF, HERBERT.** Born Sept. 13, 1909, in Vienna where he was educated and was a leading actor for several years. Made Broadway bow in 1942 in "Nathan The Wise." Has also appeared in "The Russian People," "Innocent Voyage," "Jacobowsky and The Colonel," "Temper The Wind," "The Whole World Over," "Miss Liberty," revivals of "Ghosts," "Hedda Gabler" and "Tovarich," "The Deep Blue Sea."

**BERLINGER, WARREN.** Born in Brooklyn, Aug. 31, 1937. Educated at P.S. 208 and Professional Children's School. Has appeared on Broadway in "Annie Get Your Gun," "The Happy Time," "Bernardine," "Take A Giant Step," "Anniversary Waltz."

**BEST, EDNA.** Born in Hove, Sussex, Eng., March 3, 1900. Studied for stage at Guildhall School. Made N.Y. debut in 1925 in "These Charming People." Other Broadway appearances include "The High Road," "Melo," "There's Always Juliet," "Delicate Story," "Yankee Point," "The Browning Version," "A Harlequinade," revivals of "Captain Brassbound's Conversion" (1950) and "First Lady" (1952), "Jane," "The Ladies of The Corridor," "Mlle. Colombe."

**BEVANS, PHILIPPA.** Born in London, Eng., Feb. 10, 1916. Educated at Miss Woodward's School, Boston. Appeared on Broadway in "Ah, Wilderness" (revival), "Harriet," "Dream Girl," "Temporary Island," "Harvest of Years," "S. S. Glencairn," "The Relapse," "Buy Me Blue Ribbons," "Mr. Pickwick," "The Starcross Story."

**BIGLEY, ISABEL.** Born in N.Y.C. Studied at Julliard and Royal Academy of Dramatic Art. Played in London production of "Oklahoma" before making her Broadway debut, Nov. 24, 1950, in "Guys and Dolls." Has appeared since in "Me and Juliet."

**BIRCH, PAUL.** Born in Atmore, Ala., Jan. 13, 1912. Educated at Georgia Military Academy and Univ. of Alabama. Made Broadway debut Jan. 20, 1954, in "The Caine Mutiny Court Martial."

**BLACKMER, SIDNEY.** Born in Salisbury, N.C., July 13, 1898. Educated at Warrenton High and Univ. of N.C. Appeared in stock and on tour before making Broadway bow in 1917 in "The Morris Dance." Other appearances include "The Mountain Man," "The 13th Chair," "The Love Child," "The Moon Flower," "The Carolinian," "Scaramouche," "Love In A Mist," "39 East," "The Springboard," "Mima," "Chicken Every Sunday," "Wonderful Journey," "Portrait In Black," "Come Back, Little Sheba," "The Brass Ring."

**BLAINE, VIVIAN.** Born in Newark, N. J., Nov. 21, 1923. Appeared in night clubs with bands and in several motion pictures before making her Broadway debut Nov. 24, 1950, in "Guys and Dolls." She is at present repeating her roll in the London company.

**BLISS, HELENA.** Born in St. Louis, Mo., Dec. 31, 1919. Educated at Hosmer Hall and Washington Univ. Has appeared on Broadway in "Very Warm For May," "Du Barry Was A Lady," "Song of Norway," "Gypsy Lady," "Show Boat" (1954 revival).

Harry Belafonte        Vivian Blaine        Charles Boyer

**BOAZ, CHARLES.** Born in Massena Springs, N.Y., June 19, 1919. Educated at Morris High. Studied at American Academy and American Theatre Wing. Made Broadway bow in 1946 in "A Joy Forever." Has appeared since in "Mister Roberts" (on tour), "A Flag Is Born," "The Big Two," "Gramercy Ghost," "The Male Animal" (1952 revival).

**BOLAND, MARY.** Born in Philadelphia, Jan. 28, 1885. Educated at Sacred Convent, Detroit. Was John Drew's leading lady in "Inconstant George," "Smith," "The Single Man," "The Perplexed Husband," "The Will," "The Tyranny of Tears," "Much Ado About Nothing." Among her many appearances on Broadway are "My Lady's Dress," "Clarence," "The Torch Bearers," "Ada Beats The Drum," "The Vinegar Tree," "Jubilee," "The Rivals," "Open House," "Lullaby."

**BOLGER, RAY.** Born in Dorchester, Mass., Jan. 10, 1906. Made Broadway bow in 1926 in "The Merry World." Has appeared since in "A Night in Paris," "The Passing Show of 1926," "Heads Up" (on tour), "George White's Scandals of 1931," "Life Begins at 8:40," "On Your Toes," "Keep Off The Grass," "Three To Make Ready," "Where's Charley?".

**BOND, SHEILA.** Born in N.Y.C., Mar. 16, 1928. Began stage training at four. Made Broadway debut in 1942 in "Let Freedom Sing," followed by "Allah Be Praised," "Artists and Models," "Street Scene," "Inside U.S.A.," "Make Mine Manhattan," "The Live Wire," "Wish You Were Here."

**BOOTH, SHIRLEY.** Born in N.Y.C. Made Broadway debut in 1925 in "Hell's Bells." Has appeared since in "Bye, Bye, Baby," "Laff That Off," "The War Song," "Too Many Heroes," "Three Men On A Horse," "Excursion," "The Philadelphia Story," "My Sister Eileen," "Tomorrow The World," "Hollywood Pinafore," "Land's End," "Goodbye, My Fancy," "Love Me Long," "Come Back, Little Sheba," "A Tree Grows In Brooklyn," "The Time of The Cuckoo," "By The Beautiful Sea."

**BOURNEUF, PHILIP.** Has appeared on Broadway in "Dead End," "Two Bouquets," "One For The Money," "Native Son," "Winged Victory," "Flamingo Road," ART revivals of "Henry VIII," "What Every Woman Knows," "Androcles and The Lion," "Yellow Jack" and "Alice In Wonderland," "The Last Dance," Whorf's "Richard III," "Miss Liberty," "Faithfully Yours," "The Strong Are Lonely," City Center revivals of "Rip Van Winkle," "Love's Labour's Lost" and "The Merchant of Venice."

**BOYER, CHARLES.** Born in Figeac, France, Aug. 28, 1899. Appeared on stage and in films in France before coming to U.S. Made Broadway debut Dec. 4, 1948, in "Red Gloves." Has appeared since with the Drama Quartette in "Don Juan In Hell" (in N.Y. and on tour), and in "Kind Sir."

**BRANDO, MARLON.** Born April 3, 1924, in Omaha, Neb. Studied at New School of Social Research. Made Broadway debut Oct. 19, 1944, in "I Remember Mama." Has appeared since in "Truckline Cafe," "Candida" with Cornell, "A Flag Is Born," "A Streetcar Named Desire."

**BRANDON, PETER.** Born in Berlin, Germany, July 11, 1926. Trained for stage at Neighborhood Playhouse. Made Broadway debut April 11, 1950, in "Cry of The Peacock." Has appeared since in 1952 revivals of "Come of Age" and "Tovarich," and in "Ondine."

**BRIDGES, LLOYD.** Born in San Leandra, California, Jan. 15th. Received B.A. Degree from U.C.L.A. Made Broadway debut Dec. 23, 1953, in "Dead Pigeon."

**BROOKS, GERALDINE.** Born in N.Y.C. Made Broadway debut in 1944 in "Follow The Girls." Has appeared since in "The Winter's Tale" and "The Time of The Cuckoo."

**BROOKS, MARTIN.** Born in the Bronx, N.Y.C., Nov. 30, 1925. Educated at Penn. State. Received stage training at American Theatre Wing. Made N.Y. debut in 1950 in "That Lady." Has appeared since in "Smile of The World," "Burning Bright," "An Enemy of The People," "I Am A Camera."

**BROTHERSON, ERIC.** Born in Chicago, May 10, 1911. Educated at Univ. of Wisc. Made Broadway debut in 1937 in "Between The Devil." Has appeared since in "Set To Music," "Lady In The Dark," "My Dear Public," "Gentlemen Prefer Blondes," "Room Service," (1953 revival).

**BROUN, HEYWOOD HALE.** Born in N.Y.C., March 10, 1918. Received B.A. Degree from Swarthmore. Has appeared on Broadway in "Love Me Long," "The Bird Cage," "The Live Wire," "The Small Hours," "The Pink Elephant," "His and Hers."

**BRYCE, EDWARD.** Born in Allentown, Pa., Sept. 24, 1921. Educated at Univ. of Denver and Columbia. Made Broadway debut in 1948 in "The Cradle Will Rock." Has appeared since in "The Liar."

**BRYNNER, YUL.** Born in Sakhalin Island, Japan, June 15, 1915. Educated in France and received B.S. Degree from Sorbonne. Came to America in 1940. Made Broadway debut in 1946 in "Lute Song." Became T.V. director. "The King and I" lured him back to the stage.

Jean Carson

Carleton Carpenter

Carol Channing

**BURKE, BILLIE.** Born in Washington, D.C., Aug. 7, 1885. Made stage debut in Eng. in 1903. Made N.Y. debut opposite John Drew in "My Wife" in 1907. Also appeared in "Love Watches," "Mrs. Dot," "The Runaway," "The Mind-The-Paint Girl," "The Amazons," "The Land of Promise," "Rose Briar," "The Marquise," "The Happy Husband," "Family Affairs," "The Truth Game." Began film career in 1916 and subsequently made many films. Has been seen more recently on stage in "This Rock," "Mrs. January and Mr. X," "Accidentally Yours" and "Life With Mother" on tour.

**BURTON, RICHARD.** Born in Pontrhydyfen, South Wales, Nov. 10, 1925. Educated at Port Talbot School and Exeter College, Oxford. Received stage training with Oxford Dramatic Society. Made Broadway bow Nov. 10, 1950, in "The Lady's Not For Burning." Has appeared since in "Legend of Lovers."

**CALLAHAN, BILL.** Born in N.Y.C., Aug. 23, 1926. Educated at Barnard School for Boys and Fordham Univ. Made Broadway debut in 1943 in "Something For The Boys." Has appeared since in "Mexican Hayride," "Call Me Mister," "Annie Get Your Gun," "As The Girls Go," "Top Banana," "Two's Company."

**CALVIN, HENRY.** Born May 25, 1918, in Dallas, Texas. Was Soloist at Radio City Music Hall, and appeared on concert and operatic stages before making Broadway debut in 1947 revival of "The Chocolate Soldier." Has appeared since in "Sally" (revival), "Kismet."

**CAREY, MACDONALD.** Born in Sioux City, Iowa, March 15th. Educated at Phillips Exeter Academy and received M.A. degree from Univ. of Iowa. Has appeared on Broadway in "Lady In The Dark" and "Anniversary Waltz."

**CARLISLE, KITTY.** Born in New Orleans, Sept. 3, 1914. Studied for stage at Royal Academy of Dramatic Arts, London. Has appeared in N.Y. in "Champagne Sec," "White Horse Inn," "Three Waltzes," "Walk With Music," "The Rape of Lucretia," "Anniversary Waltz."

**CARPENTER, CARLETON.** Born in Bennington, Vt., July 10, 1926. Educated at Bennington High School. Made Broadway debut March 2, 1944, in "Bright Boy." Has appeared since in "Career Angel," "Three To Make Ready," "Magic Touch," "John Murray Anderson's Almanac."

**CARROLL, LEO G.** Born in Weedon, Eng., in 1892. Made stage debut in 1911 in "The Prisoner of Zenda." Made N.Y. debut in 1925 with Noel Coward in "The Vortex." Has appeared since in "The Constant Nymph," "The Perfect Alibi," "The Green

Bay Tree," "Petticoat Fever," "The Masque of Kings," "The Two Bouquets," "Angel Street," "The Late George Apley," "The Druid Circle," "You Never Can Tell," "Jenny Kissed Me," "Mary Rose," "Lo and Behold!," "On Borrowed Time" (1953 revival).

**CARROLL, ROBERT.** Born in North Carolina, March 22, 1920. Educated at Univ. of N.C. Made first N.Y. appearance in 1946 revival of "Cyrano de Bergerac." Has appeared since in "Music In My Heart," City Center revivals of "A Tragedian In Spite of Himself," "The Wedding," "The Alchemist," "S.S. Glencairn," and "The Insect Comedy," "The Silver Whistle," "Twentieth Century," "My Three Angels."

**CARSON, JEAN.** Born in Charleston, W. Va., Feb. 28, 1925. Received training in Drama Dept. of Carnegie Tech. Made Broadway debut in 1948 in "Bravo." Has appeared since in "Metropole," "The Bird Cage," "Men of Distinction," "Anniversary Waltz."

**CHALMERS, THOMAS.** Sang leading roles at Metropolitan Opera for several seasons before making Broadway debut as an actor. Has appeared in "The Wild Duck," "Beyond The Horizon," "Mourning Becomes Electra," Players Club revival of "Uncle Tom's Cabin," "Outward Bound," "Antony and Cleopatra," "Hamlet," "Bathsheba," "Death of A Salesman," "The Remarkable Mr. Pennypacker."

**CHANNING, CAROL.** Born in Seattle, Wash., Jan. 31, 1921. Educated at Bennington College. Appeared on Broadway in "No For An Answer," "Let's Face It," "So Proudly We Hail," "Lend An Ear," "Gentlemen Prefer Blondes," "Wonderful Town."

**CHASE, STEPHEN.** Born in Huntington, L. I., Apr. 11, 1902. Educated at Loomis School, Conn. Among his many Broadway appearances are "Wooden Kimono," "The Silver Chord," "Zeppelin," "People On The Hill," "Reflected Glory," "Uncle Harry," "Strange Fruit," "Allegro," "The Caine Mutiny Court Martial."

**CHATTERTON, RUTH.** Born in N.Y.C., Dec. 24, 1893. Made Broadway debut in 1911 in "The Great Name," followed by "Standing Pat," "Daddy Long Legs," "Come Out Of The Kitchen," "A Bit of Love," "A Marriage of Convenience," "Moonlight and Honeysuckle," "Mary Rose," "La Tendresse," "The Changelings," "The Little Minister," "The Man With A Load of Mischief," "The Devil's Plum Tree." After many years in Hollywood returned to the stage in "West of Broadway," "Private Lives" on tour, "Leave Her To Heaven," "Second Best Bed," "Idiot's Delight" (1951 revival).

| Ina Claire | Ralph Clanton | Patricia Collinge |

**CHRISTIE, AUDREY.** Born in Chicago, June 27, 1911. Educated at Lake View High, Chicago. Has appeared on Broadway in "Follow Thru," "Sweet and Low," "Sailor Beware," "Sons of Guns," "The Women," "I Married An Angel," "Banjo Eyes," "Without Love," "The Voice of The Turtle," "The Duchess Misbehaves," "Light Up The Sky," "Buy Me Blue Ribbons."

**CLAIRE, INA.** Born in Washington, D.C., Oct. 15, 1895. Educated at Holy Cross Academy. First stage appearance in 1907 in vaudeville. Later appeared in "Jumping Jupiter," "The Quaker Girl," "Honeymoon Express," "Follies of 1915-16," "Polly With A Past," "The Gold Diggers," "Bluebeard's Eighth Wife," "Grounds For Divorce," "The Last of Mrs. Cheyney," "Our Betters," "Biography," "Ode To Liberty," "Love Is Not So Simple," "Barchester Towers," "The Talley Method," "The Fatal Weakness," "The Confidential Clerk."

**CLANTON, RALPH.** Born in Fresno, Cal., Sept. 11, 1914. Trained at Pasadena Playhouse. Appeared on Broadway in "Victory Belles," "Evans' "Macbeth," "Richard III," "Othello," "Lute Song," Ferrer's "Cyrano de Bergerac" (and 1953 City Center revival), "Antony and Cleopatra," "Design For A Stained Glass Window," "The Taming of The Shrew" (1951), "The Burning Glass."

**CLARK, BOBBY.** Born in Springfield, Ohio, June 16, 1888. With Paul McCullough appeared for many years in vaudeville. Has been seen on Broadway in "The Music Box Revue of 1922," "The Ramblers," "Strike Up The Band," "Here Goes The Bride," "Walk A Little Faster," "Thumbs Up," "Ziegfeld Follies," "Streets of Paris," "All Men Are Alike," "Love For Love," "The Rivals," "Star and Garter," "Mexican Hayride," "The Would-Be Gentleman," "Sweethearts," "As The Girls Go."

**CLARK, DORT.** Born Oct. 1, 1917, in Wellington, Kan. Graduate of Kansas State Teachers College. Made Broadway bow in 1942 in "Sweet Charity," and subsequently appeared in "The First Million," "Lower North," "Snafu," "Happy Birthday," "South Pacific," "Wonderful Town."

**CLARK, KENDALL.** First appeared on stage in support of Eva LeGallienne in "L'Aiglon" and "Camille." Has appeared since in "End of Summer," "Ghost of Yankee Doodle," "The Fifth Column," "George Washington Slept Here," "Home of The Brave," "The Eagle Has Two Heads," "St. Joan" (1951), "The Shrike," 1953 City Center revivals of "The Shrike" and "Richard III."

**CLARKE, LYDIA.** Born in Two Rivers, Wisc., Apr. 14, 1923. Educated at Northwestern Univ. Received stage training in summer stock. Made Broadway debut March 4, 1950, in "Detective Story." Is currently in Chicago company of "The Seven Year Itch."

**CLIFT, MONTGOMERY.** Born in Omaha, Neb., Oct. 17, 1920. Made N.Y. debut in 1935 in "Fly Away Home." Has appeared since in "Jubilee," "Yr. Obedient Husband," "Dame Nature," "The Mother," "There Shall Be No Night," "Mexican Mural," "The Skin of Our Teeth," "Our Town" (revival), "The Searching Wind," "Foxhole In The Parlor," "You Touched Me," "The Wild Duck" (1954 revival).

**COLLINGE, PATRICIA.** Born in Dublin, Ire., Sept. 20, 1894. Made stage debut in Eng., and first N.Y. appearance in 1908 in "The Queen of The Moulin Rouge." Has appeared since in "The Girl and The Wizard," "The Bluebird," "The Thunderbolt," "Everywoman," "The New Henrietta," "Billy," "Pollyanna," "Tillie," "Golden Days," "Just Suppose," "Tarnish," "Dark Angel," "The Lady With The Lamp," "Another Language." "Autumn Crocus," "The Little Foxes," "The Heiress," "Mary Rose," "I've Got Sixpence."

**COLLINS, RUSSELL.** Born in Indianapolis, Oct. 6, 1897. Educated at Ind. State Univ. and Carnegie Tech. Trained at Cleveland Playhouse. Has appeared in "Men In White," "Gold Eagle Guy," "Waiting For Lefty," "Star Wagon," "Morning's At Seven," "The Moon Is Down," "Juno and The Paycock," "Carousel," "The Iceman Cometh," "The Survivors," "The Enchanted," "The Grass Harp," "Sabrina Fair."

**COMPTON, FRANCIS.** Born in Malvern, Eng., May 4, 1890. Made Broadway debut in 1912 in "The Whip." More recent appearances include "Idiot's Delight," "The Play's The Thing," "Red Gloves," "Montserrat," "Ring Round The Moon," "The Green Bay Tree" (1951) "Gigi."

**CONLOW, PETER.** Born in Philadelphia, July 2, 1929. Studied at American Theatre Wing. Made Broadway debut Nov. 13, 1948, in "As The Girls Go." Has appeared since in "Lend An Ear," "Razzle Dazzle," "Courtin' Time," "Three Wishes For Jamie."

**CONNOR, WHITFIELD.** Born in Ireland, Dec. 3, 1916. Educated at Wayne Univ. and Univ. of Mich. Made Broadway debut in 1946 in Maurice Evans' "Hamlet." Has appeared since in "The Duchess of Malfi," "Kathleen," Redgrave's "Macbeth," "The Winner."

**CONROY, FRANK.** Born in Derby, Eng., Oct. 14, 1890. Appeared in Eng. before making N.Y. bow in 1915 in "Helena's Husband." Has appeared since in "The Bad Man," "The Constant Wife," "On Borrowed Time," "The Little Foxes," "For Keeps," "One Man Show," "Hear That Trumpet," "Bravo," "Point of No Return," "Kind Sir."

| Jackie Cooper | Ann Crowley | John Cromwell |

**COOK, DONALD.** Born in Portland, Ore., Sept. 26, 1901. Trained with Kansas City Community Playhouse. Has appeared on Broadway in "N.Y. Exchange," "Paris Bound," "Rebound," "Wine Of Choice," "American Landscape," "Skylark," "Claudia," "Foolish Notion," "Made In Heaven," "Portrait In Black," "Private Lives". (1948), "The Moon Is Blue," "King of Hearts."

**COOKSON, PETER.** Born May 8, 1915, in Milwaukee, Ore. Received stage training with Pasadena Community Playhouse. Made Broadway debut in 1947 in "Message For Margaret." Has appeared since in "The Heiress," "The Little Blue Light," "Can-Can."

**COOLIDGE, PHILIP.** Born Aug. 25, 1908, in Concord, Mass. Made Broadway debut in 1938 in "Our Town." Has appeared since in "Merchant of Yonkers," "Family Portrait," "Margin For Error," "Jacobowsky and The Colonel," "Sing Out, Sweet Land," "Barefoot Boy With Cheek," "The Traitor," "Darkness At Noon," "Barefoot In Athens," "The Crucible," "Kismet."

**COOPER, JACKIE.** Born in Los Angeles, Sept. 15, 1922. Spent 23 years in films before making Broadway debut, Apr. 18, 1949, in "Magnolia Alley." Has appeared since in National and London companies of "Mister Roberts," and in "Remains To Be Seen," "King of Hearts."

**COOPER, MELVILLE.** Born in Birmingham, Eng., Oct. 15, 1896. Made N.Y. bow in 1935 in "Laburnum Grove." Has appeared in "Jubilee," "The Merry Widow," "While The Sun Shines," "Firebrand of Florence," "Pygmalion," "Gypsy Lady," "The Haven," "An Inspector Calls," "The Liar," "The Day After Tomorrow," "Make A Wish," "Much Ado About Nothing" (1952), "Escapade."

**CORDNER, BLAINE.** Born in Jacksonville, Fla., Aug. 21, 1901. Has appeared on Broadway in "We, The People," "Bridal Quilt," "Blow, Ye Winds," "The World Waits," "First Flight," "A New Life," "Arsenic and Old Lace," "Bloomer Girl," "Set My People Free," and in Australia in "The Moon Is Blue."

**CORNELL, KATHARINE.** Born in Berlin, Ger., Feb. 16, 1898. Made N.Y. debut in 1916 in "Bushido" with Wash. Sq. Players. Has appeared since in "Nice People," "A Bill of Divorcement," "Will Shakespeare," "The Enchanted Cottage," "The Outsider," "Candida," "The Green Hat," "The Letter," "The Age of Innocence," "The Barretts of Wimpole Street," "Romeo and Juliet," "St. Joan," "Wingless Victory," "No Time For Comedy," "The Doctor's Dilemma," "The Three Sisters," "Lovers and Friends," "Antigone," "Antony and Cleopatra," "That Lady," "The Constant Wife," "The Prescott Proposals."

**COTSWORTH, STAATS.** Born in Oak Park, Ill., Feb. 17, 1908. Received training with Eva LeGallienne's Civic Repertory Theatre where he played in "Romeo and Juliet," and "Alice In Wonderland." Other appearances include "Rain From Heaven," "Murder At The Vanities," "First Episode," "Moon Over Mulberry Street," "Madame Capet," Evans' "Macbeth" (1941), and City Center revivals of "She Stoops To Conquer" (1949) and "Richard III" (1953).

**COURTNEIDGE, CICELY.** Born in Sydney, Aust., April 1, 1893. One of England's foremost comediennes, she has made only two N.Y. appearances in "By The Way" (1925) and "Under The Counter" (1947).

**CRAIG, HELEN.** Born in San Antonio, Tex., May 13, 1914. Educated at Scarborough School. Received stage training at Hedgerow Theatre. Made Broadway debut in 1936 in "Russet Mantle." Other appearances include "New Faces," "Julius Caesar," "Soliloquy," "Family Portrait," "The Unconquered," "Johnny Belinda," "As You Like It," "Lute Song," "Land's End," "The House of Bernarda Alba," "Maya."

**CRAVEN, ROBIN.** Born in London, Sept. 20, 1910. Educated at Oxford and Royal Academy of Dramatic Art. Made N.Y. debut in 1938 in "Dear Octopus." Has appeared since in "Foreigners," "Glamour Preferred," "Claudia," "Hand In Glove," "Present Laughter," "Strange Bedfellows," "The King and I."

**CROMWELL, JOHN.** Born in Toledo, Ohio, Dec. 23, 1887. Educated at Howe School, Ind. Made N.Y. debut in 1910 in "Baby Mine." Produced or coproduced "Tarnish," "Bewitched," "Devils," "Women Go On Forever," "Lucky Sam McCarver." Has appeared in "Little Women," "The Man Who Came Back," "Major Barbara," "The World We Live In," "The Silver Cord," "Gentlemen of The Press," "Yankee Point," "Point of No Return," "The Climate of Eden," "Sabrina Fair."

**CRONYN, HUME.** Born in London, Ontario, Can., July 18, 1911. Educated at Ridley College and Univ. of McGill. Trained at American Academy of Dramatic Art and Barter Theatre. Made N.Y. bow in "Hippers Holiday." Has appeared since in "High Tor," "Escape This Night," "Three Men On A Horse," "Boy Meets Girl," "Room Service," "The Three Sisters," "Mr. Big," "Retreat To Pleasure," "The Fourposter," "Madam, Will You Walk."

**CROWLEY, ANN.** Born in Scranton, Pa., Oct. 17, 1929. Graduate of Julia Richmond High, N. Y. Played leads in "Oklahoma," "Carousel," "Miss Liberty," "Seventeen."

Lili Darvas       Charles Dingle       Leora Dana

**CROWLEY, PAT.** Born in Scranton, Pa., Sept. 17, 1934. Educated at West Scranton High School. Appeared on Broadway in "Carousel," "Southern Exposure," "Four Twelves Are 48," "Tovarich" (1952).

**CUMMINGS, VICKI.** Born in Northampton, Mass. Has appeared in "The Time, The Place and The Girl," "Sunny River," "Mrs. Kimball Presents," "Lady In Danger," "The Voice of The Turtle," "For Love Or Money," "Oh, Mr. Meadowbrook," "Mr. Barry's Etchings," "A Phoenix Too Frequent," "Buy Me Blue Ribbons," "Hook 'N' Ladder," "I've Got Sixpence," "Mid-Summer."

**DAHL, ARLENE.** Born in Minneapolis, Minn., Aug. 11. Educated at Washburn High., Univ. of Minn. and Minneapolis College of Music. Has appeared on Broadway in "Mr. Strauss Goes To Boston" and "Cyrano De Bergerac" (1953 revival).

**DALTON, DORIS.** Born Mar. 18, 1912, in Sharon, Mass. Educated at Wellesley. Appeared in stock before making N.Y. debut in "Petticoat Fever." Has appeared since in "Sweet Aloes," "Blow, Ye Winds," "The Fabulous Invalid," "Another Love Story," "The Ryan Girl," "Present Laughter," "Seventeen."

**DALY, JAMES.** Born in Wisconsin, Oct. 23, 1918. Educated at Cornell. Has appeared in "Born Yesterday," "Man and Superman," "The Devil's Disciple," "Billy Budd," "Mary Rose," "Major Barbara," "St. Joan," "Dark Legend," "The Merchant of Venice" (City Center, 1953).

**DANA, LEORA.** Born in N.Y.C., Apr. 1, 1923. Educated at Lenox School and Barnard College. Trained for stage at Royal Academy of Dramatic Art, London. Has appeared on Broadway in "The Madwoman of Chaillot," "The Happy Time," "Point of No Return," "Sabrina Fair."

**DANIELL, HENRY.** Born in London, Mar. 5, 1894. Appeared in Eng. before making N.Y. bow in 1921 in "Claire de Lune." Has appeared here in "Serena Blandish," "Kind Lady," "Murder Without Crime," "Lovers and Friends," "That Lady," "The Cocktail Party," "My Three Angels."

**DARVAS, LILI.** Born in Budapest, Hungary. Discovered by and played in many Max Reinhardt productions. Made Broadway debut in 1944 in "Soldier's Wife." Has appeared since in Evans' "Hamlet," "Bravo," "Cry of The Peacock," "Horses In Midstream."

**DAWSON, MARK.** Born in Philadelphia, Mar. 23, 1920. Studied at Phila. Conservatory of Music. Made Broadway debut in 1942 in "By Jupiter." Has appeared since in "Dancing In The Streets," "Sweethearts," "High Button Shoes," "Great To Be Alive," "Me and Juliet."

**DAYKARHANOVA, TAMARA.** Born in Moscow, Russia, Jan. 14, 1894. Trained at Moscow Art Theatre with Stanislavsky. Has appeared in "The House of Bernarda Alba," "The Emperor's Clothes," "Bullfight."

**DEAN, JAMES.** Born in Fairmont, Ind., Feb. 8, 1931. Made Broadway debut Dec. 3, 1953, in "See The Jaguar." Has appeared since in "The Immoralist."

**DEEBANK, FELIX.** Born in Farnworth, Lancashire, Eng., Aug. 28, 1920. Educated at Manchester Grammar School and University. Studied at Royal Academy of Dramatic Art, London. Made N.Y. bow in 1952 in "The Deep Blue Sea." Has appeared since in "Escapade."

**DEIGHTON, MARGA ANN.** Born in British India. Has appeared on Broadway in "Masks and Faces," "Love On The Dole," "Summer and Smoke," "Mrs. McThing."

**DE LUCE, VIRGINIA.** Born in San Francisco, Oct. 25th. Educated at Newton High School, Mass. Trained for stage at Bishop-Lee School of The Theatre, Boston. Made Broadway debut, May 16, 1952, in "New Faces."

**DERR, RICHARD.** Born in Norristown, Pa., June 15, 1917. Received training at Hedgerow Theatre. Made N. Y. debut in 1949 in "The Traitor." Has appeared since in "The Closing Door," "A Phoenix Too Frequent," "The Grand Tour," "Dial 'M' For Murder."

**DEVEREAUX, JOHN DREW.** Born in N.Y.C., June 15, 1918. Educated at N.Y. Military Academy. Made Broadway debut in 1935 in "Remember The Day." Has appeared since in "Bright Honor," "Ghost of Yankee Doodle," "Life With Father," "Medea," "Life With Mother," "To Be Continued," "The Prescott Proposals," "King of Hearts."

**DE WOLFE, BILLY.** Born in Wollaston, Mass., Feb. 18th. Appeared in vaudeville, night clubs and motion pictures before making Broadway debut Dec. 10, 1953, in "John Murray Anderson's Almanac."

**DIENER, JOAN.** Educated at Sarah Lawrence College where she majored in psychology. Has appeared on Broadway in "Small Wonder," "Season In The Sun," "Kismet."

Val Dufour           Mildred Dunnock           Harry Ellerbe

**DINGLE, CHARLES.** Born in Wabash, Ind., Dec. 28, 1887. Among his many Broadway appearances are "The Little Foxes," "Miss Liberty," "The Immoralist."

**DOUGLAS, LARRY.** Born in Philadelphia, Feb. 17, 1914. Educated at Brooklyn College. Made Broadway bow in "Jumbo" in 1935. Has appeared since in "Frederika," "Three Waltzes," "Panama Hattle," "Star and Garter," "What's Up," "The Duchess Misbehaves," "Hold It," "All For Love," "The King and I."

**DOUGLAS, MELVYN.** Born in Macon, Ga., Apr. 5, 1901. Made N.Y. bow in 1928 in "A Free Soul." Has appeared since in "Back Here," "Recaptured," "Tonight Or Never," "No More Ladies," "Mother Lode," "Tapestry In Gray," "Two Blind Mice," "The Bird Cage," "Glad Tidings," "Time Out For Ginger."

**DOUGLASS, STEPHEN.** Born in Mt. Vernon, Ohio, Sept. 27, 1921. Received training at Papermill Playhouse. Appeared in London and on Broadway in "Carousel." Has appeared since in "Make A Wish," "The Golden Apple."

**DRAKE, ALFRED.** Born Oct. 7, 1914, in N.Y.C. Graduate of Brooklyn College. Has appeared on Broadway in "White Horse Inn," "Babes In Arms," "Two Bouquets," "One For The Money," "Straw Hat Revue," "Two For The Show," "Out of The Frying Pan," "As You Like It," "Yesterday's Magic," "Oklahoma," "Sing Out, Sweet Land," "Beggar's Holiday," "The Cradle Will Rock," "Joy To The World," "Kiss Me, Kate," "The Gambler," "Kismet."

**DUFOUR, VAL.** Born in New Orleans, Feb. 5, 1923. Educated at Louisiana State Univ. Appeared in ELT's "Babes In Arms," and made Broadway debut in 1952 in "The Grass Harp." Has appeared since in "Frankie and Johnny", "Elektra."

**DUGGAN, ANDREW.** Born in Franklin, Ind., Dec. 28, 1923. Received B.A. from Indiana Univ. Has appeared on Broadway in "Dream Girl," "The Innocents," "The Rose Tatoo," "Gently Does It," "Anniversary Waltz."

**DUKE, ROBERT.** Born in Washington, D.C., June 22, 1917. Educated at American Univ. and Mozarteum, Salzburg, Austria. Made Broadway debut in 1946 in "The Winter's Tale." Has appeared since in "Antony and Cleopatra," "Anne of The Thousand Days," DeHavilland's "Romeo and Juliet," "Gertie," "Sabrina Fair."

**DUNNOCK, MILDRED.** Born in Baltimore. Educated at Goucher College, Johns Hopkins and Columbia Univ. Made Broadway debut in 1932 in "Life Begins." Has appeared since in "The Corn Is Green," "Richard III," "Only The Heart," "Foolish Notion," "Lute Song," "Another Part of The Forest," "The Hallams," "Death of A Salesman," "Pride's Crossing," "The Wild Duck" (1951), "In The Summer House."

**ELLERBE, HARRY.** Born in Columbia, S.C. Made first N.Y. appearance in "Philip Goes Forth." Has appeared since in "Thoroughbred," "Strange Orchestra," "Ghosts" and "Hedda Gabler" with Nazimova, "Outward Bound," "Whiteoaks," "Sleep, My Pretty One," "Oh, Mr. Meadowbrook," "The Cocktail Party" on tour. Has directed "For Love Or Money," "Oh, Mr. Meadowbrook," "The Pink Elephant."

**ELSOM, ISOBEL.** Born in Chesterton, Cambridge, Eng., Mar. 16, 1893. Appeared in many English plays and movies before making N.Y. debut in 1926 in "The Ghost Train." Has appeared since in "The Mulberry Bush," "The Behavior of Mrs. Crane," "Ladies In Retirement," "Hand In Glove," "The Innocents," "The Curious Savage," De Havilland's "Romeo and Juliet," "The Climate of Eden," "The Burning Glass."

**EMERSON, FAYE.** Born in Elizabeth, La., July 8, 1917. Educated at San Diego State College. Appeared in many films and on TV before making N.Y. debut in 1948 revival of "The Play's The Thing." Has appeared since in "Parisienne."

**EMMETT, ROBERT.** Born in Monterey, Calif., Sept. 28, 1921. Educated at Univ. of Calif. Studied at Neighborhood Playhouse. Has appeared in "Peer Gynt" (1951), "Two On The Aisle," "Mid-Summer," "Madam, Will You Walk."

**EVANS, EDITH.** Born in London, Feb. 8, 1888. Educated at St. Michael's School. Has appeared on Broadway in "The Lady With A Lamp," Cornell's "Romeo and Juliet," "Daphne Laureola."

**EVANS, MAURICE.** Born in Dorchester, Dorset, Eng., June 3, 1901. Made first professional appearance in Eng. in 1926 in "Orestia." First N.Y. appearance was as Romeo to Cornell's Juliet in 1935. Has appeared since in "St. Helena," "Richard II," "St. Joan," "Henry IV, Part I," "Hamlet," "Macbeth," "Man and Superman," "The Browning Version," "Harlequinade," "The Devil's Disciple," "The Wild Duck" (1951), "Dial 'M' For Murder."

**EVANS, REYNOLDS.** Began stage career as an extra with Sothern and Marlowe. Has appeared since with Walter Hampden in "Cyrano de Bergerac," with Evans in "Richard II" and "Henry IV," and more recently in "The Doughgirls," "The Late George Apley," "Metropole," "Fancy Meeting You Again," "The Solid Gold Cadillac."

Anne Francine       Eddie Firestone       Bijou Fernandez

**EVANS, WILBUR.** Born in Philadelphia in 1905. Educated at Curtis Institute of Music. Made stage debut in San Francisco in 1930 in "Bambina." Was in Carnegie Hall productions of "The Merry Widow and "The New Moon." Sang in New Opera Co. production of "La Vie Parisienne." Most recent roles were in "Mexican Hayride," "Up In Central Park," London company of "South Pacific," "By The Beautiful Sea."

**EVELYN, JUDITH.** Born in Seneca, S. D., Mar 13, 1913. Educated at Univ. of Manitoba. Appeared in several plays in England before making Broadway debut in 1941 in "Angel Street." Has appeared since on tour in "State of The Union," "On Approval," and "A Streetcar Named Desire," and in N.Y. in "The Overtons," "The Rich Full Life," "Craig's Wife," (1947), "The Ivy Green," "The Shrike," "The Sea Gull" (1954).

**EVERS, HERBERT.** Born in N.Y.C., Jan. 2, 1922. Appeared with Jitney Players before making Broadway bow in 1941 in "Popsy." Has appeared since in "All Gaul Is Divided," "Grandma's Diary," "Angel In The Pawnshop," "A Date With April."

**FABRAY, NANETTE.** Born in San Diego, Cal., Oct. 27, 1922. Educated at Hollywood High and Max Reinhardt Workshop. As a child, danced in Fanchon and Marco vaudeville unit and appeared in "Our Gang" comedies. Made N.Y. debut in 1940 in "Meet The People." Has appeared since in "Let's Face It," "By Jupiter," "Jackpot," "My Dear Public," "Bloomer Girl," "High Button Shoes," "Love Life," "Arms and The Girl," "Make A Wish."

**FERNANDEZ, BIJOU.** Born in N.Y.C., Nov. 4, 1877. Made stage debut in 1884 in "May Blossom." Has had a long and illustrious career, appearing with both the old Austin Daly and the Empire Theatre companies. More recent stage appearances include "Masque of Kings," "I'd Rather Be Right," "My Sister Eileen," "The Prescott Proposals."

**FERRER, JOSE.** Born in Santurce, P.R., Jan. 8, 1912. Educated at Princeton. First N.Y. appearance in 1935 in "A Slight Case of Murder." Has appeared since in "Brother Rat," "In Clover," "Missouri Legend," "Mamba's Daughters," "Key Largo," "Charley's Aunt," "Vickie," "Let's Face It," "Othello," "Cyrano de Bergerac," "The Silver Whistle," "Twentieth Century" (1951), "The Shrike," City Center revivals of "Volpone," "Angel Street," "Four Chekhov Comedies," "The Alchemist," "S.S. Glencairn," "The Insect Comedy," "Cyrano," "Charley's Aunt," "The Shrike" and "Richard III."

**FERRER, MEL.** Born in N.Y.C. Educated at Princeton. Has appeared on Broadway in "You Never Know," "Kind Lady" revival, "Strange Fruit," "Ondine."

**FIEDLER, JOHN.** Born in Plateville, Wisc., Feb. 3, 1925. Graduate of Shorewood High, Milwaukee. Studied at Neighborhood Playhouse. Made first N.Y. appearance in Phoenix Theatre revival of "The Sea Gull," May 11, 1954.

**FIELD, BETTY.** Born in Boston, Feb. 8, 1918. Studied at American Academy of Dramatic Arts. First stage appearance was in London company of "She Loves Me Not" in 1934. Has appeared since in N.Y. in "Page Miss Glory," "Three Men On A Horse," "Room Service," "What A Life," "The Primrose Path," "Two On An Island," "Flight To The West," "A New Life," "The Voice of The Turtle," "Dream Girl," "The Rat Race," "Not For Children," "The Fourposter," "The Ladies of The Corridor."

**FINNEY, MARY.** Born in Spokane, Wash. Educated at St. Joseph's Academy, Brighton, Mann. Trained at Margo Jones' Dallas Theatre. Has appeared on Broadway in "Southern Exposure," "The Cellar and The Well," "Make A Wish," "Gentlemen Prefer Blondes," "The Children's Hour" (1952), "The Magic and The Loss."

**FIRESTONE, EDDIE.** Born in San Francisco, Dec. 11, 1920. Educated at Northwestern Univ. Received stage training under Preston Sturgis Players. Made Broadway bow, Jan. 20, 1954, in "The Caine Mutiny Court Martial."

**FLETCHER, BRAMWELL.** Born Feb. 20, 1904, in Bradford, Yorkshire, Eng. Made N.Y. bow in 1929 in "Scotland Yard." Has appeared since in "Ten Minute Alibi," "Lady Precious Stream," "Within The Gates," "Storm Operation," "Rebecca," "The Day After Tomorrow," "Maggie," revivals of "Outward Bound," "The Doctor's Dilemma," "Getting Married," "Candida" (1952) and, "Misalliance" (1953).

**FONDA, HENRY.** Born in Grand Island, Neb., May 16, 1905. Educated at Univ. of Minn. Made first N.Y. appearance in "The Game of Love and Death" in 1929. Has appeared since in "I Loved You Wednesday," "Forsaking All Others," "New Faces" (1934), "The Farmer Takes A Wife," "Blow, Ye Winds," "Mister Roberts," "Point of No Return," "The Caine Mutiny Court Martial."

**FONTANNE, LYNN.** Born in London, Dec. 6, 1887. Made first stage appearance in 1905 with Ellen Terry in "Alice-Sit-By-The-Fire." Made N.Y. debut in 1910 in "Mr. Preedy and The Countess." Among her many appearances since are "Dulcy," "The Guardsman," "Goat Song," "At Mrs. Beam's," "The Second Man," "Strange Interlude," "Caprice," "Elizabeth The Queen," "Reunion In Vienna," "Design For Living," "Idiot's Delight," "Amphitryon 38," "The Sea Gull," "There Shall Be No Night," "The Pirate," "O Mistress Mine," "I Know My Love."

| Richard France | Luella Gear | Robert Gallagher |

**FORBES, SCOTT.** Born in High Wycombe, Eng., Sept. 11, 1921. Appeared with English repertory companies and in London before making Broadway bow, April 2, 1953, in "Horses In Midstream." Has appeared since in "The Burning Glass."

**FORD, PAUL.** Born in Baltimore, Md., Nov. 2, 1901. Educated at Dartmouth. Made N.Y. debut in "Decision." Has appeared since in "Lower North," "Kiss Them For Me," "Flamingo Road," "On Whitman Avenue," "Another Part of The Forest," "Command Decision," "The Teahouse of The August Moon."

**FORSYTHE, JOHN.** Born in Penn's Grove, N. J., Jan. 29, 1918. Made Broadway debut in 1942 in "Yankee Point." Has appeared since in "Vickie," "Winged Victory," "Yellow Jack" (1944), "It Takes Two," "All My Sons," "Mister Roberts," "The Teahouse of The August Moon."

**FOY, EDDIE, JR.** Born in New Rochelle, N.Y., Feb. 4, 1905. Educated at St. Gabriel's School. Appeared on Broadway in "Smiles," "Show Girl," "Ripples," "The Cat and The Fiddle," "At Home and Abroad," "Orchids Preferred," "The Red Mill" (1945), "High Button Shoes," "The Pajama Game."

**FRANCE, RICHARD.** Born in Chicago, Jan. 6, 1930. Educated at Senn High, Chicago and Y.M.C.A. Professional School. Made N.Y. debut in 1951 in "Seventeen." Has appeared since in "Wish You Were Here," "By The Beautiful Sea," replaced Harold Lang in London company of "Pal Joey."

**FRANCINE, ANNE.** Born in Philadelphia. Well known as night club entertainer. Made Broadway debut in 1945 in "Marriage Is For Single People." Has appeared since in "By The Beautiful Sea."

**FRANCIS, ARLENE.** Born in Boston in 1908. Educated at Finch Finishing School. Has appeared in N.Y. in "One Good Year," "Horse Eats Hat," "The Women," "All That Glitters," "Michael Drops In," "Journey To Jerusalem," "The Doughgirls," "The Overtons," "The French Touch," "The Cup of Trembling," "My Name Is Aquilon," "Metropole," "The Little Blue Light," "Late Love."

**FREY, NATHANIEL.** Born in N.Y.C., Aug. 3, 1918. Educated at DeWitt Clinton High and NYU. Studied at American Theatre Wing. Made Broadway bow in 1947 in "Barefoot Boy With Cheek." Has appeared since in "High Button Shoes," "Touch And Go," "Call Me Madam," "A Tree Grows In Brooklyn," "Wonderful Town."

**GALLAGHER, ROBERT.** Born in Chicago, Aug. 28, 1920. Educated at Univ. of New Mexico. Studied at Pasadena Playhouse. Made N.Y. bow in 1948 in "I Gotta Get Out." Has appeared since in "Make Mine Manhattan," "Two On The Aisle," "Hazel Flagg," "Show Boat" (1954 City Center revival).

**GATES, LARRY.** Born in St. Paul, Minn., Sept. 24, 1915. Educated at Univ. of Minn. Made Broadway debut in 1939 in "Speak of The Devil." Has appeared since in "Twelfth Night" (1940), "Bell, Book and Candle," "The Taming of The Shrew" (1951), "The Love of Four Colonels," "The Teahouse of The August Moon."

**GATESON, MARJORIE.** Born in Brooklyn. Educated at Pacific Collegiate Institute and Brooklyn Conservatory of Music. Made Broadway debut in 1913 in "Little Simplicity," "Love Letter," "For Goodness Sake," "As Good As New." Appeared in many films and returned to N.Y. in 1947 revival of "Sweethearts." Has appeared since in revival of "Show Boat" (1954).

**GAXTON, WILLIAM.** Born in San Francisco, Dec. 2, 1893. Educated at Univ. of Cal. Made N.Y. bow in second "Music Box Revue." Has appeared since in "Betty Lee," "Miss Happiness," "All For You," "Connecticut Yankee," and teamed with Victor Moore in "Of Thee I Sing," "Let 'Em Eat Cake," "Anything Goes," "Leave It To Me," "Louisiana Purchase," "Hollywood Pinafore," "Nellie Bly."

**GAYNES, GEORGE.** Born in Helsinki, Finland, May 3, 1917. Studied at Milan Conservatory and appeared in opera in France. Has appeared with City Center Opera Company and on Broadway in "The Consul," "Out Of This World," "Wonderful Town."

**GAZZARA, BEN.** Born in N.Y.C., Aug. 28, 1930. Educated at Stuyvesant High and City College of N.Y. Trained at Dramatic Workshop. Toured in "Jezebel's Husband" and had lead in "Day of Grace" for Theatre Guild at Westport (1953) before making Broadway debut Oct. 14, 1953, in "End As A Man."

**GEAR, LUELLA.** Born in N.Y.C., Sept. 5, 1897. Made Broadway debut in 1917 in "Love O' Mine." Has appeared since in "The Gold Diggers," "Elsie," "Poppy," "Queen High," "The Optimist," "Ups-A-Daisy," "The Gay Divorcee," "Life Begins At 8:40," "On Your Toes," "Crazy With The Heat," "The Streets of Paris," "Count Me In," "That Old Devil," "My Romance," "To Be Continued," "Sabrina Fair."

**GEER, WILL.** Born Mar. 9, 1902, in Frankfort, Ind. Educated at Univ. of Chicago and Columbia. Most recent appearances on Broadway include "Tobacco Road," "Abe Lincoln In Illinois," "The Cradle Will Rock," "Of Mice and Men," "Sophie," "Flamingo Road," "On Whitman Avenue," "The Cradle Will Rock" (1948), "Hope's The Thing," Phoenix revivals of "Coriolanus" and "The Sea Gull" (1954).

Ben Gazzara

Hermione Gingold

John Granger

**GHOSTLEY, ALICE.** Born in Eve, Mo., Aug. 14, 1926. Educated at Univ. of Okla. Appeared in Off-Broadway and ELT productions before making Broadway debut in "New Faces of 1952."

**GIELGUD, JOHN.** Born Apr. 14, 1904, in London, where he studied at Lady Benson's School and the Royal Academy of Dramatic Art. Made London debut in 1921 at the Old Vic and achieved great success on British stage. Made N.Y. bow in 1928 in "The Patriot." Has appeared since in "Hamlet" (1936), "The Importance of Being Earnest," "Love For Love," "Medea," "Crime and Punishment," "The Lady's Not For Burning"

**GILBERT, LOU.** Born in Sycamore, Ill., Aug. 1, 1909. Made Broadway bow in 1945 in "Common Ground." Other appearances include "Beggars Are Coming To Town," "Truckline Cafe," "The Whole World Over," "Volpone," "Hope's The Thing," "Detective Story," "His and Hers."

**GILLETTE, PRISCILLA.** Born in Tenafly, N.J., Nov. 27, 1925. Educated at Tenafly High and Syracuse Univ. Has appeared on concert stage and TV. Made Broadway debut in 1948 in "Brigadoon." Has appeared since in "Regina," "Out Of This World," City Center revival of "Regina," "The Children's Hour" on tour, "The Golden Apple."

**GILLMORE, MARGALO.** Born in London, May 31, 1897. Studied at American Academy of Dramatic Arts. Made N. Y. debut in 1917 in "The Scrap of Paper." Has appeared since in "The Famous Mrs. Fair," "He Who Gets Slapped," "Outward Bound," "The Green Hat," "Berkeley Square," "The Barretts of Wimpole Street," "Flowers of The Forest," "Valley Forge," "The Women," "No Time For Comedy," "State of The Union," "Kind Sir."

**GINGOLD, HERMIONE.** Born in London, Dec. 9th. Says her education was slight. Has had a long and popular career on the English stage. Made Broadway debut Dec. 10, 1953, in "John Murray Anderson's Almanac."

**GISH, DOROTHY.** Born in Massilon, Ohio, Mar. 11, 1898. Made first stage appearance in 1903 in "East Lynne." After an eminent career in films, returned to the stage in 1928 in "Young Love." Has appeared since in "The Inspector General," "Getting Married," "The Streets of New York," "Pillars of Society," "The Bride The Sun Shines On," "Foreign Affairs," "Brittle Heaven," "Missouri Legend," "Life With Father," "The Great Big Doorstep," "The Magnificent Yankee," "The Story of Mary Surratt," "The Man."

**GISH, LILLIAN.** Born in Springfield, Ohio, Oct. 14, 1896. First appeared on stage at age of 6. After a long and successful screen career, returned to Broadway in 1930 in "Uncle Vanya." Has appeared since in "Camille," "Nine Pine Street," "The Joyous Season," "Within The Gates," "Hamlet," "The Star Wagon," "Dear Octopus," "Life With Father," "Mr. Sycamore," "Crime and Punishment," "The Curious Savage," "The Trip To Bountiful."

**GLEASON, THOMAS.** Born in South Bend, Ind., Feb. 11, 1915. Has appeared on N.Y. stage in "Ziegfeld Follies" (1936), "Let's Face It," "Magdalena," "South Pacific."

**GOLDSTEIN, JENNIE.** Born in N.Y.C., May 8, 1899. Attended P.S. 122 and 79. Started on stage as child actress. Well known in Yiddish theatre. Had own theatre at 19. Has appeared on Broadway in "The Number" and "Camino Real."

**GOODNER, CAROL.** Born in N.Y.C., May 20, 1904. Has appeared on Broadway in "They Walk Alone," "Let's Face It," "Blithe Spirit," "The Man Who Came To Dinner," "The Wookey," "The Family," "Lovers and Friends," "Deep Are The Roots," "How I Wonder," "The Autumn Garden," "The Brass Ring," "Horses In Midstream."

**GORDON, RUTH.** Born in Wollaston, Mass., Oct. 30, 1896. Educated at Quincy High. Studied at American Academy of Dramatic Arts. Made stage debut in 1915 with Maude Adams in "Peter Pan." Has appeared since in "Seventeen," "Clarence," "Saturday's Children," "Serena Blandish," "Hotel Universe," "A Church Mouse," "Three Cornered Moon," "Ethan Frome," "The Country Wife," "A Doll's House," "The Three Sisters," "Over 21," "The Leading Lady," "The Smile of The World," Authored "Over 21," "Years Ago," "The Leading Lady."

**GOSSETT, LOUIS.** Born in Brooklyn, May 27, 1936. Educated at Abraham Lincoln High School. Made Broadway debut Sept. 24, 1953, in "Take A Giant Step."

**GOUGH, LLOYD.** Has appeared on Broadway in "Yellow Jack," "The Ghost of Yankee Doodle," "Shadow and Substance," "My Dear Children," "Tanyard Street," "Golden Wings," "Heart of A City," "Deep Are The Roots," "Ondine."

**GRAHAM, RONNY.** Born in Philadelphia, Aug. 26, 1919. Educated at Germantown Grammar and High Schools. Appeared in night clubs and Brattle Theatre revue "It's About Time" before making Broadway debut in "New Faces of 1952."

**GRANGER, JOHN.** Born in Oklahoma, Feb. 21, 1924. Educated at Culver, Univ. of Tex. and Rice Univ. Received stage training with Margo Jones in Texas. Made Broadway debut Oct. 7, 1953, in "The Little Hut."

Joan Greenwood  Will Hare  Carol Haney

**GRAY, DOLORES.** Born in Hollywood, Calif., June 7, 1924. Made Broadway debut in 1944 in "Seven Lively Arts," followed by "Are You With It?" Had London success in title role of "'Annie Get Your Gun." Has appeared in N.Y. since in "Two On The Aisle," "Carnival In Flanders."

**GRAY, JOAN.** Born in N.Y.C. Educated at Univ. of Denver. Made Broadway debut Sept. 21, 1948, in "A Story For Strangers." Has appeared since in "Oh, Men! Oh, Women!"

**GREENWOOD, JOAN.** Born in London in 1919. Received stage training at the Royal Academy of Dramatic Art and the Oxford Repertory group. Appeared in many English films and on the English stage before making her Broadway debut Feb. 11, 1954, in "The Confidential Clerk."

**GREGORY, JAMES.** Born in N.Y.C., Dec. 23, 1911. Received training in stock. Appeared on Broadway in "Key Largo," "Journey To Jerusalem," "In Time To Come," "Glamour Preferred," "Autumn Hill," "Dream Girl," "All My Sons," "Death of A Salesman," "Dinosaur Wharf," "Collector's Item," "Dead Pigeon."

**HAGEN, UTA.** Born June 12, 1919, in Goettingen, Ger. Made N.Y. debut in 1938 with the Lunts in "The Sea Gull." Has appeared since in "The Happiest Years," "Key Largo," "Vickie," "Othello," "The Whole World Over," "Angel Street" (1948), "A Streetcar Named Desire," "The Country Girl," "St. Joan" (1951), "Tovarich" (1952), "In Any Language," "The Magic and The Loss."

**HAMILTON, NEIL.** Born in Lynn, Mass., Sept. 9, 1897. Had long career in movies. Most recently appeared on Broadway in "Many Happy Returns," "The Deep Mrs. Sykes," "The Men We Marry," "State of The Union," "To Be Continued," "Late Love."

**HAMPDEN, WALTER.** Born in Brooklyn, June 30, 1879. Educated at Brooklyn Polytechnic Inst. and Harvard. Made stage debut in 1901 in Benson's Shakespearean Co. Has appeared in almost all plays by Shakespeare and Ibsen, and in "Caponsacchi," "Seven Keys To Baldpate," "Cyrano de Bergerac," "The Rivals," "The Strings, My Lord, Are False," "The Patriots," 1946-7 ART productions, "The Traitor," "The Velvet Glove," "The Crucible."

**HANEY, CAROL.** Born in New Bedford, Mass., Dec. 24, 1924, and educated in local grammar and high schools. Made her Broadway debut May 13, 1954, in "The Pajama Game."

**HANLEY, ELLEN.** Born in Lorain, Ohio, May 15, 1926. Attended Juil. School of Music. Made Broadway debut in "Annie Get Your Gun." Has appeared since in "Barefoot Boy With Cheek," "High Button Shoes" on tour, "Two's Company."

**HANSEN, WILLIAM.** Born Mar. 2, 1911, in Tacoma, Wash. Graduate of Univ. of Wash. Studied with Ouspenskaya and at Group Theatre School. Made N.Y. bow in "My Heart's In The Highlands." Has appeared since in "Night Music," "Medicine Show," "Twelfth Night," Evans' "Macbeth," "The Assassin," "Brigadoon," "Montserrat," "The Member of The Wedding," "Barefoot In Athens," "Golden Boy" (1952), "The Teahouse of The August Moon."

**HARDIE, RUSSELL.** Born in Griffin Mills, N.Y., May 20, 1906. Educated at St. Mary's College. Made N.Y. bow in "The Criminal Code." Has appeared since in "Pagan Lady," "The Constant Sinner," "Remember The Day," "The Ghost of Yankee Doodle," "Primrose Path," "Snafu," "Foxhole In The Parlor," "The Doughgirls" and "My Sister Eileen" on tour, "Home of The Brave," "The Bees and The Flowers," "Streetcar Named Desire" on tour, "Love Me Long."

**HARDWICKE, CEDRIC.** Born in Lye, Eng., Feb. 19, 1893. Recent N.Y. appearances include "Promise," "The Amazing Dr. Clitterhouse," "Shadow and Substance," "Antigone," "Candida" (1946), "Caesar and Cleopatra" (1949) "Don Juan In Hell," "Horses In Midstream," "The Burning Glass."

**HARE, WILL.** Born in Elkins, W. Va., Mar. 30, 1919. Trained at American Actors Theatre. Has appeared in "The Eternal Road," "The Moon Is Down," "Suds In Your Eye," "Only The Heart," "The Visitor," "The Trip To Bountiful."

**HARENS, DEAN.** Born in South Bend, Ind., June 30. Studied at Goodman Theatre, Chicago. Made Broadway debut in 1941 in "The Talley Method." Has appeared since in "Papa Is All," "Men In Shadow," "Those Endearing Young Charms," "Tenting Tonight," "Be Your Age," "A Girl Can Tell."

**HARRIS, JULIE.** Born in Grosse Point, Mich., Dec. 25, 1925. Attended Yale Drama School. Made Broadway debut in 1945 in "It's A Gift." Has appeared since in "Henry IV" and "Oedipus" with Old Vic Co., and in "The Playboy of The Western World," "Alice In Wonderland," Redgrave's "Macbeth," "Sundown Beach," "The Young and Fair," "Magnolia Alley," "Montserrat," "The Member of The Wedding," "I Am A Camera," "Mademoiselle Colombe."

**HARRISON, REX.** Born in Huyton, Lancs., Eng., Mar. 5, 1908. Educated at Uppingham. Has appeared on English stage and in many English and American films. Made Broadway bow in 1936 in "Sweet Aloes." Has appeared since in "Anne of The Thousand Days," "Bell, Book and Candle," "Venus Observed," "The Love of Four Colonels."

Julie Harris      Alan Hewitt      Diana Herbert

**HARTMAN, PAUL.** Born in San Francisco. Has appeared in "Red, Hot and Blue," "You Never Know," "Top-Notchers," "Keep Laughing," "Angel In The Wings," "All For Love," "Tickets, Please," "Of Thee I Sing" (1952).

**HAVOC, JUNE.** Born in Seattle, Wash., Nov. 1916. Made N.Y. debut in 1936 in "Forbidden Melody." Has appeared since in "The Women," "Pal Joey," "Mexican Hayride," "Sadie Thompson," "The Ryan Girl," "Dunnigan's Daughter." Replaced Betty Field in "Dream Girl" and Celeste Holm in "Affairs of State."

**HAWKINS, JACK.** Born in London, Sept. 14, 1910. Educated at Trinity County School, Middlesex. Made N.Y. debut in 1929 in "Journey's End." Has appeared since in "Dear Octopus," "Romeo and Juliet" (1951).

**HAYDON, JULIE.** Born in Oak Park, Ill., June 10, 1910. Educated at Gordon School for Girls, Hollywood. Has appeared in "Bright Star," "Shadow and Substance," "The Time of Your Life," "Magic," "Hello, Out There," "The Glass Menagerie," "Miracle of The Mountains," "Our Lan'," "The Cocktail Party" on tour.

**HAYES, BILL.** Born in Harvey, Ill., June 5, 1925. Educated at DePauw Univ. and Northwestern. Has appeared in summer theatre musicals and on TV before making Broadway debut May 28, 1953, in "Me and Juliet."

**HAYES, HELEN.** Born in Washington, D.C., Oct. 10, 1900. Educated at Sacred Heart Academy. Made first stage appearance in 1908 in Washington in "Babes In The Wood." Made N.Y. debut in 1909 with Lew Fields in "Old Dutch." Among her many appearances are "The Summer Widowers," "Penrod," "Dear Brutus," "Clarence," "Bab," "To The Ladies," "We Moderns," "Dancing Mothers," "Caesar and Cleopatra," "What Every Woman Knows," "Coquette," "Mary of Scotland," "Victoria Regina," "Ladies and Gentlemen," "Twelfth Night," "Candle In The Wind," "Harriet," "Happy Birthday," "The Wisteria Trees," "Mrs. McThing."

**HECKART, EILEEN.** Born in Columbus, Ohio, Mar. 29. Educated at Ohio State Univ. Studied at American Theatre Wing. Made N.Y. debut in 1944 City Center revival of "Our Town." Has appeared since in "They Knew What They Wanted," (1949), "The Traitor," "Hilda Crane," "In Any Language," "Picnic."

**HELMORE, TOM.** Born in London, Jan. 4, 1912. Educated at Tonbridge School, Kent. Has appeared on Broadway in "No Time For Comedy," "The Day Before Spring," "You Never Can Tell," "Clutterbuck," "Legend of Sarah," "The High Ground," "Love and Let Love," "The Winner."

**HEPBURN, AUDREY.** Born in Brussels, Belgium, in 1929. Made first stage appearance in 1948 in London production of "High Button Shoes." Made Broadway debut Nov. 24, 1951, in "Gigi." Has appeared since in "Ondine."

**HEPBURN, KATHARINE.** Born in Hartford, Conn., Nov. 9, 1909. Educated at Bryn Mawr. Made Broadway debut in 1928 in "Night Hostess" using name of Katherine Burns. Has appeared since in "These Days," "A Month In The Country," "Art and Mrs. Bottle," "The Warrior's Husband," "The Lake," "The Philadelphia Story," "Without Love," "As You Like It" (1950), "The Millionairess."

**HERBERT, DIANA.** Born in Hollywood, Calif. Dec. 25, 1928. Educated at UCLA. Made Broadway debut in 1948 when she replaced June Lockhart in "For Love Or Money." Has appeared since in "The Number," "Men of Distinction," "Wonderful Town."

**HESTON, CHARLTON.** Born in Evanston, Ill., Oct. 4, 1922. Educated at Northwestern Univ. Made Broadway bow Nov. 26, 1947, in "Antony and Cleopatra." Has appeared since in "Leaf and Bough," "Design For A Stained Glass Window."

**HEWITT, ALAN.** Born in N.Y.C., Jan. 21, 1915. Educated at Dartmouth. Made Broadway debut in 1935 in "The Taming of The Shrew." Has appeared since in "Idiot's Delight," "The Masque of Kings," "Amphitryon 38," "The Sea Gull," "The American Way," "The Moon Is Down," "Death of A Salesman," "Call Me Madam," "Ondine."

**HICKS, RUSSELL.** Born in Baltimore, Md., June 4, 1895. Educated at Baltimore Polytechnic Inst. Appeared with Vagabond Players and many stock companies before making N. Y. debut in 1925 in "Wisecrackers." Has appeared since in "No Trespassing," "Torch Song," "Goin' Home," "All The King's Horses," "Nona," "Time For Elizabeth," "On Borrowed Time" (1935), "The Caine Mutiny Court Martial."

**HILL, PHYLLIS.** Born in N.Y.C., Oct. 27, 1925. Educated at Friends Seminary, N.Y.C. Has appeared on Broadway in "Rosalinda," "Sons and Soldiers," "What's Up," "Helen Goes To Troy," "Cyrano de Bergerac" (1946), City Center revivals of "Volpone," "Angel Street," "The Alchemist" and "The Insect Comedy," "The Shrike," "The Fifth Season."

John Hodiak          Laurel Hurley          Earle Hyman

**HILL, STEVEN.** Born in Seattle, Feb. 24, 1922. Educated at Univ. of Wash. Has appeared on Broadway in "A Flag Is Born," "Mister Roberts," "Sundown Beach," "The Lady Frem The Sea," "The Country Girl."

**'HODIAK, JOHN.** Born in Pittsburgh, Apr. 16, 1914. Educated at Hamtramck High, Mich. Began career as radio actor in Detroit, then went to Hollywood. Made Broadway debut in 1952 in "The Chase." Has appeared since in "The Caine Mutiny Court Martial."

**HOLDEN, JAMES.** Born in Birmingham, Ala., Dec. 12, 1923. Studied at Pasadena Playhouse. Made Broadway debut in 1947 in "Command Decision." Has appeared since in "The Member of The Wedding," "The Remarkable Mr. Pennypacker."

**HOLLIDAY, JUDY.** Born June 21, 1921, in the Bronx, N.Y. Spent several years with The Revuers, a night club act. Made Broadway debut in 1945 in "Kiss Them For Me." Has appeared since in "Born Yesterday," "Dream Girl" (1951 revival).

**HOLM, CELESTE.** Born in N.Y.C., Apr. 29, 1919. Made Broadway debut in 1938 in "Glorianna." Has appeared since in "The Time of Your Life," "Another Sun," "The Return of The Vagabond," "Papa Is All," "The Damask Cheek," "Oklahoma," "Bloomer Girl," "She Stoops To Conquer," "Affairs of State," "Anna Christie" (1951), "His and Hers."

**HUBER, GUSTI.** Born in Vienna, Austria, July 27, 1914. Educated at Academie siie Musek und Darstellende Kunst. One of Vienna's leading actresses, made N.Y. debut in 1952 in "Flight Into Egypt." Has appeared since in "Dial 'M' for Murder."

**HUBER, PAUL.** Born in Wilkes-Barre, Pa., Nov. 26, 1895. Has appeared on Broadway in Barrymore's "Hamlet," "The Constant Sinner," "Sailor, Beware!," "Everywhere I Roam," "Johnny Belinda," "Strip For Action," "Decision," "Mr. Peebles and Mr. Hooker," "Miss Liberty," "Point of No Return," "The Immoralist."

**HULL, HENRY.** Born in Louisville, Ky., Oct. 3, 1890. Among his many Broadway appearances are "The Man Who Came Back," "39 East," "The Cat and The Canary," "Lulu Belle," "Michael and Mary," "Springtime For Henry," "The Youngest," "Tobacco Road," "Masque of Kings," "Foolish Notion," "Mister Roberts."

**HULL, JOSEPHINE.** Born in Newton, Mass., Jan. 3, 1886. Educated at Radcliffe College. Her many Broadway appearances include "Fata Morgana," "Craig's Wife," "March Hares," "Fresh Fields," "American Dream," "An International Incident," "You Can't Take It With You," "Arsenic and Old Lace," "Harvey," "Minnie and Mr. Williams," "The Golden State," "Whistler's Grandmother," "The Solid Gold Cadillac."

**HUNTER, KIM.** Born in Detroit, Nov. 12, 1922. Educated at Miami Beach High. Made Broadway debut in 1947 in "A Streetcar Named Desire." Has appeared since in "Darkness At Noon," "The Chase," "The Children's Hour" (1952).

**HURLEY, LAUREL.** Born in Allentown, Pa., Feb. 14, 1927, and educated at local high school. Made Broadway debut in 1943, as Kathie in "The Student Prince." Has appeared since then with the New York City Opera Company and in the 1954 City Center revival of "Show Boat."

**HUSTON, PHILIP.** Born in Goshen, Va., Mar. 14, 1910. Educated at Blair Academy. Made Broadway debut in 1934 in "Strange Orchestra." Has appeared since in "Macbeth," "Twelfth Night," "Othello," "Catherine Was Great," "The Tempest," "The Winter's Tale," "The Father," "With A Silk Thread," "Tower Beyond Tragedy," "The Shrike," 1953 City Center revivals of "Cyrano de Bergerac," "Richard III," "The Shrike."

**HYMAN, EARLE.** Born in Rocky Mount, N.C., Oct. 11, 1926. Educated at Franklin Lane High, Brooklyn. Received stage training at New School and Davenport Theatre. Appeared with American Negro Theatre in "Three's A Family," "Anna Lucasta." Has also appeared in "Run Little Chillun," "Climate of Eden," City Center revival of "The Merchant of Venice" (1953), and played title role in Off-Broadway production of "Othello."

**IRVING, GEORGE S.** Born in Springfield, Mass., Nov. 1, 1922. Has appeared on Broadway in "Oklahoma," "Call Me Mister," "Along Fifth Avenue," "Two's Company," "Me and Juliet."

**IVES, BURL.** Born in Hunt Township, Ill. Well known for folk songs. Has appeared on Broadway in "The Boys From Syracuse," "I Married An Angel," "Heavenly Express," "Sing Out, Sweet Land," "She Stoops To Conquer" (1950), "Paint Your Wagon," 1954 City Center revival of "Show Boat."

**JACKSON, ANNE.** Born in Alleghany, Pa., Sept. 3, 1926. Studied at Neighborhood Playhouse. Made Broadway debut in 1945 in "Signature." Has appeared since in "Yellow Jack," "John Gabriel Borkman," "The Last Dance," "Summer and Smoke," "Magnolia Alley," "Love Me Long," "The Lady From The Sea," "Never Say Never," "Oh, Men! Oh, Women!"

**Page Johnson**          **Edith King**          **James Jewell**

**JACKSON, HARRY.** Born in Pelham Manor, N.Y., March 21, 1923. Educated at Syracuse Univ. and studied for stage at American Theatre Wing. Has appeared on Broadway in "Texas Lil' Darlin'," "Mid-Summer," "The Teahouse of The August Moon."

**JAFFE, SAM.** Born in N.Y.C., Mar. 8, 1898. Made stage debut in 1915 in "The Clod." Has appeared since in "Samson and Delilah," "The Main Line," "The Jazz Singer," "Grand Hotel," "The Eternal Road," "A Doll's House," "The Gentle People," "Thank You, Svoboda," "This Time Tomorrow," "An Enemy of The People," "Mlle. Colombe," "The Sea Gull" (1954).

**JANIS, CONRAD.** Born in N.Y.C., Feb. 11, 1928. Made Broadway debut in 1942 in "Junior Miss." Has appeared since in "Dark of The Moon," "The Next Half Hour," "The Brass Ring," "Time. Out For Ginger."

**JANNEY, LEON.** Born in Ogden, Utah, Apr. 1, 1917. Educated at Hollywood Professional Children's School. After career as child film star, made N.Y. debut in 1934 in "Every Thursday." Has appeared since in "The Simpleton of The Unexpected Isles," "Parade," "Mulatto," "Foreigners," "Ghost For Sale," "Days of Our Youth," "The Victors," "Madam, Will You Walk."

**JEANMAIRE.** Born in Paris, France. Danced with the Monte Carlo Ballet and Ballet Russe before making her Broadway debut with Roland Petit's "Ballets de Paris." Has starred since in "The Girl In Pink Tights."

**JEFFREYS, ANNE.** Born in Goldsboro, N.C., Jan. 26, 1923. Educated at Anderson College. Made Broadway debut in 1947 musical version of "Street Scene." Has appeared since in "My Romance," "Kiss Me, Kate," "Three Wishes For Jamie."

**JEWELL, JAMES.** Born in Gainesville, Ga., Oct. 20, 1925. Educated at Rollins College. Made Broadway debut in 1944 in "Song of Norway." Has appeared since in "Razzle Dazzle," "Allegro," "John Murray Anderson's Almanac."

**JOHNSON, PAGE.** Born in Welch, W. Va., Aug. 25, 1927. Educated at Ithaca College. Made Broadway debut March 10, 1950, in "Romeo and Juliet." Has appeared since in "Elektra" and "Oedipus" with Greek National Theatre, and in "Camino Real."

**JONES, BARRY.** Born in Guernsey, Channel Islands, Mar. 6, 1893. Educated at Elizabeth College. Made N.Y. Bow in 1924 in "Man and The Masses." Other N.Y. appearances were in "The Bully," "The Sport of Kings," "The Constant Nymph," "The Road To Rome," "Love For Love" (1940), "The Doctor's Dilemma," "Barefoot In Athens," "Misalliance."

**JONES, HENRY.** Born in Philadelphia, Aug. 1, 1912. Educated at St. Joseph's College. Trained at Hedgerow Theatre. Has appeared in Evans' "Hamlet" and "Henry IV," "The Time of Your Life," "Village Green," "My Sister Eileen," "This Is The Army," "Joan of Lorraine," "How I Wonder," "Town House," "They Knew What They Wanted" (1949), "A Story For A Sunday Evening," "The Solid Gold Cadillac."

**JOURDAN, LOUIS.** Born in Marseilles, France. Appeared in many Hollywood films before making Broadway debut Feb. 24, 1954, in "The Immoralist."

**KALLMAN, DICK.** Born in N.Y.C., July 7, 1933. Educated at Tilton Academy and Professional Children's School. Made Broadway debut June 21, 1951, in "Seventeen." Has appeared since in "The Fifth Season."

**KANE, WHITFORD.** Born in Larne, Ire., Jan. 30, 1882. Made stage debut in Belfast in 1903 in "Ticket-Of-Leave Man," N.Y. debut in 1912 in "The Drone." Among his many appearances are "The First Legion," "The Doctor's Dilemma," "Excursion," "The Moon Is Down," "St. Helena," "Hamlet" (1st grave digger with Barrymore and Evans), "Lifeline," "Career Angel," "Meet A Body," "It's A Gift," "The Winter's Tale," "As You Like It" (1950).

**KEITH-JOHNSTON, COLIN.** Born in London, Oct. 8, 1896. Made N.Y. debut in 1929 in "Journey's End." Has appeared since in "Hamlet," "The Warrior's Husband," "Dangerous Corner," "Noah," "Pride and Prejudice," "The Doctor's Dilemma," "The Winter's Tale," "The Autumn Garden," "Point of No Return."

**KELLEY, PETER.** Born in Indianapolis, Ind., Dec. 17, 1925. Graduate of Purdue Univ. Made Broadway debut in 1951 in "South Pacific." Has appeared since in "Two's Company," "Wish You Were Here."

**KELLY, GRACE.** Born in Philadelphia, Nov. 12, 1929. Educated at Ravenhill Academy and Stevens School. Received stage training at American Academy of Dramatic Arts. Made Broadway debut in 1949 in "The Father." Has appeared since in "To Be Continued."

Peter Kelley

Cloris Leachman

Richard Kiley

**KENNEDY, ARTHUR.** Born in Worcester, Mass., Feb. 17, 1914. Educated at Carnegie Tech. Has appeared on Broadway in Evans' productions of "Henry IV" and "Richard II," "All My Sons," "Death of A Salesman," "See The Jaguar," "The Crucible."

**KERR, JOHN.** Born in N.Y.C., Nov. 15, 1931. Graduate of Harvard. Received training at Brattle Theatre where he appeared in many productions. Made Broadway debut Oct. 16, 1952, in "Bernardine." Has appeared since in "Tea and Sympathy."

**KILBURN, TERRANCE.** Born in London, Nov. 25, 1928. Educated at UCLA. Received stage training with Circle Players in Hollywood. Made Broadway debut in 1952 in "Candida." Has appeared since in "Sherlock Holmes," 1953 City Center revival of "Charley's Aunt."

**KILEY, RICHARD.** Born in Chicago, Mar. 31, 1922. Educated at Loyola Univ. Studied at Barnum Dramatic School, Chicago. Played Stanley in National Co. of "A Streetcar Named Desire." Made Broadway debut in 1953 in "Misalliance." Has appeared since in "Kismet."

**KING, DENNIS.** Born in Coventry, Eng., Nov. 2, 1897. Made N.Y. debut in 1921 in "Claire de Lune." Has appeared since in Cowl's "Romeo and Juliet," "Antony and Cleopatra," "The Vagabond King," "The Three Musketeers," "I Married An Angel," "A Doll's House," "The Three Sisters," "Dunnigan's Daughter," "He Who Gets Slapped," "Medea," "Edward, My Son," "The Devil's Disciple," "Billy Budd," "Music In The Air," "The Strong Are Lonely."

**KING, EDITH.** Made first Broadway appearance in 1915 in "The Boomerang." Has appeared since in "Amphitryon 38," "The Taming of The Shrew," "A Kiss For Cinderella," "Othello," "Legend of Lovers," "Ondine."

**LAHR, BERT.** Born in N.Y.C., Aug. 13, 1895. Played in vaudeville and burlesque before making Broadway bow in "Delmar's Revels." Has appeared since in "Hold Everything," "Flying High," "Hot-Cha," "George White's Varieties," "The Show Is On," "DuBarry Was A Lady," "Seven Lively Arts," "Burlesque," "Make Mine Manhattan," "Two On The Aisle."

**LANDIS, JESSIE ROYCE.** Born in Chicago, Nov. 25, 1904. Made N.Y. debut in 1926 in "The Honor of The Family." Has appeared since in "Command Performance," "Solid South," "Merrily We Roll Along," "Love From A Stranger," "Brown Danube," "Dame Nature," "Love's Old Sweet Song," "Papa Is All," "Kiss and Tell," "The Winter's Tale," "Little A," "The Last Dance," "Magnolia Alley," "Richard III" (1953).

**LANG, HAROLD.** Born in Daly City, Calif., Dec. 21, 1923. Appeared with Ballet Russe and Ballet Theatre before making Broadway bow in "Mr. Strauss Goes To Boston." Has appeared since in "Three To Make Ready," "Look, Ma, I'm Dancin'," "Kiss Me, Kate," "Make A Wish," "Pal Joey" (1952 N.Y. and London company).

**LAURENCE, PAULA.** Born in Brooklyn, Jan. 25, 1916. Began stage career in "Horse Eats Hat" and "Dr. Faustus." In addition to becoming one of N.Y.'s most popular night club entertainers, she has appeared in "Junior Miss," "Something For The Boys," "One Touch of Venus," "Cyrano de Bergerac," "Volpone," "The Insect Comedy," "The Liar," "Season In The Sun," "Tovarich," "Coriolanus."

**LAUTNER, JOE.** Born in Cambridge, Mass., Sept. 29, 1924. Educated at Purdue Univ. Studied at Neighborhood Playhouse and American Theatre Wing. Has appeared on Broadway in "Oklahoma," "Angel In The Pawnshop," "Make A Wish," "New Faces of 1952."

**LEACHMAN, CLORIS.** Born in Iowa and educated at Northwestern Univ. Studied with Actors Studio Group. Made Broadway debut in 1948 in "Sundown Beach." Has appeared since in "As You Like It," "A Story For A Sunday Evening," "Lo and Behold!" "Dear Barbarians," "South Pacific," "King of Hearts."

**LE GALLIENNE, EVA.** Born in London, Jan. 11, 1899. Studied at Royal Academy of Dramatic Art. Made N.Y. debut in 1915 in "Mrs. Boltay's Daughters." Among her many appearances are "Liliom," "The Swan," "The Master Builder." In 1926 organized Civic Repertory Co. and presented many productions before disbanding in 1933. Has appeared since in "L'Aiglon," "Prelude To Exile," "Madame Capet," "Uncle Harry," "The Cherry Orchard," "Therese," "Henry VIII," "What Every Woman Knows," "Alice In Wonderland," "Ghosts," "Hedda Gabler," "The Corn Is Green" (1950).

**LEIGH, CAROL.** Born in N.Y.C., Nov. 4, 1933. Graduate of George Washington High School. Studied at American Theatre Wing and Neighborhood Playhouse. Made Broadway debut in 1949 revival of "Sally." Has appeared since in "All For Love," "Make A Wish," "Texas Lil' Darlin'," "By The Beautiful Sea."

**LEIGH, VIVIEN.** Born in Darjeeling, India, in Nov., 1913. Educated at Convent of The Sacred Heart, Eng. Studied at Comedie Francaise under Mlle. Antoine and at Royal Academy, London. Made N.Y. debut in 1940 in "Romeo and Juliet." Has appeared since in "Caesar and Cleopatra," "Antony and Cleopatra."

| Phyllis Love | Jonathan Lucas | Carol Leigh |

**LE MASSENA, WILLIAM.** Born in Glen Ridge, N.J., May 23, 1916. Educated at NYU. Has appeared on Broadway in "The Taming of The Shrew," "There Shall Be No Night," "The Pirate," Evans' "Hamlet," "Call Me Mister," "Inside U.S.A.," "I Know My Love," "Dream Girl" (1951), "Nina," "Ondine."

**LENYA, LOTTE.** Born in Vienna and trained at Zurich Municipal Theatre. Is well known on the stages of Vienna and Berlin. Made her American debut in "Candle In The Wind." Has appeared since in "The Firebrand of Florence," "Barefoot In Athens," "The Threepenny Opera."

**LEVENE, SAM.** Born in N.Y.C. in 1907. Graduate of American Academy of Dramatic Arts. Has appeared on Broadway in "Three Men On A Horse," "Dinner At Eight," "Room Service," "Margin For Error," "A Sound of Hunting," "Light Up The Sky," "Guys and Dolls."

**LEVERSEE, LORETTA.** Born in Chicago, March 26, 1928. Studied at Dramatic Workshop and Actor's Studio. Made first N.Y. appearance Jan. 12, 1954, in "Bullfight."

**LEWIS, DAVID.** Born in Pittsburgh, Oct. 19, 1916. Trained for stage with Erie, Pa., Civic Theatre. Made N.Y. debut in 1943 in "Goodbye Again." Has appeared since in "The Streets Are Guarded," "Little Women" (1944), "The Taming of The Shrew" (1951), "The Wild Duck" (1951), "King of Hearts."

**LILLIE, BEATRICE.** Born in Toronto, Can. Educated at St. Agnes' College, Belleville, Ont. Made N. Y. debut in 1924 in "Charlot's Revue." Has appeared since in "Oh, Please," "This Year of Grace," "She's My Baby," "The Third Little Show," "Too True To Be Good," "At Home Abroad," "The Show Is On," "Set To Music," "Seven Lively Arts," "Inside U.S.A.," "An Evening With Beatrice Lillie."

**LINN, BAMBI.** Born in Brooklyn, Apr. 26, 1926. Educated at Professional Children's School and studied with Agnes de Mille. Has appeared on Broadway in "Oklahoma," "Carousel," "Alice In Wonderland," "Sally," "Great To Be Alive."

**LLOYD, NORMAN.** Born in Jersey City, N.J., Nov. 8, 1914. Trained with Eva Le Gallienne's Civic Repertory Theatre. Has appeared in Mercury Theatre productions of "Julius Caesar" and "The Shoemaker's Holiday," and in "Everywhere I Roam," "Medicine Show," "Village Green," "Liberty Jones," "King Lear" (1950), "Madam, Will You Walk."

**LOGAN, ELLA.** Born in Glasgow, Scot., Mar. 6, 1913. Appeared first in British and European music halls and musical comedies. Made N.Y. debut in 1934 in "Calling All Stars." Has appeared since in "Scandals of 1939," "Hiya, Gentlemen," "Sons O' Fun," "Show Time," "Finian's Rainbow."

**LOVE, PHYLLIS.** Born in Des Moines, Iowa, Dec. 21, 1929. Educated at Carnegie Tech. Has appeared on Broadway in "The Member of The Wedding," "The Country Girl," "The Rose Tattoo," "The Remarkable Mr. Pennypacker."

**LUCAS, JONATHAN.** Born in Sherman, Tex., Aug. 14, 1922. Educated at Southern Methodist Univ. Made N.Y. bow in 1945 in "A Lady Says Yes." Has appeared since in "Bloomer Girl," "Billion Dollar Baby," "Around The World," "Finian's Rainbow," "Small Wonder," "Touch and Go," "Of Thee I Sing" (1952), "The Golden Apple."

**LUCE, CLAIRE.** Born Oct. 15, 1903, on a train passing thru Syracuse, N.Y. Made Broadway debut in 1923 in "Little Jessie James," followed by "Music Box Revue," "Ziegfeld Follies," "Society Girl," "The Gay Divorcee," "Of Mice and Men." Appeared successfully for several years on English stage. Returned to Broadway in "Portrait In Black," "With A Silk Thread," "The Taming of The Shrew" (1951), "Much Ado About Nothing" (1952).

**LUMB, GEOFFREY.** Born in Batley, Yorkshire, Eng., July 13, 1905. Educated at New College, Harrogate. Made N.Y. debut in 1943 in "Harriet." Has appeared since in "For Keeps," "Dunnigan's Daughter," "Hope's The Thing," "Minnie and Mr. Williams," "Two Blind Mice," "The Solid Gold Cadillac."

**LUND, JOHN.** Born in Rochester, N.Y., Feb. 6, 1913. Began stage career in Railroad Pageant at World's Fair. Understudied Alfred Drake in 1941 revival of "As You Like It." In 1942 appeared in "New Faces" followed by "Early To Bed," "The Hasty Heart."

**LUNT, ALFRED.** Born Aug. 19, 1893, in Milwaukee. Educated at Carroll College and Harvard. First stage appearance with Boston stock company in 1913. Among his many appearances are "Clarence," "The Intimate Strangers," "Outward Bound," "The Guardsman," "Arms and The Man," "Goat Song," "At Mrs. Beam's," "Juarez and Maximilian," "Ned McCobb's Daughter," "The Brothers Karamazov," "The Second Man," "The Doctor's Dilemma," "Marco Millions," "Volpone," "Caprice," "Elizabeth The Queen," "Reunion In Vienna," "Design For Living," "Idiot's Delight," "The Taming of The Shrew," "Amphitryon 38," "The Sea Gull," "There Shall Be No Night," "The Pirate," "O Mistress Mine," "I Know My Love."

Murray Matheson      Lucille Marsh      Arthur Maxwell

**LYNN, DIANA.** Born in Los Angeles, Oct. 7, 1926. Appeared in many motion pictures and in stock before making Broadway debut Dec. 26, 1951, in City Center revival of "The Wild Duck." Has appeared since in "Horses In Midstream" and in London Company of "The Moon Is Blue."

**MacGRATH, LEUEEN.** Born in London, July 3, 1914. Studied at Royal Academy of Dramatic Art. Made N.Y. debut in 1948 in "Edward, My Son." Has appeared since in "The Enchanted," "The High Ground," "Fancy Meeting You Again" which she co-authored, "The Love of Four Colonels."

**MacMAHON, ALINE.** Born in McKeesport, Pa., May 3, 1899. Educated at Barnard College. Made N.Y. debut in 1921 in "The Madras House." Has appeared since in "The Green Ring," "The Exciters," "The Grand Street Follies," "Beyond The Horizon," "Maya," "Once In A Lifetime," "Heavenly Express," "The Eve of St. Mark," "The Confidential Clerk."

**MARCH, FREDRIC.** Born in Racine, Wisc., Aug. 31, 1897. Educated at Univ. of Wisc. Made Broadway debut in 1920 in "Deburau." In 1932 went to Hollywood and made films for 10 years. Returned to N.Y. stage for "Yr. Obedient Husband," "The American Way," "Hope For A Harvest," "The Skin of Our Teeth," "A Bell For Adano," "Years Ago," "Now I Lay Me Down To Sleep," "An Enemy of The People," "The Autumn Garden."

**MARCH, LORI.** Born in Hollywood, Calif. Studied at American Theatre Wing. Has appeared in 1953 City Center revivals of "Cyrano de Bergerac" and "Charley's Aunt," and in the Phoenix Theatre's "Coriolanus."

**MARKEY, ENID.** Born in Dillon, Colo. Was star in silent films before making Broadway debut in 1919 in "Up In Mabel's Room." Has appeared in "Barnum Was Right," "The Women," "Morning's At Seven," "Ah, Wilderness," "Mr. Sycamore," "Beverly Hills," "Snafu," "Happy Birthday," "The Silver Whistle," "Buy Me Blue Ribbons," "Mrs. McThing."

**MARLOWE, GLORIA.** Born and educated in Brooklyn. Has appeared on Broadway in "South Pacific," "The King and I," "In Any Language."

**MARSH, LUCILLE.** Born in Chicago and graduated from Highland Park High School. Studied at Goodman Theatre and Max Reinhardt Workshop. Has appeared in "Janie," "School For Brides," "Set 'Em Up, Tony," and revivals of "Abie's Irish Rose," "Ladies' Night," "The Late Christopher Bean," "You Can't Take It With You."

**MARSHALL, E. G.** Born June 18, 1910, in Owatonna, Minn. Educated at Carlton College and Univ. of Minn. Has appeared on Broadway in "Jason," "The Skin of Our Teeth," "The Petrified Forest," "Jacobowsky and The Colonel," "The Iceman Cometh," "Hope's The Thing," "The Survivors," "The Crucible."

**MARSHALL, SARAH.** Born in London, May 25, 1933. Educated at Westlake School, Los Angeles. Studied with Constance Collier. Made N.Y. debut in 1949 in "The Browning Version." Has appeared since in City Center revivals of "Dream Girl," "Idiot's Delight" and "Charley's Aunt," and in "Jane," "Mr. Pickwick," Phoenix Theatre's "The Sea Gull."

**MARTIN, MARY.** Born in Weatherford, Tex., Dec. 1, 1914. Educated at Ward-Belmont, Nashville. Made Broadway debut in 1938 in "Leave It To Me." Has since starred in "One Touch of Venus," "Lute Song," "Annie Get Your Gun" on tour, "South Pacific" (also in London), "Kind Sir."

**MASON, REGINALD.** Born in San Francisco, June 27, 1882. Educated at Bedford, Eng. Made N.Y. debut in 1907 in "Caught In The Rain." More recently has appeared in "Dear Octopus," "Jupiter Laughs," "The Doughgirls," "Rebecca," "The Love of Four Colonels."

**MASSEY, RAYMOND.** Born in Toronto, Can., Aug. 30, 1896. Educated at Toronto Univ. and Balliol College, Oxford. After successful career in Eng., made N.Y. debut in 1931 as Hamlet. Has appeared since in "The Shining Hour," "Ethan Frome," "Abe Lincoln In Illinois," "The Doctor's Dilemma," "Pygmalion," "The Father," "John Brown's Body."

**MATHESON, MURRAY.** Born in Casterton, Aust., April 1, 1912. Appeared in many London stage productions before making N.Y. debut in 1950 in "The Relapse." Has appeared since in "Escapade."

**MAXWELL, ARTHUR.** Born in San Antonio, Tex., Oct. 13, 1919. Educated at Univ. of Tex. Has appeared on Broadway in "Ziegfeld Follies of 1943," "A Lady Says Yes," "Lend An Ear," "Alive and Kicking," "Me and Juliet."

**McCARTHY, KEVIN.** Born in Seattle, Wash., Feb. 15, 1914. Educated at Georgetown Univ. and Univ. of Minn. Made Broadway bow in 1938 in "Abe Lincoln In Illinois." Has appeared since in "Flight To The West," "Winged Victory," "Truckline Cafe," "Joan of Lorraine," "Death of A Saleman" in London, "Anna Christie" (1952), "Love's Labour's Lost," "The Deep Blue Sea," "The Sea Gull" (1954 Phoenix production).

| Scott Merrill | Edith Meiser | Donald McKee |
|---|---|---|

**McCORMICK, MYRON.** Born in Albany, Ind., Feb. 8, 1907. Made N.Y. debut in 1932 in "Carrie Nation." Has appeared since in "Goodbye Again," "Yellow Jack," "Small Miracle," "Paths of Glory," "The Damask Cheek," "Thunder Rock," "Storm Operation," "Soldier's Wife," "State of The Union," "Joy To The World," "South Pacific."

**McCRACKEN, JOAN.** Born in Philadelphia, Dec. 31, 1922. Educated at West Phila. High. Studied and appeared with Catherine Littlefield Ballet. Appeared on Broadway in "Oklahoma," "Bloomer Girl," "Billion Dollar Baby," "Galileo," "The Big Knife," "Dance Me A Song," "Angel In The Pawnshop," "Me and Juliet."

**McDOWALL, RODDY.** Born in London, Sept. 17, 1928. Educated at St. Joseph's College, London, and 20th-Century-Fox Studio School. Appeared in many films and in stock before making Broadway debut Feb. 18, 1953, in "Misalliance." Has appeared since in "Escapade."

**McGAVIN, DARREN.** Born in Spokane, Wash., May 7, 1922. Educated at College of the Pacific, Stockton, Calif. Made N.Y. debut in 1948 as extra with Dublin Gate Theatre's "The Old Lady Says No!" Has appeared since in "Death of A Salesman," "My Three Angels."

**McGRATH, PAUL.** Born in Chicago and educated at Carnegie Tech. Made N.Y. debut in 1920 in "The First Year." Has appeared since in "Ned McCobb's Daughter," "John Ferguson," "The Green Bay Tree," "Ode To Liberty," "Susan and God," "Lady In The Dark," "Tomorrow The World," "Common Ground," "Command Decision," "The Big Knife," "The Small Hours," "Love and Let Love," "Touchstone," "A Girl Can Tell."

**McKAY, SCOTT.** Born in Pleasantville, Iowa, May 28, 1917. Educated at Univ. of Colo. Made N.Y. debut in 1938 in "Good Hunting." Has appeared since in "The American Way," "Letters To Lucerne," "The Moon Is Down," "The Eve of St. Mark," "Dark Eyes," "Pillar To Post," "Another Part of The Forest," "Born Yesterday," "Bell, Book and Candle," "Sabrina Fair."

**McKEE, DONALD.** Born in Hatboro, Pa., Aug. 29, 1898. Has appeared on Broadway in "Lady of The Lamp," "Fashions For Men," "Dancing Mothers," "The Merchant of Venice" (1927), "Command Decision," "The Ladies of The Corridor," "His and Hers."

**McLERIE, ALLYN.** Born in Grand Mere, Quebec, Dec. 1, 1926. Educated at Ft. Hamilton High, Brooklyn. Made N.Y. debut in 1943 in "One Touch of Venus." Has appeared since in "On The Town," "Finian's Rainbow," "Where's Charley?," "Miss Liberty."

**MEEKER, RALPH.** Born in Minneapolis, Nov. 21, 1920. Educated at Northwestern Univ. Made N.Y. debut in 1945 in "Strange Fruit." Has appeared since in "Cyrano de Bergerac," "Mister Roberts," "A Streetcar Named Desire," "Picnic."

**MEISER, EDITH.** Born in Detroit. Educated at Vassar. Has appeared in "Fata Morgana," "The Guardsman," three editions of "Garrick Gaieties," "Mexican Hayride," "The Stars Weep," "I Gotta Get Out," "Getting Married" (1951), "The Magic and The Loss."

**MERANDE, DORO.** Born in Columbia, Kan. Has appeared on Broadway in "Our Town," "Love's Old Sweet Song," "The More The Merrier," "Junior Miss," "The Naked Genius," "Pick-Up Girl," "Violet," "Hope For The Best," "Apple of His Eye," "The Silver Whistle," "The Rat Race," "4 Twelves are 48," "Lo and Behold!"

**MEREDITH, BURGESS.** Born in Cleveland, Ohio, Nov. 16, 1908. Educated at Amherst. Joined Eva LeGallienne's Repertory Co. in 1930. Has appeared on Broadway in "Little Ol' Boy," "She Loves Me Not," "Barretts of Wimpole Street," "Flowers of The Forest," "Winterset," "High Tor," "Liliom," "Candida," "The Playboy of The Western World," "The Fourposter," "The Remarkable Mr. Pennypacker."

**MERIVALE, JOHN.** Born in Toronto, Can., Dec. 1, 1917. Educated at Rugby and New College, Oxford. Made N.Y. bow in 1938 in "Lorelei." Has appeared since in "Journey's End," "Romeo and Juliet," "Lady Windermere's Fan," "An Inspector Calls," "Anne of The Thousand Days," "The Day After Tomorrow," "Getting Married," "Venus Observed," "The Deep Blue Sea."

**MERMAN, ETHEL.** Born in Astoria, L.I., Jan. 16, 1908. Appeared in vaudeville with Clayton, Jackson and Durante. Made Broadway debut in 1930 in "Girl Crazy." Has appeared since in "George White's Scandals," "Take A Chance," "Anything Goes," "Red, Hot and Blue," "Stars In Your Eyes," "Panama Hattie," "Something For The Boys," "Annie Get Your Gun," "Call Me Madam."

**MERRILL, SCOTT.** Born in Baltimore, Md., July 14, 1922. Educated at Baltimore City College. Made Broadway bow in "Oklahoma." Has appeared since in "Love Life," "Guys and Dolls," "Small Wonder," "Lady In The Dark," "Paint Your Wagon," "Pal Joey," "Threepenny Opera."

**MIDDLETON, ROBERT.** Born in Cincinnati, May 13, 1911. Educated at Hughes High School, Univ. of Cincinnati and Carnegie Tech. Has appeared in 1951 City Center revival of "The Wild Duck," "A Red Rainbow."

Elizabeth Montgomery        Morris Miller        Pauline Myers

**MILLER, MORRIS.** Born in San Francisco, July 13, 1927. Educated at Los Angeles City College. Studied at American Theatre Wing and played in stock. Has appeared in "The Royal Family" (1950 revival), "Picnic."

**MILLER, SKEDGE.** Born in Greenville, Ohio, May 8, 1918. Educated at Univ. of Akron. Trained at Cleveland Playhouse. Made Broadway debut in 1943 in "Victory Belles." Has appeared since in "The Relapse," "The Wild Duck" (1952).

**MITCHELL, JAMES.** Born in Sacramento, Cal., Feb. 29, 1920. Graduate of Los Angeles City College. Made Broadway bow in "Bloomer Girl." Has appeared since in "Billion Dollar Baby," "Brigadoon," "Paint Your Wagon."

**MITCHELL, LATHROP.** Born in Thomasville, Ga., Apr. 9, 1907. Educated at Univ. of Ga. Received training with Avon Shakespearean Co. Has appeared in "The Barretts of Wimpole Street," Cornell's "Romeo and Juliet," "A Regular Guy," "Cabbages and Kings," "Aries Is Rising," "Plan M," "Major Barbara."

**MONTGOMERY, EARL.** Born in Memphis, Tenn., Apr. 17, 1921. Graduate of Harvard. Made N.Y. debut in 1947 Experimental Theatre production of "Galileo." Has appeared since in "Summer and Smoke," "The Relapse," "Mr. Pickwick," City Center revivals of "Love's Labour's Lost" and "The Merchant of Venice," "The Strong Are Lonely."

**MONTGOMERY, ELIZABETH.** Born in Los Angeles, April 15, 1933. Educated at Westlake and Spence Schools. Trained for stage at American Academy of Dramatic Arts. Made Broadway debut Oct. 13, 1953, in "Late Love."

**MOORE, LEON.** Born in Raleigh, N.C., Apr. 7, 1926. Studied at New School and with Piscator's Dramatic Workshop. Made Broadway debut in 1952 in "The Climate of Eden."

**MOORE, MARY ALICE.** Born Dec. 5, 1923, in Florence, Ariz. Educated at Northwestern Univ. Made Broadway debut in 1944 in "School For Brides." Has appeared since in "Henry VIII," "What Every Woman Knows," "John Gabriel Borkman," "Androcles and The Lion," "A Red Rainbow."

**MOORE, VICTOR.** Born in Hammonton, N.J., Feb. 24, 1876. Made first stage appearance in 1893 in "Babes In The Woods" at Boston Theatre. For 25 years toured in vaudeville in "Change Your Act Or Back To The Woods." Then appeared in "The Talk of New York," "Shorty McCabe," "Patsy On The Wing," "Oh, Kay," "Hold Everything," "Of Thee I Sing," "Let 'Em Eat Cake," "Anything Goes," "Leave It To Me," "Louisiana Purchase," "Hollywood Pinafore," "Nellie Bly," "On Borrowed Time" (1953).

**MORISON, PATRICIA.** Born in N.Y.C., in 1919. Made Broadway debut in 1938 in "Two Bouquets." Made many films before returning to N.Y. stage in "Kiss Me, Kate" which she re-created in London. Has appeared since in "The King and I."

**MORROW, DORETTA.** Born in N.Y.C., Jan. 27, 1928. Has appeared on Broadway in "The Red Mill" (1945), "Where's Charley?," "The King and I," "Kismet."

**MUNDY, MEG.** Born in London, educated at Wadleigh High and Inst. of Musical Art. Made Broadway debut in 1936 in "Ten Million Ghosts." Has appeared since in "Hoorah For What," "The Fabulous Invalid," "Three To Make Ready," "How I Wonder," "The Respectful Prostitute," "Detective Story," "Love's Labour's Lost."

**MUNSHIN, JULES.** Born in N.Y.C. Appeared in night clubs and vaudeville before making Broadway debut in 1943 in "The Army Play-By-Play." Has appeared since in "Call Me Mister," "Bless You All," "Mrs. McThing."

**MURPHY, DONALD.** Born Jan. 29, 1920, in Chicago. Educated at Rollins College. Made N.Y. debut in 1943 in "The Moon Vine." Has appeared since in "Janie," "Try and Get It," "For Keeps," "Common Ground," "Wonderful Journey," "A Young Man's Fancy," "Dear Barbarians," "The Time of The Cuckoo."

**MURRAY, DON.** Born in Hollywood, Cal., July 31, 1929. Studied at American Academy of Dramatic Arts. Made N.Y. debut in 1948 in "The Insect Comedy." Has appeared since in "The Rose Tattoo."

**MYERS, PAULINE.** Born in Ocilla, Ga., Nov. 9th. Studied at New Theatre School. Made Broadway debut in 1933 in "Growin' Pains." Has appeared since in "Plumes In The Dust," "The Willow and I," "The Naked Genius," "Dear Ruth," "Take A Giant Step," "Anniversary Waltz."

**NAGEL, CONRAD.** Born in Keokuk, Iowa, Mar. 16, 1897. Made Broadway bow in 1918 in "Forever After." Devoted many years to making films. Returned to N.Y. stage for "The First Apple," "The Skin of Our Teeth," "Tomorrow The World," "Susan and God," "A Goose For The Gander," "State of The Union," "Goodbye, My Fancy," "Music In The Air," "Be Your Age."

**NALDI, NITA.** Born in Washington, D.C., Apr. 1, 1900. Appeared in Ziegfeld and Shubert productions before becoming motion picture star. Has appeared on Broadway in "Firebird," "Queer People," "In Any Language."

209

| Paul Newman | Mariko Niki | Arthur O'Connell |

**NAPIER, ALAN.** Born in Birmingham, Eng., Jan. 7, 1903. Educated at Clifton College and Birmingham Univ. Studied at Royal Academy of Dramatic Art. Made N.Y. debut in 1940 in "Lady In Waiting." Has appeared since in "Gertie," Phoenix production of "Coriolanus."

**NATWICK, MILDRED.** Born in Baltimore, June 19, 1908. Made N.Y. debut in 1932 in "Carrie Nation." Has appeared since in "The Wind and The Rain," "The Distaff Side," "End of Summer," "Love From A Stranger," "Candida," "The Star Wagon," "Missouri Legend," "Blithe Spirit," "The Playboy of The Western World," "The Grass Harp," Phoenix production of "Coriolanus."

**NEAL, PATRICIA.** Born in Kentucky in 1926. Educated at Univ. of Tenn. and Northwestern Univ. Received training at Barter Theatre. Has appeared in "The Voice of The Turtle," "Another Part of The Forest," "The Children's Hour" (1952), 1953 De Lys revival of "A School For Scandal."

**NELSON, BARRY.** Born in San Francisco. Educated at Univ. of Calif. Made N.Y. debut in "Winged Victory" in 1943. Has appeared since in "Light Up The Sky," "The Rat Race," "The Moon Is Blue."

**NELSON, HERBERT.** Born in Stillwater, Minn., Dec. 17, 1913. Educated at Univ. of Minn. Has appeared in "The Night Before Christmas," "The First Crocus," "His and Hers."

**NESBITT, CATHLEEN.** Born in Cheshire, Eng., Nov. 24, 1889. Educated at Victoria College, Belfast. Studied at Rosina Filippi's School. Made N.Y. debut in 1911 with Irish Players in "The Well of The Saints." Other N.Y. appearances include "Justice," "Hush," "Such Is Life," "Magic," "The Garden of Paradise," "General Post," "The Saving Grace," "Diversion," "The Cocktail Party," "Gigi," "Sabrina Fair."

**NEWMAN, PAUL.** Born in Cleveland, Ohio, Jan. 26, 1925. Graduate of Kenyon College. Studied at Yale Drama School. Appeared in stock before making Broadway debut, Feb. 19, 1953, in "Picnic."

**NEWTON, RICHARD.** Born in Vancouver, Can., July 5, 1911. Educated at McGill Univ. Studied at Royal Academy of Dramatic Art, London. Made N.Y. debut in 1946 in "The Duchess of Malfi." Has appeared since in "Edward, My Son," "The Deep Blue Sea," "The Confidential Clerk."

**NIELSEN, LESLIE.** Born in Regina, Saskatchewan, Can., Feb. 11, 1926. Educated at Matriculation High, Alberta. Received stage training at Neighborhood Playhouse. Made Broadway debut in 1952 in "Seagulls Over Sorrento."

**NIKI, MARIKO.** Born in Tokyo, Japan. Educated at Sacred Heart School and Bungaku-za School of Modern Theatre, Tokyo. Appeared in Tokyo's little theatre group in modern Japanese versions of "Hamlet" and "Our Town." Made Broadway debut Oct. 15, 1953, in "The Teahouse of The August Moon."

**NOLAN, LLOYD.** Born in San Francisco, Aug. 11, 1902. Educated at Stanford Univ. Studied at Pasadena Playhouse. Has appeared on Broadway in "Cape Cod Follies," "Sweet Stranger," "Americana," "One Sunday Afternoon," "Ragged Army," "Gentlewoman," and more recently in "The Caine Mutiny Court Martial."

**NOLTE, CHARLES.** Born in Duluth, Minn., Nov. 3, 1926. Educated at Univ. of Minn. and Yale. Made Broadway debut in 1947 in "Antony and Cleopatra." Has appeared since as Billy Budd in Experimental Theatre's "Uniform of Flesh," in "Caesar and Cleopatra," "Design For A Stained Glass Window," "Mister Roberts," title role in "Billy Budd," "The Caine Mutiny Court Martial."

**NORTH, SHEREE.** Born in Los Angeles, Jan. 17, 1933. Educated at Santa Monica High and UCLA. Appeared in Hollywood's Greek Theatre musical productions for 5 years before making Broadway debut Feb. 11, 1953, in "Hazel Flagg."

**O'CONNELL, ARTHUR.** Born in N.Y.C., Mar. 29, 1908. Educated at St. John's College, Brooklyn. Made Broadway bow in 1943 in "The Army Play-By-Play." Has appeared since in "Summer Will Never Come," 1952 revivals of "Anna Christie" and "Golden Boy," "Picnic."

**OLIVER, ANTHONY.** Born in Abersychan, Wales, July 4, 1924. Educated at Monmouth School. Made Broadway debut Oct. 28, 1953, in "Gently Does It."

**OLIVIER, LAURENCE.** Born in Dorking, Surrey, Eng., May 22, 1907. Educated at St. Edward's School, Oxford, and studied with Elsie Fogarty. Made N.Y. debut in 1929 in "Murder On The Second Floor." Has appeared since in "Private Lives," "The Green Bay Tree," "No Time For Comedy," "Romeo and Juliet," 1946 Old Vic's productions, and in 1951 with his own productions of "Antony and Cleopatra" and "Caesar and Cleopatra."

**O'MALLEY, REX.** Born in London, Jan. 2, 1901. Received training with Birmingham Repertory Co. Broadway appearances include "The Marquise," "The Apple Cart," "Wonder Bar," "The Mad Hopes," "Revenge With Music," "You Never Know," "Matrimony Pfd.," "The Simpleton of The Unexpected Isles," "The Taming of The Shrew," "No More Ladies," "Many Happy Returns," "Lady Windermere's Fan," "Charley's Aunt" (1953).

Herbert Nelson          Geraldine Page          Charles Nolte

**O'NEAL, FREDERICK.** Born in Brooksville, Miss., Aug. 27, 1905. In 1940, co-founded American Negro Theatre and appeared in seven of their productions before making Broadway debut in 1944 in "Anna Lucasta." Has appeared since in "Take A Giant Step," "The Winner."

**OSTERWALD, BIBI.** Born in New Brunswick, N.J., Feb. 3, 1921. Educated at Catholic Univ. Made N.Y. debut in 1944 in "Sing Out, Sweet Land." Has appeared since in "Three To Make Ready," "Sally" (1948), "Magnolia Alley," "Gentlemen Prefer Blondes," "The Golden Apple."

**OVERTON, FRANK.** Born in Babylon, L.I., Mar. 12, 1918. Graduate of Bard College. Made Broadway debut in 1943 in "Counterattack." Has appeared since in "Jacobowsky and The Colonel," "Truckline Cafe," "All My Sons," "The Trip To Bountiful."

**PAGE, GERALDINE.** Born in Kirksville, Mo., Nov. 22, 1924. Educated at Englewood High, Chicago. Studied at Goodman School, Chicago. Appeared in stock and many Off-Broadway productions before making Broadway debut Jan. 21, 1953, in "Mid-Summer." Has appeared since in "The Immoralist."

**PAIGE, JANIS.** Born in Tacoma, Wash., Sept. 16, 1922. Educated at Stadium High. Appeared in films before making Broadway debut in 1951 in "Remains To Be Seen." Has appeared since in "The Pajama Game."

**PALANCE, JACK.** Born in Lattimer, Pa., Feb. 18, 1920. Educated at Univ. of N.C. and Stanford Univ. Has appeared on Broadway in "The Big Two," "Temporary Island," "The Vigil," "Darkness At Noon."

**PALMER, BYRON.** Born in Los Angeles, June 21, 1921. Educated at Fairfax High and Occidental College. Has appeared with Greek Theatre Light Opera Co., Hollywood. Made N.Y. debut in 1948 in "Where's Charley?". Has appeared since in "Bless You All."

**PALMER, LILLI.** Born in Posen, Austria, May 24, 1914. Trained for stage at Ilka Gruning School, Berlin. Appeared in Berlin, Paris and London and made films in Ger., Eng. and Hollywood before making Broadway debut in 1949 in "My Name is Aquilon." Has appeared since in "Caesar and Cleopatra" (1949), "Bell, Book and Candle," "Venus Observed," "The Love of Four Colonels."

**PARKHILL, DALE.** Born in Greenville, Tex., Oct. 2, 1925. Educated at Univ. of Tex. Studied at Royal Academy of Dramatic Art, London. Made Broadway debut in 1950 in "The Tower Beyond Tragedy."

**PATRICK, DENNIS** (formerly Dennis Harrison) Born in Philadelphia, Mar. 14, 1918. Received stage training in stock. Has appeared in "Harvey," "Cock-a-Doodle Doo" (Experimental Theatre), and in title role of "The Liar" on tour.

**PATTERSON, ELIZABETH.** Born in Savannah, Tenn., Nov. 22, 1882. Educated in Paris. Gained stage training with Ben Greet and Stuart Walker Companies. Has appeared on Broadway in "Magnolia," "Intimate Strangers," "Candida" (1923), "Lazy Bones," "Charm," "Solid South," "Her Master's Voice," "But Not Goodbye," "Spring Freshet," "Yankee Point," "His and Hers."

**PATTERSON, NEVA.** Born in Nevada, Iowa., Feb. 10, 1922. Made Broadway debut in 1947 in "The Druid Circle." Has appeared since in "The Ivy Green," "Ring Round The Moon," "The Long Days," "Lace On Her Petticoat," "The Seven Year Itch."

**PAXINOU, KATINA.** Born in Peiraeus, Greece, where with her husband, Alexis Minotis, she helped found the Greek National Theatre. Her greatest triumph was in 1939 when she toured Europe in "Electra." Appearances on Broadway include "Hedda Gabler," "Sophie," "House of Bernarda Alba," "Electra," "Oedipus Tyrannis."

**PEARSON, BEATRICE.** Born in Denison, Tex., July 27, 1920. Made Broadway debut in 1940 in "Liliom." Has appeared since in "Life With Father," "Free and Equal," "Get Away Old Man," "Over 21," "The Mermaids Singing," "The Voice of The Turtle," "The Day After Tomorrow."

**PENN, LEO.** Born in Lawrence, Mass., Aug. 27, 1921. Educated at UCLA. Made Broadway debut in 1951 in "Dinosaur Wharf." Has appeared since in DeLys productions of "Maya" and "School For Scandal", and in "The Girl on The Via Flaminia."

**PETERSON, MARJORIE.** Born in Houston, Tex. Has appeared on Broadway in "Greenwich Village Follies," "Earl Carroll's Vanities," "Annie Dear," "Contess Maritza," "The Red Robe," "The Perfumed Lady," "Creeping Fire," "Pre-Honeymoon," "It's A Gift," "Great To Be Alive," "A Date With April."

**PHILLIPS, MARGARET.** Born in Wales, July 6, 1923. Received training in summer theatres. Has appeared on Broadway in "Cry Havoc," "The Late George Apley," "Another Part of The Forest," "Summer and Smoke," "The Cocktail Party," "Second Threshold," "The Merchant of Venice" (1953), "Dial 'M' For Murder."

| Ainslie Pryor | Margaret Phillips | George Reich |

**PHILLIPS, WENDELL K.** Born in Illinois, Nov. 27, 1907. Educated at Univ. of Wisc. Studied at Goodman Theatre, Chicago. Made Broadway debut in 1931 in "Incubator." Has appeared since in "Mother Sings," "Many Mansions," "Abe Lincoln In Illinois," "The Fifth Column," "Anne of The Thousand Days," "The Solid Gold Cadillac."

**PIERPONT, LAURA.** Born in Cincinnati, Feb. 14, 1890, and educated in public schools there. Has been on stage since age of six. Created Mrs. Pinkerton in Belasco's "Madame Butterfly." More recent appearances include "Winged Victory," "The Women," "State of The Union," Sleepy Hollow," "The Leading Lady," "The Smile of The World," "Two Blind Mice," "Time Out For Ginger."

**PINE, PHILLIP.** Born in Hanford, Cal., July 16, 1925. Trained at Actor's Lab, Hollwood. Has appeared in "Janie," "Counterattack," "Lower North," "But Not Goodbye," "All You Need Is One Good Break," "One Bright Day," "See The Jaguar," "The Immoralist."

**POST, WILLIAM, JR.** Attended Phillips-Exeter Academy and Yale. Made Broadway debut in 1929 in "The Criminal Code." Has appeared since in "When The Bough Breaks," "Richard II," "Ah, Wilderness," "A Touch of Brimstone," "Three Wise Fools," "My Sister Eileen," "Calico Wedding," "Love Goes To Press," "Richard III" (1953).

**POVAH, PHYLLIS.** Born in Detroit, Mich. Has appeared in "Mr. Pim Passes By," "Windows," "Minnick," "Blood Money," "The Tale of The Wolf," "Hotel Universe," "The Women," "The Naked Genius," "Dear Ruth," "Light Up The Sky," "Gently Does It," "Anniversary Waltz."

**POWER, TYRONE.** Born in Cincinnati, May 5, 1914. Educated at Purcell High. Received training with Stuart Walker Stock Co. Made Broadway debut in 1931 with his father in Shakespearean repertoire. Has appeared since in Cornell's productions of "Flowers of The Forest," "Romeo and Juliet" and "St. Joan," and in "John Brown's Body."

**PRESTON, EDNA.** Born in N.Y.C., July 19, 1892. Has appeared on many radio and TV shows. Made Broadway debut in 1951 in "Out West of Eighth." Has appeared since in 1952 revival of "Tovarich," "Madamoiselle Colombe."

**PRESTON, ROBERT.** Born in Newton Highlands, Mass., June 8, 1913. Educated at Lincoln High. Studied at Pasadena Playhouse. Made Broadway debut in 1951 in "Twentieth Century." Has appeared since in "The Male Animal" (1951), "Men of Distinction," "His and Hers," "The Magic and The Loss."

**PRICE, GERALD.** Born in Hollywood, Calif., June 29, 1921. Educated at Fairfax High. Received stage training at New School's Dramatic Workshop. Has appeared in "Romeo and Juliet" (1951), "Diamond Lil," "Threepenny Opera," on tour in "Show Boat" and "Kiss Me, Kate."

**PRICE, VINCENT.** Born in St. Louis, Mo., May 27, 1911. Educated at Univ. of London and Yale. Made Broadway bow in 1935 in "Victoria Regina." Has appeared since in Mercury Theatre's "Shoemaker's Holiday" and "Heartbreak House," "The Lady Has A Heart," "Outward Bound" (1938), "Angel Street," "Richard III" (1953 City Center revival).

**PRINCE, WILLIAM.** Born in Nicholas, N.Y., Jan. 26, 1913. Educated at Cornell. Made Broadway debut in Evans' "Richard II." Has appeared since in "Hamlet," "Henry IV," "Ah, Wilderness," "Guest In The House," "Across The Board On Tomorrow Morning," "The Eve of St. Mark," "John Loves Mary," "Forward The Heart," "As You Like It" (1950), "I Am A Camera."

**PROCTOR, CHARLES.** Born in Dallas, Tex., Mar. 12, 1925. Educated at Southern Methodist Univ. Trained with Margo Jones. Made Broadway debut in 1951 in "Twilight Walk." Has appeared since in 1953 revival of "The Bat."

**PRYOR, AINSLIE.** Born in Memphis, Tenn., Feb. 1, 1921. Educated at Va. Polytechnic Inst. and Southwestern Univ. Director-Manager of Raleigh, N.C., Little Theatre for six years. Made Broadway debut Jan. 20, 1954, in "The Caine Mutiny Court Martial."

**RANDOLPH, JOHN.** Born in N.Y.C., June 1, 1915. Educated at CCNY. Has appeared on Broadway in "Medicine Show," "Hold On To Your Hats," "Native Son," "Command Decision," "Come Back, Little Sheba," "The Golden State," "Peer Gynt," "Paint Your Wagon," "Seagulls Over Sorrento," "The Grey-Eyed People," "Room Service" (1953), Phoenix Theatre's "Coriolanus" (1953).

**RASUMNY, MIKHAIL.** Born in Odessa, Russia, May 13, 1898. Arrived in America in 1935 with the Moscow Art Theatre. Went to Hollywood and appeared in more than 40 films. Recently appeared on Broadway in "Madamoiselle Colombe."

**RATHBONE, BASIL.** Born June 13, 1892, in Johannesburg, Transvaal. Educated at Repton College. Made N.Y. debut in 1912 with Benson's Shakespearean Repertory Co. Returned to London and achieved considerable success. Returned to Broadway in 1922 in "The Czarina." Has appeared since in "R.U.R.," "The Swan," "The Grand Duchess and The Waiter," "The Captive," "Julius Caesar," "The Command To Love," "Romeo and Juliet" with Cornell, "Obsession," "The Heiress," "Julius Caesar" (1950 revival), "The Gioconda Smile," "Jane," "Sherlock Holmes."

Mark Richman          Marita Reid          Steve Reeves

**REDFIELD, WILLIAM.** Born in N.Y.C., Jan. 26, 1927. Made Broadway debut in 1936 in "Swing Your Lady." Has appeared since in "Excursion," "Virginia," "Stop-Over," "Our Town," "Second Helping," "Junior Miss," "Snafu," "Barefoot Boy With Cheek," "Montserrat," "Miss Liberty," "Out Of This World," "Misalliance."

**REED, FLORENCE.** Born in Philadelphia, Jan. 10, 1883. Made stage debut in 1901 at Fifth Ave. Theatre in a monologue. Made Broadway debut in 1908 as Ophelia with E. H. Sothern's Co. Among her many appearances are "Seven Days," "Painted Woman," "The Yellow Ticket," "A Celebrated Case," "The Wanderer," "Chu Chin Chow," "Roads of Destiny," "The Mirage," "East of Suez," "The Shanghai Gesture," "Macbeth," "Romeo and Juliet," "Outward Bound" (1939), "The Flying Gerardos," "The Skin of Our Teeth," "Rebecca," "The Winter's Tale" (1946), "Medea," "Richard III" (1953).

**REEVES, STEVE.** Born in Glasgow, Mont., Jan. 21, 1928. Appeared in films and TV before making Broadway debut Dec. 3, 1953, in "Kismet."

**REICH, GEORGE.** Born in Patchogue, N. Y., Dec. 15, 1926. Educated at Patchogue High. Has appeared on Broadway in "The Chocolate Soldier" (1946), "Inside U.S.A.," "Touch and Go," "Roland Petit's Ballet de Paris."

**REID, FRANCES.** Born in Wichita Falls, Tex. Studied at Pasadena Playhouse. Made N.Y. debut in 'Where There's A Will." Has appeared since in "The Rivals," "Bird In Hand," "The Patriots," "Listen, Professor," "A Highland Fling," "The Wind Is Ninety," "Cyrano de Bergerac," Evans' "Hamlet," "Richard III" (1949), "Twelfth Night" (1949).

**REID, MARITA.** Born in Gibraltar, Spain, Aug. 29, 1895. Educated at Conservatory of Madrid. Has appeared in N.Y. in "Malvaloca," "Passion Flower," "In The Summer House."

**RHODES, ERIK.** Born in El Reno, Okla., Feb. 10, 1906. Educated at Univ. of Okla. Made Broadway debut in 1928 in "A Most Immoral Lady." Has appeared since in "The First Little Show," "Hey, Nonny, Nonny," "A Gay Divorcee," "Dance Me A Song," "Collector's Item," "Can-Can."

**RICHARDS, PAUL.** Born in Annapolis, Md., July 8, 1924. Educated at Thomas Jefferson High, Brooklyn. Studied at American Theatre Wing and Actor's Studio. Made N.Y. debut Oct. 15, 1953, in "End As A Man."

**RICHARDSON, RALPH.** Born in Cheltenham, Gloucestershire, Dec. 19, 1902. Made English debut in 1921 in "The Merchant of Venice." In 1935, toured U.S. and made N.Y. debut with Cornell in "Romeo and Juliet." Returned in 1946 with the Old Vic Company in repertory.

**RICHMAN, MARK.** Born in Philadelphia, Apr. 16, 1927. Graduate of Phila. College of Pharmacy and Science. Appeared in many summer theatres before making his Broadway bow Oct. 15, 1953, in "End As A Man."

**RITCHARD, CYRIL.** Born in Sydney, Aust., Dec. 1, 1898. Educated at St. Aloysius College and Sydney Univ. Since 1917 has appeared on both London and Australian stages. Made N.Y. bow in 1947 in "Love For Love." Has since directed several plays and appeared in "Make Way For Lucia," "The Relapse."

**ROBERTS, RALPH.** Born in Salisbury, N.C., Aug. 17, 1918. Educated at Univ. of N.C. Made Broadway bow in 1948 revival of "Angel Street." Has appeared since in "Four Checkhov Comedies," "S.S. Glencairn," "The Madwoman of Chaillot."

**ROBINSON, BARTLETT.** Born in N.Y.C., Dec. 9, 1912. Appeared on Broadway in "Naughty Naught '00," "Fireman's Flame," "Merchant of Yonkers," "Dear Ruth," "Another Part of The Forest," "Light Up The Sky," "Point of No Return," "Room Service" (1953), "South Pacific," "The Prescott Proposals."

**ROBSON, FLORA.** Born Mar. 28, 1902, in South Shields, Durham, Eng. Educated at Palmer's Green High. Studied at Royal Academy of Dramatic Art. Had distinguished career in Eng. before making N.Y. debut in 1940 in "Ladies In Retirement." Has appeared since in "Anne of England," "The Damask Cheek," "Macbeth" with Redgrave, "Black Chiffon."

**ROELAND, AUGUSTA.** Born in Richmond, Va. Made Broadway debut in 1937 in 'Lady Jane." Has appeared since in "Victoria Regina," "Embezzled Heaven," "Heart of A City," "For Love Or Money," "The Heiress," "Red Gloves," "The Fifth Season."

**ROERICK, WILLIAM.** Born in N.Y.C., Dec. 17, 1912. Educated at Hamilton College. Made Broadway debut in 1935 in Cornell's "Romeo and Juliet." Has appeared since in "St. Joan," Gielgud's "Hamlet," "Our Town," "The Importance of Being Earnest," "The Land Is Bright," "Autumn Hill," "This Is The Army," "The Magnificent Yankee," "Tonight at 8:30" (1948), "Madam, Will You Walk," "The Burning Glass."

**ROONEY, PAT, SR.** Born in N.Y.C., July 4, 1880. Has appeared on Broadway in "Roger Bros. In Washington," "Roger Bros. In Harvard," starred with his wife, Marion Bent, in "Love Birds," "The Daughter of Rosie O'Grady," and in vaudeville for many years. More recently appeared in "Guys and Dolls."

Eva Marie Saint        Jack Ruth        Mira Rostova

**ROSS, ANTHONY.** Born in N.Y.C. in 1906. Graduate of Brown Univ. Made Broadway debut in 1932 in "Whistling In The Dark." Has appeared since in "Bury The Dead," "Arsenic and Old Lace," "This Is The Army," "The Glass Menagerie," "It Takes Two," "The Cup of Trembling," "Season In The Sun," "Sunday Breakfast," "The Emperor's Clothes," "In Any Language," "The Frogs of Spring."

**ROSS, ELIZABETH.** Born in Morristown, N.J., Aug. 28, 1926. Educated at Catholic Univ. Made Broadway debut in 1946 in "The Song of Bernadette." Has appeared since in "The Story of Mary Surratt," "Minnie and Mr. Williams," "In The Summer House."

**ROSTOVA, MIRA.** Born in Leningrad, Russia, Apr. 10, 1919. Educated in Switzerland. Appeared in Germany and Austria before coming to America. Made N.Y. debut May 11, 1954, in Phoenix Theatre production of "The Sea Gull."

**ROUNSEVILLE, ROBERT.** Born in Attleboro, Mass., Mar. 25, 1919. Educated at Deerfield and Tufts Colleges. Has appeared on Broadway in "Babes In Arms," "Knickerbocker Holiday," "Two Bouquets," "Higher and Higher," "Up In Central Park," 1952 Gilbert and Sullivan revivals, "Show Boat" (1954 revival).

**ROWLES, POLLY.** Born in Philadelphia and educated at Carnegie Tech. Has appeared on Broadway in Whorf's "Richard III," "Anne of The Thousand Days," "The Golden State," "The Small Hours," "Gertie," "Time Out For Ginger."

**RUSSELL, ANNA.** Born in London, Dec. 27, 1913. Studied at Conservatory, Brussels, and Royal College of Music, London. Appeared on the concert stage in America before making Broadway debut on Sept. 7, 1953, in "Anna Russell's Little Show."

**RUTH, JACK.** Born in Wilmington, Del., Nov. 11, 1921. Educated at Rollins College. Has appeared on Broadway in "Ramshackle Inn," "Little Women," "The Deep Mrs. Sykes," "The Next Half Hour," "The Solid Gold Cadillac."

**RYAN, ROBERT.** Born in Chicago, Nov. 11, 1913. Educated at Loyola Academy, Chicago, and Dartmouth. Studied at Max Reinhardt Workshop and Vladimir Sokoloff Beechwood Studio. Made Broadway debut in 1941 in "Clash By Night." Recently appeared in 1953 Phoenix Theatre production of "Coriolanus."

**RYDER, ALFRED.** Born in N.Y.C., Jan. 5, 1919. Educated at Professional Children's School. Made Broadway debut in 1929 in "Peter Pan." Has appeared since in "All The Living," "Jeremiah," "Awake and Sing," "Medicine Show," "Man With Blonde Hair," "Nathan, the Wise," "Skydrift," "Yellow Jack," "Ghosts," "Julius Caesar" (1950), "The Tower Beyond Tragedy."

**SAINT, EVA MARIE.** Born in Newark, N.J., July 4, 1924. Educated at Bowling Green State Univ., Ohio. Studied at American Theatre Wing and the Actor's Studio. Made Broadway debut Nov. 3, 1953, in "The Trip To Bountiful."

**SANDS, DOROTHY.** Born Mar. 5, 1900, in Cambridge, Mass. Educated at Radcliffe College. Studied at Neighborhood Playhouse. Has appeared in "The Grand Street Follies" (1927-8-9), "The Sea Gull," "The Stairs," "All The Comforts of Home," "Papa Is All," "Tomorrow The World," "A Joy Forever," "Bell, Book and Candle," "Misalliance."

**SARNOFF, DOROTHY.** Born in N.Y.C., May 25, 1919. Educated at Cornell. Has sung with N.Y. City Center, New Orleans and Philadelphia Opera Companies. Her Broadway roles include "Rosalinda," "Magdalena," "The King and I," "My Darlin' Aida."

**SAVO, JIMMY.** Born in N.Y.C. in 1895. Prominent in vaudeville for many years before making Broadway debut in "Vanities of 1923." Has appeared since in "Hassard Short's Ritz Revue," "Murray Anderson's Almanac," "Parade," "The Boys From Syracuse," "Wine, Women and Song," "What's Up?"

**SCHEERER, BOB.** Born in Santa Barbara, Cal., Dec. 28, 1928. Educated at Fairfax High, Hollywood. Studied at Actor's Lab, Hollywood. Made Broadway debut in 1948 in "Lend An Ear." Has appeared since in "Dance Me A Song," "Top Banana."

**SCHILDKRAUT, JOSEPH.** Born in Vienna, Mar. 22, 1895. Studied for stage in Germany and at American Academy of Dramatic Arts. Made first stage appearance in 1910 in his father's company. Has appeared since in "Pagans," "Liliom," "Peer Gynt," "The Firebrand," "Anatole," Civic Repertory Co., "Uncle Harry," "The Cherry Orchard," "The Green Bay Tree" (1951), "Love's Labour's Lost" (1953).

**SCOTT, KEVIN.** Born in Oakland, Cal., Dec. 10, 1928. Received stage training at Little Theatre in Denver. Made Broadway debut in 1952 in "Wish You Were Here." Has appeared since in "Carnival In Flanders."

| Marian Seldes | Kevin Scott | Dorothy Sands |

**SCOTT, MARTHA.** Born in Jamesport, Mo., Sept. 22, 1914. Educated at Univ. of Mich. First N.Y. appearance in 1938 in "Our Town." Has appeared since in "Foreigners," "The Willow and I," "Soldier's Wife," "The Voice of The Turtle," "It Takes Two," "Design For A Stained Glass Window," "The Remarkable Mr. Pennypacker."

**SELDES, MARIAN.** Born in N.Y.C., Aug. 23, 1928. Educated at Dalton School. Studied at Neighborhood Playhouse. Has appeared in "Medea," "Crime and Punishment," "That Lady," "The Tower Beyond Tragedy," "The High Ground," "Come of Age" (1952), "Ondine."

**SEYMOUR, JOHN D.** Born in Boston, Oct. 24, 1897. Educated at Colgate Univ. Made Broadway debut in 1918 in "Out There." Has appeared since in Barrymore's "Richard III," "Dearest Enemy," "Blood Money," "Sweet Adeline," "The Barretts of Wimpole Street," "Cyrano de Bergerac," "Pride and Prejudice," "Susan and God," "The Moon Is Down," "Eastward in Eden," "The Vigil," "Light Up The Sky," "The Sacred Flame."

**SHARP, HENRY.** Born Feb. 19, 1889, in Riga, Latvia. Studied at American Academy of Dramatic Arts. Has appeared in "A Gentleman From Mississippi," "Over Night," "Madame X," "Escape Me Never," "Morning Star," "Arsenic and Old Lace," "The Assassin," "Oh, Men! Oh, Women!."

**SHAW, RETA.** Born in South Paris, Maine, Sept. 13, 1912. Studied at Leland Powers School of The Theatre. Has appeared on Broadway in "It Takes Two," "Virginia Reel," "Gentlemen Prefer Blondes," "Picnic," "The Pajama Game."

**SHAYNE, ALAN.** Born in Brooklin. Mass.. Nov. 21, 1925. Educated at Brookline High. Studied at Tributary Theatre, Boston. Has appeared on Broadway in Evans' "Hamlet," "Antony and Cleopatra" (1947), "The Madwoman of Chaillot."

**SHELLEY, JOSHUA.** Born in Brooklyn and educated at NYU. Made N.Y. debut in 1935 in "Black Pit." Has appeared since in "One Touch of Venus." "On The Town," "Tid-Bits of '46," "Tenting Tonight," "Barefoot Boy With Cheek," "Make Mine Manhattan," "The Liar," "4 Twelves Are 48," "The Girl In Pink Tights."

**SHERMAN, HIRAM.** Born in Boston, Feb. 11, 1908. Educated at Univ. of Ill. Has appeared in "Shoemaker's Holiday," "Sing Out The News." "Very Warm For May," "Boyd's Daughter." "The Talley Method," "Cyrano de Bergerac," "The Alchemist." "4 Twelves Are 48," "The Moon Is Blue," "Two's Company," "The Frogs of Spring."

**SILVERS, PHIL.** Born in Brooklyn, May 11, 1911. Educated at New Utrecht High. Appeared in burlesque and vaudeville before making Broadway bow in 1939 in "Yokel Boy." Has appeared since in "High Button Shoes," "Top Banana."

**SINCLAIR, ERIC.** Born in Burkburnett, Tex., Apr. 26, 1922. Educated at Baylor Univ. Made Broadway debut in 1951 in "Legend of Lovers." Has appeared since in 1952 revival of "Much Ado About Nothing."

**SKINNER, CORNELIA OTIS.** Born in Chicago, May 30, 1902, while her father, Otis Skinner, was appearing there. Made stage debut with him in 1921 in "Blood and Sand," followed by "Will Shakespeare," "The Wild Westcotts," "White Collars." Became own dramatist, costumer, director in series of character sketches and monologues which were so successful that she appeared in them almost exclusively for 15 years. Recent N.Y. appearances include "Love For Love," "Theatre," "The Searching Wind," "Lady Windermere's Fan," her one-woman show "Paris '90."

**SMITH, ARCHIE.** Born in Richmond, Va., and educated at Univ. of Va. Studied at Chekhov Theatre Studio. Has appeared in "Harriet," "The Late George Apley," "The Madwoman of Chaillot," "The Show-Off."

**SMITH, HOWARD.** Born in Attleboro, Mass., Aug. 12, 1895. Educated at McGill Univ. Has appeared in "The Eternal Magdalene," "Miss Quis," "Solitaire," "The Life of Reilly," "Decision," "Dear Ruth," "Mr. Peebles and Mr. Hooker," "Death of A Salesman," "Mid-Summer," "The Pink Elephant," "A Red Rainbow," "Anniversary Waltz."

**SMITH, KENT.** Born in N.Y.C., Mar. 19, 1907. Educated at Phillips Exeter and Harvard. Made Broadway debut in 1934 in "Spring In Autumn." Has appeared since in "Dodsworth," "Candida," "Wingless Victory," "St. Joan," "Star Wagon," "Old Acquaintance," "The Story of Mary Surratt," "Antony and Cleopatra," "The Wisteria Trees," "Burning Bright," "Richard II," "The Autumn Garden," "The Wild Duck" (1952), "Charley's Aunt" (1953).

**SMITH, LORING.** Born in Stratford, Conn., Nov. 18, 1895. Made Broadway bow in 1917 in "Leave It To Jane." Has appeared since in "Kiss The Boys Goodbye," "Glamour Preferred," "George Washington Slept Here," "All For All," "A Joy Forever," "Junior Miss," "Over 21," "John Loves Mary," "The Happiest Years," "Texas Lil' Darlin'," "Of Thee I Sing" (1952), "Be Your Age," "The Solid Gold Cadillac."

| Susan Steell | Michael Steele | Jean Stapleton |

**SMITH, ROBERT.** Born in Brooklyn, Dec. 15, 1912. Graduate of Manhattan College and studied law at St. John's College. Made Broadway debut in 1934 in "Lost Horizons." Has appeared since in "Three Waltzes," "You Never Know," "One For The Money," "Two For The Show," "Family Affair," "Brigadoon," "Gramercy Ghost," "The Girl In Pink Tights."

**SMITHERS, WILLIAM.** Born in Richmond, Va., July 10, 1927. Educated at Hampden-Sydney College and Catholic Univ. Made Broadway debut in 1951 in "Romeo and Juliet." Has appeared since in "Legend of Lovers," "End As A Man."

**STANLEY, KIM.** Born in Tularosa, N. Mex., Feb. 11, 1921. Educated at Universities of N. Mex. and Tex. Made Broadway debut in 1949 in "Montserrat." Has appeared since in "The House of Bernarda Alba," "The Chase," "Picnic."

**STAPLETON, JEAN.** Born in N.Y.C., Jan. 19, 1923. Educated at Hunter College. Studied at American Theatre Wing and American Actors Co. Made Broadway debut Dec. 29, 1953, in "In The Summer House."

**STAPLETON, MAUREEN.** Born in Troy, N.Y., June 21, 1925. Toured with Cornell in "The Barretts of Wimpole Street" and appeared on Broadway in "The Playboy of The Western World," "Antony and Cleopatra," "Detective Story," "The Bird Cage," "The Rose Tattoo," "The Emperor's Clothes," "The Crucible," "Richard III" (1953), "The Sea Gull" (1954).

**STARR, FRANCES.** Born in Oneonta, N.Y., June 6, 1886. Educated in Albany public schools. Among her many appearances are "The Rose of The Rancho," "The Easiest Way,". "The Case of Becky," "Marie-Odile," "Tiger! Tiger!," "Shore Leave," "The Lake," "Moor Born," "Claudia," "The Young and Fair," "The Sacred Flame," "The Ladies of The Corridor."

**STEELE, MICHAEL.** Born in Berwick, Penn., Oct. 5, 1921. Educated at Penn. State College, Univ. of N.C. and UCLA. Made Broadway debut Nov. 11, 1953, in "Sabrina Fair."

**STEELL, SUSAN.** Born in N.Y.C., Nov. 7, 1906. Educated at Miss Spence's School, N.Y., and the Sorbonne, Paris. Received stage training at Vieux Colombier, Paris. Has appeared in "Johnny Johnson," "On The Town," "Crime and Punishment," "The Grass Harp," "Madam, Will You Walk."

**STEVENS, ROGER.** Born in N.Y.C., Oct. 26, 1938. Educated at Feagin School and High School of Performing Arts. Made Broadway debut Dec. 30, 1953, in "The Remarkable Mr. Pennypacker."

**STEWART, DAVID J.** Born in Omaha, Neb. Studied at Neighborhood Playhouse and Actor's Studio. Has appeared on Broadway in "Antigone," "Antony and Cleopatra," "That Lady," "The Rose Tattoo," "Barefoot In Athens," "Camino Real," "The Immoralist."

**STEWART, JOHNNY.** Born in Brooklyn, May 21, 1934. Made Broadway debut in 1947 in "High Button Shoes." Has appeared since in "Love Life," "The Happy Time," "The King and I," "The Grass Harp," "Bernardine."

**STICKNEY, DOROTHY.** Born in Dickinson, N.D., June 21, 1900. Educated at St. Catherine's College and Northwestern Dramatic School. Made N.Y. debut in 1926 in "The Squall." Has appeared since in "Chicago," "March Hares," "The Beaux Stratagem," "The Front Page," "Philip Goes Forth," "Another Language," "On Borrowed Time," "Life With Father," "Life With Mother," "The Small Hours," "To Be Continued," "Kind Sir."

**ST. JOHN, HOWARD.** Born in Chicago, Oct. 9, 1905. Educated at St. Ignatius and St. Boniface and Univ. of Ala. Made N.Y. debut in 1925 in "12 Miles Out." Has appeared since in "Under This Roof," "Cuckoos On The Hearth," "Brooklyn, U.S.A.," "The Primrose Path," "Janie," "The Late George Apley," "The Fatal Weakness," "Jane," "His and Hers."

**STODDARD, HAILA.** Born Nov. 14, 1913, in Great Falls, Mont. Graduate of Univ. of S. Calif. Made Broadway debut in 1938 in "Yes, My Darling Daughter." Has appeared since in "Susannah and The Elders," "The Rivals," "Moon Vine," "Blithe Spirit," "Dream Girl," "Dr. Social," "Springtime For Henry" (1951), "Glad Tidings," "The Frogs of Spring."

**STONE, CAROL.** Born in N.Y.C., Feb. 1, 1916. Educated at Kew-Forest School, L.I. Made Broadway debut in 1933 in "Spring In Autumn." Has appeared since in "Mackerel Skies," "The Jayhawker," "White Horse Inn," "As You Like It," "Lady Behave," "Dark of the Moon," "They Knew What They Wanted" (1949), "Desire Under The Elms" (1952), "The Fourposter" on tour.

**STORCH, ARTHUR.** Born in Brooklyn, June 29, 1925. Educated at Brooklyn College, Glasgow University, Scotland, and New School. Member of Actor's Studio. Made Broadway debut Oct. 14, 1953, in "End As A Man."

**STRAIGHT, BEATRICE.** Born in Old Westbury, L.I., Aug. 2, 1916. Educated at Dartington Hall, Eng. Made N.Y. debut in 1934 in "Bitter Oleander." Has appeared since in "Twelfth Night," "Land of Fame," "The Wanhope Building," "Eastward In Eden," "Macbeth" (1948), "The Heiress," "The Innocents," "The Grand Tour," "The Crucible."

| Donald Symington | Maureen Stapleton | William Thourlby |

**STRICKLYN, RAY.** Born in Houston, Tex., Oct. 8, 1930. Educated at Univ. of Houston. Appeared in stock and with Houston Players before making his Broadway debut Nov. 6, 1952, in "The Climate of Eden." Has appeared since in "The Grass Harp," "Stalag 17" on tour.

**STRUDWICK, SHEPPERD.** Born in Hillsboro, N.C., Sept. 22, 1907. Graduate of Univ. of N.C. Made N.Y. debut in 1929 in "The Yellow Jacket." Has appeared since in "Both Your Houses," "Let Freedom Ring," "End of Summer," "As You Like It" (1937), "Christopher Blake," "Affairs of State," "The Bat" (1952), "The Ladies of The Corridor."

**STUCKMANN, EUGENE.** Born in N.Y.C., Nov. 16, 1917. Made Broadway debut in 1943 in Coulouris' "Richard III." Has appeared since in "Counsellor-At-Law," "Othello," "The Tempest," "Foxhole In The Parlor," "Henry VIII,' "Androcles and The Lion," "Yellow Jack," "Skipper Next To God," "Richard III" (1953).

**SULLAVAN, MARGARET.** Born in Norfolk, Va., May 16, 1911. Has appeared on Broadway in "A Modern Virgin," "If Love Were All," "Happy Landing," "Chrysalis," "Bad Manners," "Dinner At Eight," "Stage Door," "The Voice of The Turtle," "The Deep Blue Sea," "Sabrina Fair."

**SYMINGTON, DONALD.** Born in Baltimore, Md., Aug. 30, 1925. Made Broadway debut in 1947 in Experimental Theatre's "Galileo." Has appeared since in "Caesar and Cleopatra" (1949), "Dream Girl" (1951), "A Girl Can Tell."

**TABBERT, WILLIAM.** Born in Chicago, Oct. 5, 1921. Made N.Y. debut in 1943 in "What's Up." Has appeared since in "Follow The Girls," "Seven Lively Arts," "Billion Dollar Baby," "South Pacific.

**TALBOT, NITA.** Born in N.Y.C., Aug. 8, 1930. Studied at Irvine Studio and with Charles Laughton. Made Broadway debut in 1951 in "Never Say Never." Has appeared since in "The Fifth Season."

**TANDY, JESSICA.** Born in London, June 7, 1909. Educated at Dame Owens Girls School. Made N.Y. debut in 1930 in "The Matriarch." Has appeared since in "The Last Enemy," "Time and The Conways," "The White Steed," "Geneva," "Jupiter Laughs," "Anne of England," "Yesterday's Magic," "A Streetcar Named Desire," "Hilda Crane," "The Fourposter," "Madam, Will You Walk."

**TAYLOR, CHARLES.** Born in Scranton, Pa., Aug. 30, 1940. Educated at Our Lady Queen of Martyrs School and Willard Mace Professional School. Has appeared on Broadway in "Annie Get Your Gun," "Peter Pan," "Point of No Return," "Richard III" (1953), "The Magic and The Loss."

**TETZEL, JOAN.** Born in N.Y.C., June 21, 1923. Educated at Professional Children's School. Made Broadway debut in 1938 in "Lorelei." Has appeared since in "Liliom," "The Happy Days," "The Damask Cheek," "Harriet," "Peep Show," "Pretty Little Parlor," "I Remember Mama," "Strange Bedfellows," "Red Gloves," "The Winner."

**THOMAS, ANN.** Born July 8, 1920, in Newport, R.I. Attended Professional Children's School and began career as child actress. Has appeared in "Doctors Disagree," "A New Life," "Having Wonderful Time," "The Man From Cairo," "Chicken Every Sunday," "The Would-Be Gentleman," "Made In Heaven," "Burlesque," "Dance Me A Song," "Not For Children."

**THOMAS, FRANK M.** Born July 13, 1890, in St. Joseph, Mo. Educated at Butler College. Made Broadway debut in 1912 in "Along Came Ruth." Has appeared since in "The House of Glass," "Red Light Annie," "The National Anthem," "Remember The Day," "Chicken Every Sunday," "The Rich Full Life," "Jeb," "Christopher Blake," "End As A Man."

**THOMPSON, MARSHALL.** Born in Peoria, Ill., Nov. 27, 1925. Educated at Occidental College. Appeared in summer stock in California and made many films before making his Broadway debut Oct. 29, 1953, in "A Girl Can Tell."

**THOMPSON, REX.** Born in N.Y.C., Dec. 14, 1942. Attends Professional Children's School. Has appeared on Broadway in "Alive and Kicking," "The Wisteria Trees," "The King and I," "Escapade," "King of Hearts."

**THOURLBY, WILLIAM.** Born in Detroit, Mich., Jan. 22, 1924. Educated at Mich. State and Tri-State College, Ind. Appeared in summer theatres before making N.Y. debut, Feb. 4, 1954, in "Stockade."

**TONE, FRANCHOT.** Born in Niagara Falls, N.Y., Feb. 27, 1906. Educated at Cornell. Made Broadway debut in 1928 in "The Age of Innocence." Has appeared since in "Cross Roads," "Red Dust," "Hotel Universe," "Green Grow The Lilacs," "Pagan Lady," "The House of Connelly," "Night Over Taos," "Success Story," "The Gentle People," "The Fifth Column," "Hope For The Best," "Oh, Men! Oh, Woman!"

**TRUEX, ERNEST.** Born in Red Hill, Mo., Sept. 19, 1890. Educated at Whittier School, Denver. Made Broadway debut in 1908 with Lillian Russell in "Wildfire." Has appeared since in "Rebecca of Sunnybrook Farm," "Good Little Devil," "The Fall Guy," "Lysistrata," "Whistling In The Dark," "George Washington Slept Here," "Helen Goes To Troy," "Androcles and The Lion," "A Temporary Island," "Oh, Mr. Meadowbrook," "The Golden State," "4 Twelves Are 48," "Flahooley."

**Anne Vernon**

**George Voskovec**

**Betsy Von Furstenberg**

**ULRIC, LENORE.** Born in New Ulm, Minn., July 21, 1894. As famous Belasco star, appeared in "Tiger Rose," "The Son-Daughter," "Lulu Belle," "Kiki," "The Harem," "Mimi." More recently appeared in "Her Man of Wax," "The Fifth Column," "The Doughgirls" on tour, "Antony and Cleopatra" (1947).

**VALENTINE, GRACE.** Born in Springfield, Ohio, Feb. 14, 1891. Made Broadway debut in 1914 in "The Yosemite." Has appeared since in "Johnny Get Your Gun," "Lombardi Ltd.," "The Fabulous Invalid," "The American Way," "George Washington Slept Here," "Happy Birthday," "A Story For Strangers," "Season In The Sun," "Anna Christie" (1952).

**VALENTINE, PAUL.** Born in N.Y.C., Mar. 23, 1919. Graduate of Commercial High. Danced with Monte Carlo Ballet Russe and St. Louis and Detroit Opera Companies. Has appeared on Broadway in "Virginia," "Sons O' Fun," "Follow The Girls," "Gypsy Lady," "Wish You Were Here."

**VAN DYKE, MARCIA.** Born in Grants Pass, Ore., and educated in its public schools. Has appeared in films and was in first violin section of San Francisco Symphony. Made Broadway debut Apr. 19, 1951, in "A Tree Grows In Brooklyn."

**VARDEN, EVELYN.** Born in Adair, Okla., June 12, 1893. Educated in Girls Collegiate School, Los Angeles. Made Broadway debut in 1910 in "The Nest Egg." Has appeared since in "Alley Cat," "Weep For The Virgins," "Russet Mantle," "Prelude To Exile," "To Quito and Back," "Our Town," "Family Portrait," "Ladies and Gentlemen," "Candle In The Wind," "Dream Girl," "Present Laughter," "Hilda Crane," "Romeo and Juliet" (1951), "A Date With April."

**VERDON, GWEN.** Born in Culver City, Calif. Has appeared on Broadway in "Alive and Kicking," "Magdalena," "Can-Can."

**VERNON, ANNE.** Born in Paris, France, Jan. 9, 1926. Educated at College of Evreux and studied for stage at Vieux Colombier, Paris. Made Broadway debut Oct. 7, 1953, in "The Little Hut."

**VON FURSTENBERG, BETSY.** Born in Westphalia, Ger., Aug. 16, 1931. Studied with Sanford Meisner. Made Broadway debut in 1951 in "Second Threshold." Has appeared since in "Dear Barbarians," "Oh, Men! Oh, Women!!"

**VOSKOVEC, GEORGE.** Born in Sazava, Czech., June 19, 1905. Educated at Dijon College, France, and Charles Univ., Prague. Made Broadway debut in 1945 in "The Tempest." Has appeared since in "The Love of Four Colonels," "His and Hers," "The Sea Gull" (1954 Phoenix revival).

**WALKER, June.** Born in Chicago, June 14, 1904. Educated at Oak Park High. Made N.Y. debut in 1918 in chorus of "Hitchy-Koo." Has appeared since in "Six Cylinder Love," "The Nervous Wreck," "Gentlemen Prefer Blondes," "Waterloo Bridge," "Green Grow The Lilacs," "The Farmer Takes A Wife," "The Merchant of Yonkers," "Truckline Cafe," "The Hallams," "Death of A Salesman" on tour, "The Ladies of The Corridor," "The Sea Gull" (1954 Phoenix revival).

**WALLACH, ELI.** Born in Brooklyn. Educated at CCNY and Univ. of Tex. Studied at Neighborhood Playhouse. Has appeared in "Henry VIII," "Androcles and The Lion," "Alice In Wonderland," "Yellow Jack," "What Every Woman Knows"—all with ART in 1947-8. Has also appeared in "Skydrift," "Antony and Cleopatra" (1947), "Mister Roberts," "The Lady From The Sea," "The Rose Tattoo," "Mlle. Colombe," "The Teahouse of The August Moon" in London.

**WALSH, TOM.** Born in New Haven, Conn., Feb. 6, 1926. Studied for stage at Theodora Irvine School. Made Broadway debut in 1947 in "Laura."

**WALSTON, RAY.** Born in New Orleans, Nov. 2, 1919. Trained at Houston Civic Theatre and Cleveland Playhouse. Made Broadway bow in Evans' "Hamlet." Has appeared since in "Front Page," "The Survivors," "Summer and Smoke," "Mrs. Gibbons' Boys," "Richard III," "The Rat Race," "South Pacific" in London, "Me and Juliet."

**WARDEN, JACK.** Born in Newark, N.J., Sept. 18, 1920. Spent 3 seasons with Margo Jones' Theatre in Dallas before making Broadway debut in 1952 revival of "Golden Boy." Has appeared since in "Lullaby."

**WARING, RICHARD.** Born in Buckinghamshire, Eng., May 27, 1912. Received stage training with Civic Repertory Co. Appeared opposite Eva Le Gallienne in "Romeo and Juliet," "Camille," "Cradle Song." Has appeared since in "Boy Meets Girl," "The Corn Is Green" (original and 1950 revival), "Henry VIII," "Androcles and The Lion," "What Every Woman Knows," "Alice In Wonderland," "Gramercy Ghost."

**WATERS, ETHEL.** Born in Chester, Pa., Oct. 31, 1900. Began career as cabaret singer. Made Broadway debut in 1927 in "Africana." Has appeared since in "Lew Leslie's Blackbirds," "Rhapsody In Black," "As Thousands Cheer," "At Home Abroad," "Mamba's Daughters," "Cabin In The Sky," "Blue Holiday," "The Member of The Wedding,' one-woman show "At Home With Ethel Waters."

Tom Walsh                    Mary Welch                    Douglas Watson

**WATSON, DOUGLAS.** Born in Jackson, Ga., Feb. 24, 1921. Educated at Univ. of N.C. Studied with Ouspenskaya. Made Broadway debut in 1947 in "Antony and Cleopatra." Has appeared since in "The Leading Lady," "Richard III," "The Happiest Years," "That Lady," "The Wisteria Trees," "Romeo and Juliet" (1951), "Desire Under The Elms" (1952) "Sunday Breakfast," "The Scarecrow" (De-Lys revival) 1953 City Center revivals of "Cyrano de Bergerac" and "Richard III," "The Confidential Clerk."

**WATSON, LUCILE.** Born in Quebec, Can., May 27, 1879. Studied at American Academy of Dramatic Arts. Made N.Y. debut in 1903 in "Hearts Aflame." Has appeared since in "The Dictator," "The City," "Under Cover," "The Eternal Magdalene," "Heartbreak House," "No More Ladies," "Pride and Prejudice," "Yes, My Darling Daughter," "Dear Octopus," "Watch On The Rhine," "Ring Round The Moon," "The Bat" (1953), "Late Love."

**WAYNE, DAVID.** Born in Traverse City, Mich., Jan. 31, 1916. Educated at Western State, Mich. Made Broadway debut in 1938 in "Escape This Night." Has appeared since in "Dance Night," "The American Way," "Scene of The Crime," "The Merry Widow," "Peepshow," "Park Avenue," "Finian's Rainbow," "Mister Roberts," "The Teahouse of The August Moon."

**WELCH, MARY.** Born in Charleston, S.C., Educated at UCLA. Made N.Y. debut in 1944 revival of "Little Women." Has appeared since in "Joy To The World," "A Streetcar Named Desire," "The House of Bernarda Alba," "Dream Girl" (1951), "The Solid Gold Cadillac."

**WEST, MAE.** Born in Brooklyn, Aug. 17, 1892. Made Broadway debut in "Folies Bergere," followed by "A La Broadway," "Vera Violetta," "The Winsome Widow," "Demi-Tasse," "The Mimic World," wrote and appeared in "Sex," "Diamond Lil," "Catherine Was Great" and "Come On Up." Has revived "Diamond Lil" several times with great success.

**WESTMAN, NYDIA.** Born in NYC. Feb. 19, 1907. Educated at Professional Children's School. As child, appeared with family in act called "The Westmans." Made legitimate debut in 1924 in "Pigs." Has appeared since in "Two Girls Wanted," "Buckaroo," "Jonesy," "Ada Beats The Drum," "Lysistrata," "The Merchant of Yonkers," "Life With Father," "Strange Bedfellows," "The Madwoman of Chaillot," "Mr. Pickwick," "The Emperor's Clothes."

**WETMORE, JOAN.** Born in Sydney, Australia. Has appeared on Broadway in "The Two Bouquets," "Two On An Island," "Kind Lady," "Counsellor-At-Law," "A New Life," "The Two Mrs. Carrolls," "For Keeps," "Hope For The Best," "The Small Hours," "A Girl Can Tell."

**WHEEL, PATRICIA.** Born in NYC. Has appeared in revivals of "Cyrano de Bergerac," "The Tempest," "Arms and The Man," "Charley's Aunt" (1953). Has also been in "Little Brown Jug," "The Stars Weep," "The Browning Version," "Cry of The Peacock," "Gertie," "The Sacred Flame."

**WHEELER, LOIS.** Born in Stockton, Cal., July 12, 1922. Studied at Pasadena and Neighborhood Playhouses. Made Broadway debut in 1943 in "The Innocent Voyage." Has appeared since in "Pick-Up Girl," "Trio," "All My Sons," "The Young and Fair," "Dinosaur Wharf," "The Fifth Season."

**WHITE, JANE.** Born in N.Y.C., Oct 30. 1922. Educated at Smith College. Studied for stage at New School. Made Broadway debut in 1945 in "Strange Fruit." Has appeared since in "Razzle Dazzle," "The Insect Comedy," "The Climate of Eden," "Take A Giant Step."

**WHITING, JACK.** Born in Philadelphia, June 22, 1901. Educated at Univ. of Pa. Made Broadway debut in "Ziegfeld Follies of 1922." Has appeared since in "Orange Blossoms," "Stepping Stones," "Hold Everything," "Heads Up," "Calling All Stars," "Hooray For What," "Very Warm For May," "Hold On To Your Hats," "The Overtons," "The Red Mill" (1945), "High Button Shoes" on tour, "Of Thee I Sing" (1952), "Hazel Flagg," "A Girl Can Tell," "The Golden Apple."

**WHITMAN, WILLIAM.** Born in Boston, Mass., July 6, 1925. Educated at Westminster School, Eng. Made Broadway debut Feb. 1, 1952, in "Jane."

**WHORF, RICHARD.** Born in Winthrop, Mass., June 4, 1906. Made stage debut in 1926 in revival of "John Ferguson." Has appeared since in "The Banshee," "Three Cornered Moon," "The Lady From The Sea," "Panic," "The Taming of The Shrew," "Idiot's Delight," "Amphitryon 38," "The Sea Gull," "There Shall Be No Night," "Angel Street" (1948), "Richard III," "Season In The Sun," "The Fifth Season."

**WILLIAMS, EMLYN.** Born in Mostyn, Flintshire, Wales, Nov. 26, 1905. Educated in Switzerland and Christ Church, Oxford. Made N.Y. debut in 1927 in "And So To Bed." Other N.Y. appearances include "Criminal At Large," "Night Must Fall," "Montserrat," "Readings From Charles Dickens," "Bleak House."

219

Martin Wolfson       Billie Worth       Gig Young

**WILLIAMS, JOHN.** Born in Chalfont St. Giles, Bucks, Eng., Apr. 15, 1903. Educated at Lancing College, Eng. Made N.Y. debut in 1924 in "The Fake." Has appeared since in "The Dark Angel," "The Ghost Train," "Mixed Doubles," "The High Road," "Petticoat Influence," "Ten Minute Alibi," "Dodsworth," "Call It A Day," "No Time For Comedy," "Claudia," "Anne of The Thousand Days," "The Velvet Glove," "Venus Observed," "Dial 'M' For Murder."

**WILSON, PERRY.** Born in Bound Brook, N.J., and attended Kent Place School and studied with Daykarhanova. Made N.Y. debut in 1940 in "Cream In The Well." Has appeared since in "Village Green," "The First Crocus," "Mexican Mural," "The Corn Is Green," "The Stranger," "On Whitman Avenue," "His and Hers."

**WINANT, HAIM.** Born in Detroit, Feb. 12, 1927. Educated at Wayne Univ. Has appeared in "High Button Shoes," "As You Like It" (1950), "Venus Observed," "Never Say Never," "The Love of Four Colonels," "The Teahouse of The August Moon."

**WINDOM, WILLIAM.** Born in N.Y.C., Sept. 28, 1923. Educated at Williams College. Made Broadway debut in 1946 ART revival of "Henry VIII." Has appeared since in "What Every Woman Knows," "John Gabriel Borkman," "Androcles and The Lion," "Yellow Jack," "Alice In Wonderland," "Bell, Book and Candle" on tour, "A Girl Can Tell," "Mlle. Colombe."

**WINTERS, LAWRENCE.** Born in Kings Creek, S.C., Nov. 12, 1915. Educated at Howard Univ. Made N.Y. debut in 1942 in "Porgy and Bess." Has appeared since in concert and with New York City Opera Co., in "Call Me Mister," "Show Boat," (1954 City Center revival).

**WINTERS, MARIAN.** Born in N.Y.C., Apr. 19, 1924. Educated in public schools in Hempstead, L.I., and Erasmus Hall, Brooklyn. Has appeared in 1951 revival of "Dream Girl," "I Am A Camera."

**WINWOOD, ESTELLE.** Born in Kent, Eng., Jan. 24, 1883. Studied at Lyric Stage Academy. Made N.Y. debut in 1916 in "Hush." Has appeared since in "A Successful Calamity," "Too Many Husbands," "The Circle," "Trelawney of The Wells," "Fallen Angels," "The Distaff Side," "The Importance of Being Earnest," "Ladies In Retirement," "Ten Little Indians," "Lady Windermere's Fan," "The Madwoman of Chaillot," "The Cocktail Party" on tour, "Mr. Pickwick," "Sabrina Fair" on tour.

**WOLFSON, MARTIN.** Born in N.Y.C., Apr. 4, 1904. Educated at CCNY. Has appeared in "Black Pit," "Counsellor-At-Law," "Co-Respondent Unknown," "The Gentle People," "Ladies and Gentlemen," "Brooklyn U.S.A.," "Counterattack," "The Cup of Trembling," "South Pacific," "Threepenny Opera."

**WOOD, PEGGY.** Born in Brooklyn, Feb. 9, 1894. Studied voice with Mme. Calve and made N.Y. debut in 1910 in "Naughty Marietta." Has appeared since in "The Lady of The Slipper," "Love O' Mike," "Maytime," "Buddies," "Marjolaine," "The Bride," "Candida," "Trelawney of The Wells," "The Merchant of Venice" with George Arliss. "Bitter Sweet" in London, "Old Acquaintance," "Blithe Spirit," "The Happiest Years," "Getting Married," 1953 City Center revival of "Charley's Aunt."

**WORLOCK, FREDERIC.** Born in London, Dec. 14, 1886. Made first N.Y. appearance in 1923 in "Sweet Nell of Old Drury." More recent appearances include "Richard II," "Henry IV," "Suspect," "Anne of England," "Portrait of A Lady," "Anne of The Thousand Days," "St. Joan" (1951), "Sabrina Fair."

**WORTH, BILLIE.** Born in Rome, N.Y., Oct. 20th. Educated at Professional Children's School. Made Broadway debut in 1940 in "Higher and Higher." Has appeared since in "Jackpot," "Bright Lights of 1943," "Seven Lively Arts," "Annie Get Your Gun," "Courtin' Time," London Company of "Call Me Madam."

**WRIGHT, MARTHA.** Born in Seattle, Wash., Mar. 23, 1926. Educated at Univ. of Wash. Made Broadway debut in 1947 in "Music In My Heart." Has appeared since in "Great To Be Alive," "South Pacific."

**WYCHERLY, MARGARET.** Born in London, Oct. 26, 1881. Made debut in 1898 in "What Dreams May Come." Has appeared since in "Everywoman," "Chashel Bryon's Profession," "The Nazarene," "The Blue Bird," "Damaged Goods," "The Thirteenth Chair," "Back To Methuselah," "The Adding Machine," "Another Language," "Tobacco Road," "Hedda Gabler," "Liliom," "Dear Judas," "Richard III" (1953 City Center revival).

**YOUNG, GIG.** Born in St. Cloud, Minn., Nov. 4, 1917. Received training at Pasadena Playhouse. Appeared in many films before making Broadway debut Dec. 17, 1953, in "Oh, Men! Oh, Women!"

Maude Adams
1872-1953

John Murray Anderson

Frankie Bailey

Bertha Belmore

**ADAMS, MAUDE**, 80, one of America's most famous and beloved actresses died of a heart attack at her home near Tannersville, N.Y., July 17, 1953. She was born in Salt Lake City, Nov. 11, 1872. Her mother, Anne Adams Kiskadden, was leading lady of the local stock company and Little Maude began her career as a child actress. She was associated with producer Charles Frohman from 1890 until his death on the Lusitania in 1915. She began her association with him as John Drew's leading lady. Her first starring role was in "The Little Minister" in 1897. Among the other famous plays in which she starred were "Peter Pan," "What Every Woman Knows," "Quality Street," "L'Aiglon," "The Jesters," "Romeo and Juliet," "Twelfth Night," "A Kiss For Cinderella," and "The Legend of Lenora." She retired in 1918, but in 1931 she toured the country playing Portia to Otis Skinner's Shylock in "The Merchant of Venice." Later she became the head of the drama department at Stephens College, Columbia, Mo., for five years. She never married. She is buried on the estate of the Cenacle Convent, Ronkonkoma, L.I., which she gave to the Roman Catholic Sisterhood of Our Lady of The Cenacle in 1922.

**ANDERSON, JOHN MURRAY**, 67, director and producer, died Jan. 30, 1954, in New York City, of a heart attack. Born in St. John's, Newfoundland, he began his theatrical career in 1919 when he presented his first Broadway offering "Greenwich Village Follies." Subsequently he staged six edition of this revue. He was involved either as producer, director, writer or creator of 29 musical productions presented on the New York stage. These include "Life Begins at 8:40," three editions of the "Ziegfeld Follies," "Jumbo," "One For The Money," "Two For The Show," "Three To Make Ready," the last edition of the "Music Box Revue," "New Faces of 1952" and the current "John Murray Anderson's Almanac." Burial was in Woodlawn Cemetery, New York City.

**BAILEY, FRANKIE**, 94, famous show girl, died July 8, 1953, in Los Angeles. At the turn of the Century, she was known as "The Girl With The Million Dollar Legs." In 1896 she left burlesque and joined the Weber and Fields Music Hall company. Among the shows in which she appeared on Broadway were "Crook," "The Potters of Texas," "Hokey-Pokey," "Fiddle-dee-dee" and "Whirl-i-gig."

**BAMBERGER, THERON**, 59, producer and former press agent, died Sept. 14, 1953, in New York City. Besides producing several plays on Broadway, he operated the Bucks County Playhouse at New Hope, Pa., for the last 13 years. Also, for the past two seasons he managed the Municipal Theatre, Fairmont Park, Philadelphia, another summer theatre venture. His wife, Phyllis Perlman, publicist, survives.

**BELMORE, BERTHA**, 70, British character actress, died Dec. 14, 1953, in Barcelona, Spain. She made her American debut in 1910 with the Ben Greet Players. Her more recent Broadway appearances were made in "Virginia," "Johnny Belinda," "Heart of A City," "By Jupiter," "The Naked Genius," "Rhapsody," "Antigone," "Harlequinade," "Caesar and Cleopatra" and "Gigi."

**BERNSTEIN, HENRI**, 77, French playwright and producer, died in Paris, Nov. 27, 1953. He had been active in the theatre for over 50 years. Among his plays produced in America were "The Thief," "Samson," "Judith," "Melo" and "The Secret."

**BRUCE, GERALDINE**, 72, retired actress, died Aug. 24, 1953, in Congers, N.Y. She appeared in the original production of "Florodora," and also in "Chinese Honeymoon," "Prince of India," "Waltz Dream," "Girl of The Barracks" and "The Chocolate Soldier."

**BRUCE, NIGEL**, 58, stage and screen actor, died Oct. 8, 1953, in Santa Monica, Calif. Before settling down in Hollywood where he made many films, he appeared on the Broadway stage in "This Was A Man" and "Springtime For Henry."

**CAMERON, KATHRYN,** 71, character actress, died in New York City, Jan. 1, 1954. She began her acting career at 16 with a touring troup of Gilbert and Sullivan operas. Her more recent Broadway appearances included "Dark of The Moon" and the revival of "Sally."

**CHAZEL, LEO,** 52, character actor, died July 16, 1953, at his home in Westport, Conn. His appearances in both musical comedies and straight plays included "Hooray For What," "Jubilee," "Polonaise," "My Sister Eileen," "The Skin of Our Teeth," "Snafu," "Arsenic and Old Lace," "My Dear Children," "Here Come The Clowns," "The Time of Your Life," and "The Iceman Cometh."

**CROPPER, ROY,** 58, musical comedy actor, died May 14, 1954, in Miami, Fla. He made his initial Broadway appearance in 1917 in "Chu-Chin-Chow." He appeared in the original production of "Blossom Time," also "Ziegfeld Follies of 1923," "The Student Prince," "Castles In The Air," "Le Maire's Affairs" and revivals of "Naughty Marietta" and "The Fortune Teller." He also sang leads in Gilbert and Sullivan repertoire for the Milton Aborn Opera Company.

**DREW, LOUISE,** 72, retired actress and daughter of the late John Drew, died April 23, 1954, in New York City. She made her stage debut in 1901 with her father in "Second In Command." Other plays in which she appeared include "Iris," "Lady Rose's Daughter," "Whitewashing Julia," "Strongheart," "Caught In The Rain," "Her Sister," "A Single Man," "It Pays To Advertise," and Ethel Barrymore revivals of "Trelawney of The Wells" and "Alice-Sit-By-The-Fire." She is survived by her actor husband Jack Devereaux and her son John Drew Devereaux.

**DUNCAN, AUGUSTIN,** 80, actor, died Feb. 20, 1954, of a heart attack at his home in Astoria, Queens, N.Y. He made his Broadway debut in 1900 in "Henry V." About 25 years ago he lost his eyesight, but continued his acting. His last stage appearance was in "Lute Song" in 1946. He appeared in and staged the Theatre Guild's 1919 production of "John Ferguson." He repeated that dual assignment in the 1928 and 1933 revivals. More recent appearances included Maurice Evans' productions of "Richard II" and "Hamlet."

**EDWARDS, ALAN,** 61, stage and screen actor, died May 8, 1954, in Los Angeles. He appeared on Broadway as leading man for such stars as Lenore Ulric, Jane Cowl, Nora Bayes, Peggy Wood and Dorothy Stone. In recent years he has devoted his career to motion pictures.

**FANCOURT, DARRELL,** 65, bass-baritone of Gilbert and Sullivan operetta fame, died Aug. 29, 1953, in London. He sang with the D'Oyly Carte Opera Co. from 1920, and during that time sang the role of the Mikado more than 3000 times. He was awarded the Order of the British Empire in Queen Elizabeth's Coronation honor list shortly before his death.

**FARNUM, WILLIAM,** 76, famous stage and screen star, died of cancer in Hollywood, June 5, 1953. Among his stage appearances were "Ben Hur," "The Littlest Rebel," "The Buccaneer," "Julius Caesar," and "Macbeth." His stage appearances were rare after 1914 when he entered motion pictures and achieved his greatest fame.

**FORTESCUE, VIOLA,** 78, retired actress, died Sept. 16, 1953, in N. Y. C. She toured the English provinces and Australia in "The Belle of New York" and appeared in America with Maxine Elliott and Mrs. Fiske, and in "Rebecca of Sunnybrook Farm." "Poor Little Rich Girl" and "The Heart of Paddy Whack."

**GRANT, SYDNEY,** 80, musical comedy actor, died in Santa Monica, Calif., July 12, 1953. Beginning his career in 1890 in "Shore Acres," he was active in the theatre for 60 years. His last role was in the national company of "Guys and Dolls." Some of his other appearances were in "Madame Sherry," "The Little Whopper," "So Long, Letty," "Pretty Mrs. Smith," "You Can't Take It With You," "The Fabulous Invalid," "The American Way" and "The Doughgirls."

Roy Cropper

Louise Drew

Augustin Duncan

Alan Edwards

Leonore Harris

Joe Laurie, Jr.

GREENSTREET, SYDNEY, 74, stage and screen character actor, died Jan. 19, 1954, in Hollywood. Born in England, he made his American stage debut with the Ben Greet Shakespearean Company. He appeared with Sir Herbert Tree, Margaret Anglin, Julia Marlowe, Viola Allen, Mitzi Hajos, Lou Tellegen and for 7 years he was with the Lunts in such plays as "The Taming of The Shrew," "Idiot's Delight," "Amphitryon 38," "The Sea Gull" and "There Shall Be No Night."

HALL, PORTER, 65, character actor, died Oct. 6, 1953, in Los Angeles. Besides appearing in many films, he appeared on Broadway in "Naked," "Loud Speaker," "Night Hostess," "It's A Wise Child," "The Dark Tower" and "As Thousands Cheer."

HARRIS, LEONORE, 74, actress, died Sept. 27, 1953, in New York City. She began her career under the management of Charles Frohman. Her many stage appearances included "The Girl From Kays," "The Whip," "Our Betters," "Bluebeard's Eighth Wife," "Dodsworth," "The Man Who Came To Dinner" and "Present Laughter."

KALMAN, EMMERICH, 71, Hungarian born composer, died in Paris, Oct. 30, 1953. He wrote such operettas as "Sari," "Countess Maritza," "The Circus Princess," "Miss Springtime," "Her Soldier Boy," "The Riviera Girl," "Golden Dawn," "The Gypsy Princess" and "The Gay Hussars." Burial was in Vienna.

KAMISARJEVSKY, THEODORE, 71, producer, director, writer and scenic designer, died Apr. 17, 1954, in Darien, Conn. He began his theatrical career in Russia in 1906. He was brought to America in 1922 by the Theatre Guild to stage their production of "Peer Gynt." In 1940 he co-authored, directed and produced "Russian Bank." His last Broadway assignment was the 1947 production of "Crime and Punishment." Recently he had been staging operas for the City Center.

LAURIE, JOE, JR., 62, actor and author, died Apr. 29, 1954, in New York City. He began his career in vaudeville and appeared in such plays as "Plain Jane," "Over The Top," "The Gingham Girl," "Swing Your Lady," "If I Was Rich," and "Weather Clear, Track Fast." He recently had success as a writer. He co-authored with Abel Green "Show Biz" and on his own wrote "Vaudeville: From The Honky Tonks to The Palace." He was cremated in Ferncliff, Hartsdale, N. Y.

LONSDALE, FREDERICK, 73, British playwright, died in London, Apr. 4, 1954. Among his plays which achieved American success were "The Last of Mrs. Cheyney," "On Approval," "Aren't We All?," "Spring Cleaning" and "The Best People."

MacMILLAN, VIOLET, 66, actress of stage and silent screen, died Dec. 28, 1953, in Grand Rapids, Mich. She was known as the "Cinderella Girl" after winning a contest to find a woman with feet small enough to wear a "Cinderella" golden slipper. Her most noted role was the lead in "The Time, The Place and The Girl."

MITCHELL, ESTHER, 56, died in New York City, Nov. 26, 1953. Born in Australia, she made her American debut in 1921 in "The Madras House." Her more recent Broadway appearances include "The Corn Is Green," "Call It A Day," "Within The Gates," "Miss Swan Expects," "O Mistress Mine" and "I Know My Love."

MITCHELL, MILLARD, 50, stage and screen actor, died of lung cancer, Oct. 13, 1953. Among his many stage appearances, after his 1925 debut in "The Holy Terror," were "Front Page," "Gentlemen of The Press," "Yellow Jack," "Three Men On A Horse," "Boy Meets Girl," "Mr. and Mrs. North," "See My Lawyer," "Kiss The Boys Goodbye," "Sons and Soldiers," "Storm Operation," "The Naked Genius," "Lovely Me" and "The Cup of Trembling."

Eugene O'Neill
1888-1953

Frederick Lonsdale

Millard Mitchell

Donald Richards

**MORLEY, VICTOR,** 82, actor and vaudevillian, died in New York City, June 29, 1953. Born in Greenwich, Eng., he made his American debut in 1902 in "Pretty Peggy." Other appearances include "The Prince of Pilsen," "The Earl and The Girl," "Three Twins," "The Quaker Girl," "Going Up," "Ziegfeld Follies of 1935," "Three Waltzes," "The Student Prince" and "Blossom Time." He retired in 1943.

**MOSCOWITZ, JENNIE,** 85, famous character actress of the Yiddish stage, died July 26, 1953, in the Bronx, N. Y. She did not confine her acting to the Yiddish-speaking theatre. Among her many appearances on the English-speaking stage were "The Melting Pot," "The Auctioneer" with David Warfield, "Partners Again," "Counselor-at-Law," "Kosher Kitty Kelly," "Excursion" and for six years she played Rose Potash in various versions of "Potash and Perlmutter."

**O'NEILL, EUGENE,** 65, America's most distinguished playwright, died in Boston, Nov. 27, 1953. He was a winner of the Nobel literary prize in 1936 and a three-time recipient of the Pulitzer award for "Beyond The Horizon" in 1920, "Anna Christie" in 1922 and "Strange Interlude" in 1928. Some of his other plays are "The Emperor Jones," "The Hairy Ape," "Ah, Wilderness!" "Marco Millions," "Desire Under The Elms," "Diff'rent," "The Straw," "Welded," "The Iceman Cometh," "All God's Children Got Wings," "The Great God Brown," "Lazarus Laughed," "Dynamo," "The Long Voyage Home," "The Moon of The Caribbees" and others.

**PAIGE, MABEL,** 74, character actress, died Feb. 8, 1954, in Van Nuys, Calif. She made her debut as a child actress in "Van The Virginian." For 30 years she had her own stock company and toured the South. Her more recent Broadway appearances were made in "Lost Horizons," "Out Of The Frying Pan," "Two Blind Mice," and "Gramercy Ghost."

**PAYNE, WILLIAM (LOU),** 80, character actor, died Aug. 14, 1953, in Hollywood. Husband of the late Mrs. Leslie Carter, he was her leading man when he married her in 1906. He played leading roles in such plays as "Eben Holden," "An American Cousin," "Her Majesty," "David Garrick," "Nazareth" and "Mrs. Leffingwell's Boots."

**RANDOLPH, LOUISE,** 83, retired actress, died Nov. 2, 1953, in Port Chester, N.Y. She made her stage debut with John Craig's Castle Square Stock Company and also appeared with Proctor's Fifth Avenue Stock Company. She was in the original Belasco production of "The Easiest Way."

**RAWLINSON, HERBERT,** 67, stage and film actor, died of lung cancer in Los Angeles, Calif., July 12, 1953. He came to America in 1910 and appeared in vaudeville and on Broadway before becoming a Hollywood star. His more recent appearances included "City Haul," "Right of Happiness," "Baby Pompadour," "A Modern Virgin" and "When Ladies Meet."

**RENNIE, HUGH,** 50, actor, died Sept. 27, 1953, in New York City. Among his Broadway appearances were "You Can't Take It With You," "Craig's Wife," "Neb McCobb's Daughter," "Pygmalion," "Goodbye Again," "They Shall Not Die," "Green Grow The Lilacs" and "Remains To Be Seen." He also directed and had been a stage manager for several summer theatres.

**RICE, VERNON,** 46, Drama Editor of the New York Post, died May 6, 1954, of a heart attack. Joining the Post in 1934, he served in several capacities before becoming Drama Editor. A staunch supporter of off-Broadway theatre, he was cited last March by the Arena Guild of America for his contribution in that field. In 1952 he served as president of the Drama Desk for a year. He is buried in Greenhill Cemetery, Muskogee, Oklahoma. Since 1947 he had been writing a summer theatre article for THEATRE WORLD.

**RICHARDS, DONALD,** 34, actor, was killed in an automobile accident Sept. 26, 1953, in Ridgewood, N.J. He began his career in 1939 with the St. Louis Grand Opera Company. His Broadway appearances included "Folies Bergere," "Count Me In," "Finian's Rainbow," and "Along Fifth Avenue."

**ROBERTS, HANS,** 80, retired actor, died in Jamaica, L.I., May 2, 1954. He was a member of the famous Augustin Daly Company. His many Broadway appearances included "Woodland," "Checkers," "The Gentlemen From Mississippi," "Ready Money," "On Trial," "The Noose," "Room Service" and "Dinner At Eight."

**ROSS, ROBERT,** 52, actor and director, died Feb. 23, 1954, in New York City. Born in Canada, he made his N.Y. debut at Eva Le Gallienne's Civic Repertory Theatre in 1926. Previous to that he directed at the Little Theatre, Berkeley, Calif. His appearances on Broadway included "Distant Drums," "The Farmer Takes A Wife," "They Shall Not Die," "Stars In Your Eyes," "Mister Roberts," "Point of No Return" and "Kind Sir." His wife, Margalo Gillmore, survives.

Fritzi Scheff
1879-1954

Lee Shubert

Godfrey Tearle

Roland Young

**SCHEFF, FRITZI,** 74, famous singer and actress, died Apr. 8, 1954, in New York City of a heart attack. Born in Vienna, she came to America in 1900 to appear with the Metropolitan Opera Company. In 1904 she switched from opera to operetta. Her most famous role was Fifi in "Mlle. Modiste" in which she sang and made famous "Kiss Me Again." Other stage appearances included "The Two Roses," "Fatinitza," "Girofle-Girofla" and "Boccaccio." She also appeared in vaudeville and summer theatres. Her last Broadway appearance was in a non-singing role in "Bravo" in 1948. She is buried in Kensico Cemetery.

**SPOONER, EDNA MAY,** 78, famous stock company actress, died July 14, 1953, in Sherman Oaks, Calif. Had her own stock company in Brooklyn from 1901 until 1914. She also appeared for several years at the Fifth Avenue Theatre, N.Y. Her sister, the late Cecil Spooner, was a stock actress too, and her father, Sprague Spooner, was a stock company manager in the 'Eighties.

**STONE, LEWIS,** 73, stage and screen actor, died in Beverly Hills, Calif., Sept. 12, 1953. In recent years he appeared exclusively in motion pictures. His earlier years included stage appearances in "The Girl of The Golden West," "The Bird of Paradise," "The Misleading Lady," and "Inside The Lines." Burial was in Rosendale Cemetery, California.

**STRAUS, OSCAR,** 83, Viennese composer, died Jan. 11, 1954, in Bad Ischl, Vienna, of a heart disease. His first successful operetta was "A Waltz Dream" and his most famous was "The Chocolate Soldier," composed in 1908 and adapted from G. B. Shaw's "Arms and The Man." Although he won fame in a similar field, he was no relation to Johann Strauss who was known as Vienna's "Waltz King."

**TEARLE, SIR GODFREY,** 68, famous British actor, died in London, June 8, 1953. Among his Broadway appearances were "The Fake," "The Flashing Stream" and Katharine Cornell's "Antony and Cleopatra." He was first president of the British Actors Equity, a post he held for 10 years. He was knighted in 1951. The late Conway Tearle was his half-brother.

**TRENT, SHEILA,** 46, actress, died May 26, 1954, in New York City. She made her stage debut at 18 in "Mister Romeo" and appeared in "Dead End," "My Sister Eileen" and a revival of Mae West's "Diamond Lil."

**VAJDA, ERNEST,** 67, Hungarian playwright, died in Woodland Hills, Calif., on Apr. 3, 1954. Among his plays produced on Broadway were "Fata Morgana," "The Harem," "Grounds For Divorce," "Crown Prince" and "Confession."

**WALLIS, GLADYS,** 80, retired actress, died Sept. 23, 1953, in Chicago. During her acting career she performed with the T. Daniel Frawley Stock Co., and appeared on Broadway in "For Money," "On Probation," "Brother John," "The Squire of Dames" and "The Lady Slavey." She married Samuel Insull, Chicago utilities leader, in 1899 and returned to the stage only once in 1926 in a revival of "A School For Scandal."

**WALTER, EDWIN,** 82, character actor, died Nov. 23, 1953, in Lenox Hill Hospital, N.Y.C. He started his career when 18 at the Comique Theatre in Harlem in "The Danger Signal." Among the many plays he appeared in were "The Tavern," "Elmer The Great," "Potash and Perlmutter," "Crime," "Seven Keys To Baldpate," "Easy Come, Easy Go" and more recently in "Tobacco Road."

**YOUNG, ROLAND,** 65, stage and screen actor, died in New York City, on June 5, 1953. Born in London, he made his American stage debut in "Hindle Wakes." He was a member of the Washington Square Players. Other plays in which he appeared were "Madame Pierre," "The Devil's Disciple," "The Last of Mrs. Cheyney," "Beggar On Horseback," "Rollo's Wild Oats," "The Queen's Husband," "A Successful Calamity," "Good Gracious, Annabelle," "Her Master's Voice," "The Distant Shore" and "A Touch of Brimstone." He became a U. S. citizen in 1918.

# INDEX